DATE DUE

BRAMANTE

ARNALDO BRUSCHI

BRAMANTE

FOREWORD BY PETER MURRAY

WITH 183 ILLUSTRATIONS

Thames and Hudson

Translated from the Italian

Frontispiece
1 Rome, Tempietto of S. Pietro in Montorio. For the metopes carved
with liturgical symbols, see pp. 132–33; for the door squeezed in
so that it overlaps the flanking pilasters, see p. 139.

Filmset and printed in England by BAS Printers Limited, Wallop, Hampshire
Bound in England

Contents

Foreword

THROUGHOUT the fifteenth century Rome was preparing itself for the
High Renaissance, an explosion of the arts rather than a revival, which
took place within an astonishingly short space of time – less, perhaps,
than a quarter of a century. The reign of Nicholas V (1447–55) saw the
first steps taken by the Papacy to encourage art and learning in Rome
since the Avignon Captivity, and, although Nicholas employed both
Alberti and Fra Angelico he had relatively little success in his artistic
aims; but at least he laid a firm foundation for the efforts of Sixtus IV
(1471–84), who, in his turn, prepared the way for the almost incredible
flowering of the arts under his nephew Julius II (1503–13) and the
almost equally great achievements of his successor, the Medici Pope
Leo X (1513–21). All this was to be cut short by the catastrophe of the
Sack of Rome in 1527, but the years between 1498, when Michelangelo began work on the *St Peter's Pietà,* and the death of Raphael in
1520 were indeed one of the greatest moments in the long history of
the visual arts.

The reign of Julius II, though not without problems in the political
field, saw the achievement, within the Vatican Palace itself, of the
great fresco cycle by Michelangelo of the Creation and Fall of Man on
the ceiling of the Sistine Chapel, completing the earlier cycles on the
walls, painted in the 1480s, which expounded the parallel between the
Lives of Moses and of Christ, illustrating the consummation of the
Mosaic Law and its universal application in the New Dispensation.
From 1508 onwards, Raphael was at work in the Stanze, and most of his
masterpieces – the *School of Athens,* the *Mass of Bolsena* – were completed in the reign of Julius, although the cycle as a whole was not
finished when Raphael himself died prematurely, in 1520. Unfortunately, what should have been Julius's crowning act of patronage on
a more than Imperial Roman scale, the total rebuilding of the millenary
Basilica of St Peter, founded by the Emperor Constantine himself,
more than eleven and a half centuries earlier, never materialized. Or,
rather, it never materialized in the form which Julius and Bramante,
his architect, intended – if indeed we can be sure what that form was.

7

There can be no doubt that Julius's vast schemes of patronage, including the tomb he commissioned from Michelangelo, were all subordinate to the truly Imperial desire to rebuild St Peter's itself in a form which would have compelled the admiration of Constantine and his architects – *Templi Petri Instauracio*, as the foundation medal of 1506 succinctly puts it. This was an ambition on an altogether different scale from a few frescoes, however distinguished, since it involved the labour of many hundreds and the financial support of millions, which, sadly, was not forthcoming: as a result, we can only guess at the grandeur of conception of the new basilica and its ideological function as the successor to Hagia Sophia and the churches of the Holy Land, but there can be no doubt that it would have been an event with far greater implications for mankind at large than even the Sistine Chapel. For this reason alone, it is necessary always to think of the High Renaissance as dominated by Bramante even more than by Raphael or Michelangelo, and so, to understand its true nature, we must understand the art of Bramante and reconstruct, as far as we can, his intentions and artistic ideals. These were certainly understood by his immediate successors – Serlio in the 1530s says: 'We should give credence to Bramante, seeing that it was he who was the inventor and light of all good architecture, which had been buried until his time . . . ', and Palladio, in his treatise published in 1570, echoes these sentiments: 'In the time of Pope Julius II that excellent man Bramante, a keen student of ancient buildings, erected some most beautiful buildings in Rome. ... Bramante was the first to bring back to the light of day the good and beautiful architecture that had been hidden since the time of the Ancients.'

It is all the stranger, therefore, that the literature on Bramante is so thin. The bibliographies on Raphael and Michelangelo are huge – some 3,000 books and articles on Michelangelo alone between 1510 and the present day – but the bibliography on Bramante is relatively tiny, and much of it is a rehash of the original *Life* by Vasari (1550 and 1568). Because of the neglect of scholars it is understandable that the general public has not realized the true greatness of this extraordinary genius, particularly since there are so few works by him still to be seen; and, worse still, those like the Tempietto or the cloister of S. Ambrogio in Milan need an experienced and sympathetic eye to discern their merit. This deplorable situation was changed in 1969, when Arnaldo Bruschi published his *Bramante architetto* (ed. Laterza, Bari and Rome). Bruschi's book must be one of the largest ever published on a single architect (nearly 1,100 pages), but far more important is the fact that it marks an epoch in Italian art-historical writing, since it departs from the tradition, so distasteful to historians bred in the Anglo-German documentary school, of total dependence on emotional response which has characterized the work of Longhi and ruined lesser men. Bruschi's book is solidly documented and gives proof of a formidable range of reading in many languages, so that his dating or his acceptance of an attribution is demonstrated with a methodological rigour which affords a rarefied joy to the pedantic historian who rates documented facts above even the most ingenious interpretations.

Yet Bruschi is an intensely Italian art historian, employing a critical vocabulary which is still almost beyond the range of English usage: we must admit that here the Longhis have the advantage in that there is an Italian terminology which, perhaps, has an English equivalent in literary criticism, but which is still lacking in the criticism of the visual arts; nor, I think, is it to be found in any other historical discipline. In the visual analysis of a work of art the Italian critic can use words or phrases like *perspective spectacle, organism, concrete universality* or *spatial dilatation* which are not easily assimilable into English but have to be paraphrased as best possible, and for this reason the task of translation has been an exceptionally difficult one. I must take some of the blame for this, since I claim the credit for asking Professor Bruschi to write a shorter version of his great work (which has turned out to be a monograph in its own right) for the English-speaking public. But if it is not always easy reading, it is worth the effort to learn the considered judgments of a man who, more than anyone for four centuries, has got close to the heart of the mystery of Bramante.

London, June 1976   PETER MURRAY

Introduction

VASARI, a fairly reliable source of information on Bramante in Rome, tells us that he died in 1514 at the age of 70. So he was born in 1444 – two years, that is, before the death of Brunelleschi. The link between the two architects is in fact made by Vasari at the beginning of his *Life* of Bramante:[1]

Of very great advantage to architecture, in truth, was the new method of Filippo Brunelleschi, who imitated and restored to the light, after many ages, the noble works of the most learned and marvellous ancients. But no less useful to our age was Bramante, in following the footsteps of Filippo, and making the path of his profession of architecture secure for all who came after him, by means of his courage, boldness, intellect, and science in that art, wherein he had the mastery not of theory only, but of supreme skill and practice.

By the sixteenth century, indeed, Brunelleschi had been largely forgotten, and it was Bramante who was regarded as (in Serlio's words) 'the inventor and light of all good architecture'.

Vasari saw Brunelleschi as the revolutionary first founder of Renaissance architecture, Bramante as the second founder, and he had certain specific parallels between the two in mind. Yet the periods in which they worked, the social, economic, political and cultural conditions against which their careers must be set, were profoundly different.

The early artistic humanism in Florence, and Brunelleschi's architecture in particular, were the product of a city of merchants, bankers and prosperous craftsmen – men proud of their republican freedom, involved in political life, busy with all kinds of varied activities, open-minded in their search for new fields for human knowledge and action; and uninterested in theoretical speculation as an end in itself. Brunelleschi's architectural and artistic revolution, achieved partly with the help of Donatello and Masaccio, was indeed closely connected with the outlook of the upper middle classes which rose in Florence between the fourteenth and fifteenth centuries. After the civil struggles and the economic crisis of the fourteenth century, the interests of this class decisively controlled the city's institutions and in particular the Greater Guilds, at least until Cosimo il Vecchio brought in the 'enlightened' tyranny of a single family. Nearly all the influences upon Brunelleschi's work can be found in the ideology of this new élite in power – a rational outlook in direct, scientific research into the natural world, functionally applied to make technical possibilities concrete, leading, in art, to the evolution of perspective, and in architecture to a break with tradition through the 'un-historical' idea that the language of the ancient world should be revived. These basic attitudes appear very clearly in Brunelleschi's work: a building project, for instance, was the representation of an idea, not the collective activity of craftsmen; it introduced into architecture the division of labour made necessary by the facts of economic life. They are made explicit in the *Vita di Filippo di Ser Brunellesco* which an anonymous biographer (probably Antonio di Tuccio Manetti) wrote several decades after his death. His treatment of the cupola of S. Maria del Fiore is especially instructive as an example of these attitudes.

This new way of regarding architecture – as an intellectual and cultural discipline, no longer a mechanical but a liberal art, one that was worthy of free men – was taken up and developed, together with the results it produced in technical methods, first of all by Alberti. It was to become a commonplace of Renaissance theory, but it had not, by the time of Brunelleschi's death, made much impression outside Florence itself. The atmosphere of the court of Urbino, in which Bramante probably spent his early years, of the Northern Italian courts such as those at Mantua or Ferrara, with which he may have come into contact, of Milan under the Sforzas and of Rome under Julius II was very different from that of Florence in Brunelleschi's day. These courts, however open they may have been to the humanistic culture which had originated in Florence, and however much they might descant on it in their own way, were still largely steeped in traditional medieval attitudes, and still ruled by princes whose political and economic power was based on war. They were feudal courts, not communal cities whose people took a passionate, conscious part in civic affairs and in the administration of the *res publica,* productive activity and trade. In this respect, the three main places Bramante knew in his life – Urbino, Milan and Rome – are alike in everything but scale. Their ambitions and interests were, in every case, essentially those of an individual – the Lord, *il Principe* as Machiavelli has defined him – or at the most those of his own small court.

In Renaissance architecture, the progress from Brunelleschi, who first formulated its ideas, to Alberti, who interpreted them, and then, in the second half of the century, to Bramante, with his new synthesis, is thus marked by the need to adapt those original ideas to a different social, economic and political context. Moreover, the years between 1465 and 1480, when it would appear that Bramante's career was starting, were a time of profound crisis within humanistic culture itself, a crisis that continued until it reached its climax in the final decade of the century. The attitude of educated people had changed profoundly since the early days. On the surface, things may not have looked very different; but the vision of the first Florentine humanism had given place, as Garin puts it, to a very 'delicate culture . . . ready to escape indulgently into an atmosphere of easy optimism'.[2] The new élite of men of letters, philosophers and artists in the service of the new princely régimes was wary of the abstract, in poetry, theology and philosophy, and often disliked any general involvement of the people in civil affairs. Cultural activities became in Florence what they had never ceased to be in the other courts, the exclusive preserve of a small ruling class. The advanced open-minded earlier generation had become academic and aristocratic, wanting a very precious, elegant culture, a culture for

initiates. Hardly any of the inheritance of early humanism seems to have been lost: ideas and hypotheses that were previously uncertain and adventurous became solid and stable, and could be amplified and developed. But instead of the sense of commitment which might have changed the world, and certainly had its effect upon city life, there was painstaking, useless activity of a cultural kind, or pure scientific research, grown abstract and theoretical. The final decade of the century brought signs of crisis: a resurgence of mysticism and the occult, of prophets and messiahs; threats of imminent disaster. In art, among the middle classes which had acquired aristocratic tastes and in the princely courts of feudal origin, there was a return to chivalric ideals, a revival of interest in the late Middle Ages, in the provincial, in regional traditions. People began to question the humanistic idea of accord with nature, the idea that man, and his activity, was in harmony with the deepest laws of the universe. The more explicitly this was expressed, the more uncertain it appeared to be. It was the first great crisis of Renaissance culture.[3]

The period when Bramante's career began was one of exhaustion and crisis in the field of architecture, despite a number of important buildings. Brunelleschi's ideas had really been understood and used only by Alberti – and by him only partially; indeed, he obviously used them with a selective bias. He interpreted Vitruvius in the light of whatever was humanistic in him, and used the idea of 'musical' proportions (which could be expressed in simple metrical, numerical relationships, rather than through geometrical arrangements) as an absolute, harking back directly to Roman architecture in a way that was both emotive and uncommitted. Above all, by developing and at the same time challenging Brunelleschi's interpretation, he put forward a different solution to the problem of the relationship between the *design* and the actual building. By reducing all architecture to design and by subscribing to the idea of the architect as an intellectual and a humanist, he removed it entirely from the field of technical skill and of practical manual work and turned it into an ideal 'perspective picture' of itself, thus on the one hand putting it into the field of the liberal arts and sciences, as an activity based on mathematics, and connected with music and geometry as well as with history, philosophy and politics; and on the other putting it into the field of art by bringing it close to painting. All that Alberti was really doing was endorsing a tendency already very much alive, particularly in Tuscany, which had characterized Italian architecture from the end of the Romanesque period and had become consolidated in the fourteenth century. After Brunelleschi, this tendency became stronger, and helped gradually to reduce architecture to the visual, figurative values of painting. In Bramante, it was continued, with important results, and it was to continue throughout the whole of the sixteenth century and the period of Italian Baroque.

Around 1445–50 was the moment when the seminal ideas of Florence began to spread further. The work of sculptors like Ghiberti, Donatello, Filarete and Agostino di Duccio, of painters like Paolo Uccello, Andrea del Castagno, 14 Filippo Lippi and Piero della Francesca, of 20 followers of Brunelleschi, such as Michelozzo and the da Maiano, and of Alberti's assistants such as Rossellino, Matteo de' Pasti and Luca Fancelli, was just as important as that of Brunelleschi himself. Alberti set up new centres of humanistic architecture outside Florence: in Ferrara, Rome, Rimini and Mantua. Some workshops, in which artists and craftsmen of various kinds came together, now formed cultural centres, as they had done in the Middle Ages. One of these was at Rimini, another at Loreto, where the influence of Giuliano da Maiano was the most important. A third was at Urbino. This saw Florentine artists like Maso di Bartolomeo around 1540; Piero della Francesca, who had already been at Ferrara and Rimini; Luciano di Laurana from 1465 to 1472; and Francesco di Giorgio Martini, of Siena, from 1474 to 1482 and again later. Images of the ancient world, more or less fantastic, began to appear in the studios; Ciriaco d'Ancona enriched them with the results of his travels, and artists and craftsmen from Tuscany and Lombardy travelled about Italy, spreading decorative motifs and subjects. One of the most active agents of change was Giuliano da Maiano (1432–90), who travelled about Italy to Siena, Faenza, Loreto, Macerata and Naples, spreading the influence of other places and ideas.

The architecture of humanism was divided into several *genres,* involving separate disciplines: there were architect-sculptors, often found among the Lombards, the Tuscans and the Venetians; architect-painters (like Piero, Mantegna, Francesco di Giorgio, and Bramante himself); architects who went in for carpentry and made models; architect-builders, who understood the problems of building technique; architects of fortifications; literary and theoretical 'architects'; and even architects who were jewellers and designers. If we exclude Alberti, the two men who were most advanced were,

paradoxically, both painters: Piero della Fran- 14 cesca and Mantegna. It is no accident that they were the main influences upon the young Bramante.

In the decade between 1480 and 1490, as the Quattrocento artistic world was coming to an end, important new architectural ideas emerged in a number of Italian centres. The most significant were expressed in church buildings (S. Maria presso S. Satiro in Milan, 17 S. Maria del Calcinaio at Cortona, S. Maria delle 34 Carceri at Prato, the cathedral of Pavia), in 46 villas (those at Poggio a Caiano, the Belvedere 53 of Innocent VIII in Rome, the villa of Poggioreale at Naples) and in plans for gigantic princely palaces (like those designed by Giuliano da 96 Sangallo).

Bramante produced some of these new plans. By 1480 the earlier generation was growing old, and together with Francesco di Giorgio and Giuliano da Sangallo he was one of the leaders of Renaissance architecture. The three men had something in common in the way they tackled problems and dealt with their work. But the works themselves, rooted in different cultures, and using different stylistic methods, are not easily compared.

During this period, the most advanced ideas nearly always appeared in plans for princes, men who were often culturally ahead of their time and in whose courts the latest ideas could be nurtured like hot-house plants. In the uneasy political balance established in Italy between the peace of Lodi in 1454 and the deaths of Lorenzo the Magnificent on 8 April 1492 and of Innocent VIII on 25 July 1492, they proved an effective *instrumentum regni,* although after 1494 the balance of political power was upset by the death of Charles VIII and in the last years of the century the economic situation also became uncertain, largely because of the failure of the Medici Bank. The figure of the fifteenth-century prince himself was also in a transitional phase – suspended eternally in a daring and delicate political game, between affirmation, supremacy, expansion, and the bare struggle to survive; that is, between power and death. The architecture produced for these courts naturally tended to retain a regional character and to reflect the individuality of their rulers.

It was only when Julius II, during his fairly short pontificate from 1503 to 1513, tried to set himself up – as a number of princes, including Ludovico il Moro and Alexander VI had already tried to do – as a single, national monarch over all the Italian rulers, large and small, that it became necessary for architecture to acquire a new national style, one which was no longer regional, but universal; just as Julius's power sought to be universal, and the old Roman Empire (and its architecture) had been universal. While other centres of architectural culture in the fifteenth century were in a state of crisis, Rome set itself up again as *caput mundi,* the centre of power and also the artistic capital of Italy and Europe.

The Renaissance grand manner was born. And Bramante alone was the founder of this new, revolutionary manner. It is quite right that he should appear in history, after Brunelleschi, as the second founder of Renaissance architecture. And Sebastiano Serlio, who inherited Bramante's ideas through Baldassare Peruzzi and Giulio Romano, was correct when, twenty years after Bramante's death, he called him 'a man of such genius in architecture that with the help and authority which the Pope gave him it might be said that he was the inventor and light of all good architecture, which had been buried until his time' (Bk III, f.64v).

Beside Bramante stood Julius II; not merely with his outstanding energy and will, and with the imperial scale of funds he had available as client, but also, and above all, with the power to give the mature manner of the architect its motivation, meaning, and renewed purpose. The second revolution of the Renaissance was thus due, as has been said, to the concerted action of two *terribili* old men who came together in a dream of 'universality' and greatness. Giuliano della Rovere, who had taken the papal name Giulio probably in memory of Julius Caesar (in 1506 he actually had a medal struck with the inscription 'IULIU[S] CAESAR PONT II'), sought to emulate the greatness of the Roman emperors on a political level, while Bramante tried, with a 'universal' architecture, to restore the physical atmosphere of ancient Rome, with all its signs of greatness. Each pursued his object with determination, imagination and unbridled ambition. But the two objects coincided, and the will and labour of both men was needed to renew the architecture of the Renaissance.

André Chastel has significantly contrasted the 'uncertainties' of Florence in the late fifteenth century with the certainties of Rome in the early years of the next century. The crisis of the last years of the fifteenth century was in fact resolved in a new, mature manner that formed the point of departure for the architecture of the sixteenth century and in general for the whole of its later development, not only in Italy but throughout Europe. However, the political and cultural crisis still loomed; the threat had merely been postponed. This was basically the crisis brought about by the change in world-view which we regard as the end of the Middle Ages and the dawn of the modern age. And so, just as Julius's efforts to be a national and universal monarch turned out to be a dream, a bold fantasy with unlooked-for, ephemeral results, so Bramante's efforts to bring in a manner suited to universal themes of glory led only to the contradictory attempts and dramatic searchings that make up Mannerism.

In Bramante's final work the crisis was still suppressed, concealed by his enthusiasm to open up a new way; an enthusiasm that came from the awareness that he was founding a new, and at the same time an ancient and 'true' architecture, embodying the aspirations of the past century. Yet his anxiety to discover and to confirm by experience the 'universal' value of the new style, the way in which nearly all his works seem to be aiming in different directions, even his wish to get through a great deal in a short time, betray how precarious was the historical situation, and show up, against a background of disquiet, only the *hope* – not the *certainty* – of a balance that was in fact unstable.

To oppose the 'natural', 'predestined' course of events; to transform history and give it a new direction – alone, humanistically, as individuals, as men able to dominate 'Fortune': this was the dream of Julius II and of Bramante. It was a dream which the architect, for all his limitations and false starts, surely realized more completely than the pope.

Chapter one

Early life: Urbino apprenticeship

DONATO, or Donino or Donnino – as his parents and his friend Leonardo da Vinci called him – Bramante was born almost certainly at Monte Asdrualdo (today Fermignano), a small town in the dukedom of Urbino. His family were peasants. The name Bramante came from his maternal grandfather, Pascuccio of Monte Asdrualdo. His father Angelo, son of Antonio from Farneta, having married Vittoria, Pascuccio's daughter, went to live in his father-in-law's house, became his heir and took his surname, handing it on to his children.[4] The families of Bramante's father and grandfather cannot have been entirely penniless, since their farmland had some value. Vasari probably exaggerates when he says that Angelo, the architect's father, was a poor man, 'who had need that [his son] should earn money'. However, the family's prosperity must have depended on all its male members working on the land. As Pascuccio, the grandfather, had no sons, he had been obliged to bring Angelo, his daughter Vittoria's husband, to live in his house. But this marriage, too, suffered from a lack of male children. Donino had only one brother, although he had seven sisters. To the parents the girls must have been a great unproductive burden, and getting them settled must have been a worry. Donino's birth was no doubt greeted in the family as a gift from heaven (Donato means 'given', so Donino probably means 'little gift'), for they naturally thought he would grow up to be a farmer, helping his father and later taking over from him, with his brother Antonio, the running of the farm. But it is likely that quite early – as we know from other sources – the young Donino showed his disinclination to work on the land and at the same time his artistic calling. Above all, his congenital restlessness must soon have made it clear that he

wanted to leave the narrow circle of Monte Asdrualdo, to see new things, and to have new experiences. The splendour of the nearby court of Urbino must have attracted him. We know nothing precisely about those early years, but having left his family Donino must have renounced his share of their wealth completely, as the wills of his father and mother, made in 1484, when he had been in Milan for several years, make clear.

Having given up his peasant background, it is likely that he had to make his way entirely on his own. Cesare Cesariano (1521) was probably going on what his master Bramante had told him when he called him 'patient son of poverty' and said that he 'suffered from poverty for a very long time'. Bramante seems never to have forgotten his peasant origins: in a document of 1510 he was still calling himself a native of Monte Asdrualdo. To those origins he no doubt owed the realism, the earthy, concrete quality he had, sometimes tinged with a kind of sharp severity; his way of going straight to essentials, and avoiding the meretricious and the merely pleasant; all this was part of his character as a person and to a great extent conditioned what he did as painter, architect and poet.

According to Vasari, 'in his boyhood, besides reading and writing, he gave much attention to arithmetic'; and also, although this is not confirmed by any document, Vasari says that his father, 'perceiving that he delighted much in drawing, applied him, when still a mere boy, to the art of painting'. The young Bramante 'gave much study to the works of Fra Bartolommeo, otherwise called Fra Carnovale da Urbino'[5] and 'delighted in architecture and perspective'. Another sixteenth-century writer, Saba da Castiglione, says in 1549 that he was a 'good painter, as a follower of Mantegna, and a great

2 Urbino, Palazzo Ducale: Cappella del Perdono, or Sacello dello Spirito Santo (see pp. 24–25)

perspectivist, as a pupil of Piero dal Borgo' (Piero della Francesca).

All this is just what we might expect, and is amply confirmed by Bramante's early works. Very likely he was first educated at Urbino, perhaps as helper and colleague of Fra Carnevale and of Piero della Francesca, who, together with Leon Battista Alberti (who dedicated his *De re aedificatoria* to Federigo da Montefeltro) was, in the field of art, the leading light of the new humanistic culture at Urbino. Federigo da Montefeltro, his secretary Ottaviano Ubaldini, and his wife Battista Sforza, were all making Urbino into a cultural centre of the very highest rank in the second half of the fifteenth century.

The ideas which characterized Urbino, although they had originated in Florence, here seemed to take a new direction, influenced by the thought and work of Piero and Alberti. In Federigo da Montefeltro's famous 'brief' in which, on 10 June 1468, he appointed Luciano di Laurana 'architect, engineer and chief of all builders', he declared that 'the quality of architecture [is] based upon the arts of arithmetic and geometry, which belong to the seven liberal and principal arts, because they are in the highest measure certain; and it is an art of great learning and great intellect . . .' This is the 'manifesto' of Urbino's culture.

Urbino became the centre of 'mathematical' humanism, of the 'civilization of perspective' in the second half of the fifteenth century; although, in the 'domestic' part of this humanistic yet still feudal court, attitudes, interests and tastes still remained at least partly rooted in late medieval traditions. Encouraged by Federigo himself, a very large number of artists, craftsmen and decorators, who varied enormously in background and education, worked uninterruptedly on the building of the palace and other works promoted by him from about 1450 until his death in 1482.[6] Federigo wished to make, as Castiglione later called it, 'a city in the form of a palace', which would be a focus for and an expression of the urban qualities of the whole of Urbino; but also a home for himself, one that answered to his tastes and requirements, a house that would be exactly right for his own family. In spite of the many influences mingling at all levels, influences upon the plan, the details, the furnishing and the decoration, the director of it all seems to have been a single person, one who, according to available sources, was himself an amateur architect: Duke Federigo. Certainly it was he who settled programmes, chose artists, approved projects, and checked the work as it progressed: from the plan of the palace and all its parts down to the decoration

and furnishing and the paintings which were to adorn the walls. Federigo's personality – that of a humanistic prince who was also a man of action, a 'medieval' condottiere, an ambitious politician and a paternalistic ruler – is almost certainly the key to an understanding of the artistic culture of Urbino and its remarkable results. But his taste was not merely cultivated and up-to-date, it was also eclectic and far-ranging: sometimes turning to what was attractive and imaginative, sometimes to decoration as an end in itself and to a rich, elaborate effect. Sometimes he failed to choose with the theoretical and critical awareness which the brief to Luciano di Laurana seems to promise. He could not always choose who would influence him: Piero della Francesca, Laurana, Francesco di Giorgio and Melozzo; many Florentine and Lombard artists and decorators, such as Ambrogio Barocci; painters like Botticelli or even foreign artists like the Fleming Justus of Ghent or the Spaniard Pedro Berruguete.

Apart from this there were strong relationships and exchanges with other centres of humanistic culture, in particular Florence and other Tuscan cities such as Siena; and with Perugia, Rimini, Ferrara, Pesaro, Mantua and Milan. But however open to and enriched by all these varied and stimulating influences, the culture of Urbino has a special character of its own, marked by a particular feeling for mathematics and perspective, which made a distinct contribution to the development of Renaissance art and architecture: witness Bramante himself and later Raphael.

Bramante's early training at Urbino – in his day he was known as 'of Urbino' – was therefore one of the fundamental influences in his life, continually reappearing throughout his artistic career. It is likely that he was employed in the workshops of the Ducal Palace, and to judge from his later works it was an experience he never forgot. Even more influential must have been his contacts with the literary men and artists who made Federigo's court their centre. The very atmosphere of Urbino, so varied and so lively, and with so many influences concentrated upon it, was an intellectual stimulant. The Duke's 'continual investigations', says Vasari, 'frequently resulted in the discovery of some useful invention, whereby the art was greatly enriched.' Luciano di Laurana began to work on the palace in 1465 and was certainly at Urbino from November 1467 to the end of 1471, or at the latest until August 1472. But it was after he had left that the most significant, that is the most constant and deliberate, results of the 'mathematical' humanism and 'perspective civilization' of Duke Federigo's court appeared. They were not real buildings, but paintings, representations and perspective fantasies of architectural space. In them, indeed, space is seen as something generated by architecture.

As these works are sometimes attributed to the young Bramante, we must mention them briefly. The earliest things of the kind at Urbino are possibly by Piero della Francesca. Next, probably shortly before 1470, come the two Barberini Panels, the *Birth of the Virgin* and 3 *Presentation of the Virgin* (formerly in the Barberini collection and now respectively in the Metropolitan Museum of Art in New York and in the Museum of Fine Arts in Boston), which may be by that mysterious Fra Carnevale whom Vasari mentions as Bramante's teacher. In these two panels, the arrangement of the townscape and figures, the quality of the colour and the light go back to Domenico Veneziano and Filippo Lippi, but the rigorous perspective plan and the careful use of buildings as a means of conveying space in depth show the new climate at Urbino. They represent a kind of synthesis of Alberti's ideas and the work of Piero della Francesca and that of Florentines like Maso di Bartolomeo, Pasquino da Montepulciano, and Giovanni da Fiesole, known as Il Greco, who were working at Urbino before Laurana. One should also note the door of S. Domenico at Urbino (designed by Maso di Bartolomeo shortly after 1450) and the chimney-piece 'della Jole' (so called because it is carved with a representation of Hercules and Iole) in the Ducal Palace.

Vivid memories of the northern world of Padua and of Mantegna appeared in 1473, in the buildings painted in the background of some of 4–8 the eight small panels which formerly decorated the *Nicchia di S. Bernardino* in the church dedicated to that saint in Perugia (now in the Galleria Nazionale in Perugia).[7] The architectural parts of these panels must be connected with Urbino and Alberti, though the figures appear to have been painted by a number of Umbrian painters, Perugino among them.

The man responsible for painting these buildings was certainly interested in architecture and its careful representation in perspective. The fact that they were painted by a single artist is proved by, among other things, the way in which they are not so much drawn as incised into the panel with remarkable care in the delineation of each architectural detail. They are self-sufficient in their compositional economy and presuppose careful preliminary planning, as is 3 the case in the Barberini Panels, mentioned earlier. The artist appears to know Alberti's

3 Master of the Barberini Panels: *Presentation of the Virgin* (Boston, Museum of Fine Arts, Charles Potter Kling Fund)

work at Rimini and Mantua, and also some of the fundamental principles of Alberti's theories. The arrangement of some of the figures – for instance, in the panels of *The Miracle of the Still-born Child, The Miracle of the Young Man gored by a bull,* and *The Miracle of the Man wounded by a Stake* – recall the Ferrara of Ercole de' Roberti (one of whose works seems to have reached Urbino before 1473, the date of these panels), while the range of decorative elements worked in shining bronze (figured capitals, acroteria, floating ribbons, putti, cornucopias, garlands, etc., and in particular two shields with busts of Classical heroes, taken with 'antiquarian' taste from medals or cameos, which appear in *The Miracle of the Man born Blind*) recalls the Paduan world of Donatello, Squarcione and above all Mantegna.

In *The Miracle of the Still-born Child,* the 5 architectural masses are set in space in a way that recalls Piero della Francesca, and the arrangement of the architectural elements is clearly taken from that in the courtyard of the palace at Urbino; but these elements are, as it

4 *Miracle of the Young Man gored by a Bull,* from the *Nicchia di S. Bernardino* (Perugia, Galleria Nazionale dell'Umbria)

5 *Miracle of the Still-born Child,* from the *Nicchia di S. Bernardino* (Perugia, Galleria Nazionale dell'Umbria)

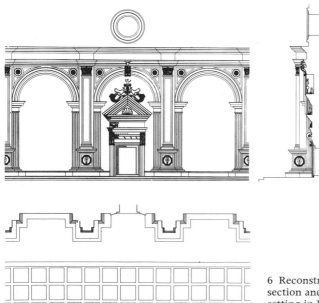

6 Reconstruction of the elevation, section and plan of the architectural setting in Ill. 4 (drawn by G. C. Miletti)

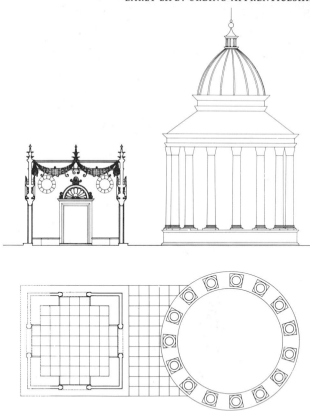

7, 8 *Miracle of the Man wounded by a Stake*, from the *Nicchia di S. Bernardino* (Perugia, Galleria Nazionale dell'Umbria), and reconstruction of the elevations and plan of the architectural setting (drawn by G. C. Miletti)

were, 'criticized' in terms of an architectural ideal which is Albertian in origin, an aesthetic of *walls* rather than columns. This ideal, which is different from the formal abstraction characteristic of buildings in Urbino in Laurana's day, is manifest in this picture in the heavier style, more robust construction and larger forms. Great emphasis is laid upon the decorative parts which are separate from the structure, imposed upon it, in a way which again conforms to Albertian theory. These characteristics appear quite clearly in the other panels as well.

In *The Miracle of the Young Man gored by a Bull* a building like Alberti's Tempio Malatestiano (with a door of the kind used by Alberti at S. Sebastiano in Mantua) is translated into terms of an architecture that is strictly one of masonry – just as happens in *The Miracle of the Curing of the Girl,* although it is remarkably independent of all current architectural ideas. Again, in *The Miracle of the Man born Blind,* the side of the Tempio Malatestiano, enormously

extended and amplified, is used to form the lower part of a building to which is added a wall pierced by aedicule windows (of the type used by Piero della Francesca and Laurana at Urbino, but expressed in unexpectedly mature forms), producing a whole that recalls the front of the Ducal Palace at Pesaro. In *The Miracle of the Man wounded by a Stake,* a perfect cubic space forms a kind of small courtyard. Beyond it is a circular temple with columns and a cupola, which, possibly inspired by the mausoleum which Federigo wished to build in the so-called Courtyard of Pasquino in the Ducal Palace, foreshadows Bramante's Tempietto in Rome.

The eclectic taste shown in the buildings in all these panels is unified by their three-dimensional character and their monumental scale, a scale which is emphasized by the tiny figures. Antiquity is suggested indirectly and in a literary way, not by the forms and arrangement of the spaces, but by their splendour and by the use of a few characteristic decorative

7, 8

4, 6

135

motifs; they are quite without the 'romantic' antiquarian hints found in Mantegna. But above all Piero's perspective system has been thoroughly mastered, and interpreted in an original way. Space is developed in depth, and the scenographic, theatrical values of the architectural plan are enhanced: so much so, that nearly all these paintings, like the Barberini Panels, suggest the scenery in a Renaissance theatre. (Renaissance stage-sets, such as those illustrated later by Peruzzi and Serlio, are also suggested by the architectural inlay-work on several doors 9 in the palace, which date from before 1474.)

It was Masaccio, perhaps in collaboration with Brunelleschi, who first partially used perspective illusionistically; this was in the fresco of the *Trinity* painted on the wall of the nave of S. Maria Novella in Florence in 1425 or a little later. Some Florentine painters, in particular Andrea del Castagno, developed this use of perspective. But the idea of defining space through the illusionistic representation of buildings, painted on all the walls to make its effect on someone standing in the middle of the room, may have been first used in the Vatican at the

9 Urbino, Palazzo Ducale: marquetry door panel in the Salotto of the Duchess. Compare the Belvedere courtyard, Ill. 102.

10 Urbino, Palazzo Ducale: Studiolo. The walls above the marquetry were originally covered with painted panels.

time of Nicholas V, in about 1453–54 (?), probably by Alberti and Castagno.[8] Mantegna, between 1465 and c. 1474, painted the Camera degli Sposi in Mantua. But it was at Urbino in the years around 1472–76 that the most successful and spectacular development took place, in 10 Federigo's small 'Studiolo' and in one room of 11 his library. Here it is no longer a matter of showing an architectural space in perspective, but of involving the spectator in a false reality that conflicts with the physical reality of the structure of the walls. The perspective representation, on walls which form the limitations of the physical space available, of buildings and scenes which both in their dimensional scale and in their lighting – from the same dim source of natural light that illumines the room – seek to appear real, 'cheats' the person watching, and creates an illusionistic space in which, as in the theatre, reality and fiction mingle to form a single spectacle.

10 In the Studiolo – the most intimate, private room in Federigo's palace – it was a matter of finding an architectural arrangement for a small,

12 Justus of Ghent?: *Music*, from the Room of the Liberal Arts of the library of the Palazzo Ducale, Urbino (London, National Gallery)

11 Urbino, Palazzo Ducale: schematic reconstruction of the position of the painted panels in the Room of the Liberal Arts of the library. *a* source of light (window), *b* focal points for the perspective lines in the paintings, A *Grammar* (?), B Rhetoric, C *Dialectic*, D *Arithmetic* (or *Geometry*?), E *Astronomy*, F *Music* (see Ill. 12), G *Geometry* (or *Arithmetic*?)

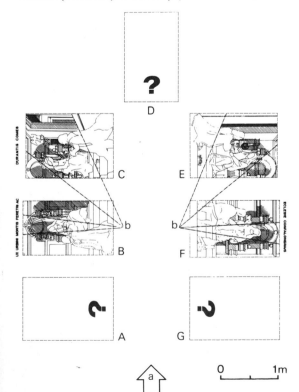

irregularly-shaped room of unattractive proportions. By simulating buildings and figures in perspective on the walls, the room was given a form that was humanistically proportioned, and although it remained intimate and small it became free and opened out into feigned niches and loggias that overcame the sense of restriction and airlessness produced by the dim lighting.

In another room of the palace at Urbino, part 11 of the library, the pretended architecture did not form part of the physical boundary of the room, but led beyond it, creating a '*spettacolo* of space', like those Bramante was to produce later.[9] Side by side on the walls, in a continuous sequence, were the thrones of the Liberal 12 Arts, represented in perspective as if on a stage or in a long loggia, and forming a single scene set in an illusory space which, to someone standing in the middle of the room, extended the actual space beyond its physical limitations in an illusionistic way. The distinction between feigned and real was destroyed: a new, un-

13 Justus of Ghent?: *A Reading,* or *Lecture at the Court of Urbino.* In the centre are Federigo da Montefeltro and his son. Compare the polygonal dome with that in the Prevedari engraving, Ill. 26. (Reproduced by gracious permission of Her Majesty Queen Elizabeth II)

expected and fantastic architectural space was produced by the use of real architectural elements – the walls, the door, the window, the large vault of the ceiling, etc. – treated as if they were also part of the imaginary space and peopled by characters theatrically engaged in 'courtly' ceremonial. As in the Studiolo, the way in which the painted figures were lit by the same natural light as the room, the very scarcity of this light and the perspective rigour and realism of the representation, must have given the scene interest and verisimilitude.

Similar illusionistic features appear in other works produced at Urbino at the time. Particu-
13 larly interesting is the so-called *Reading,* or *Lecture at the Court of Urbino* (now at Hampton Court), which may have had some connection with the Room of the Liberal Arts in the library.

These illusionistic rooms in the palace at Urbino have been dismantled and partially destroyed (some of the paintings are to be found in a number of museums in Europe), so that their original atmosphere can no longer be experienced completely. However, the parts that are left, and attempted reconstructions, allow us to see them as the most characteristic product of the culture of Urbino, seeking to translate the original message of architectural humanism from Florence into terms that would suit the social, cultural and economic context of the human-

ist courts of Central and Northern Italy. This sense of illusion, 'so well suited to chasten Gothic exuberance without killing it', as Fiocco put it,[10] may be an escape, a flight 'away from experience and true logic', a courtly cultural game that is subtly suited to the political structure in which it was born, and serves to blur the original assumptions of Florentine humanism. Perspective is no longer a scientific means of rationalizing vision, of using space in an orderly way and possessing it in a humanistic one: it becomes a precious, clever method of transferring the physical space of man's life – controlled by him in relation to his own needs – into a fantastic visual fiction.

These works were carried out by different painters, some of them known, some unknown, and each one gave his work precise, definite touches that made it entirely his own, yet within an atmosphere of close collaboration, recalling the Middle Ages. In the case of the Bar-
3 berini Panels, the man who designed the buildings, the man who drew them in perspective, and the man who painted the figures were probably a single person. But in the perspectives of the intarsia doors it is likely that the man who planned them is not the man who carried them out; certainly the architectural and the figura-
4–8 tive parts in some of the panels of the *Nicchia di S. Bernardino* were not painted by the same

10–
12 man. In the case of the Studiolo and the Room of the Liberal Arts, before the various artists carried out their individual parts, someone must of necessity have worked out a plan, even a very rough one, of the whole, possibly sketching the main outlines, the vanishing points and other elements of perspective on the walls themselves, thus achieving a fairly exact idea of the individual architectural parts to be shown. Such a project, involving a detailed cartoon, is indispensable for large-scale perspective painting.

14 At Urbino the key figure in the development of a school of 'perspective architects' was almost certainly Piero della Francesca. The treatise *De prospectiva pingendi*, which he presented to Duke Federigo in 1474, was much read by painters, and can be seen as an influence in Bramante's early works. We do not know for certain who these architects, architectural designers and painters were, who made the perspective plans for illusionistic representations, but it seems likely that they included Fra Carnevale and probably Melozzo da Forlì and the young Bramante.

We know nothing about Bramante in any certain, documented way before 1477, when he was already thirty-three and in Lombardy, at Bergamo. Where had he been before this? To judge from his later works, he must have known not only the artists at the court of Urbino (Piero, Fra Carnevale, Laurana, Melozzo and others), but also the Ferrarese school (he must have been struck, in particular, by the painting of Ercole de' Roberti); and he must certainly have studied the works of Alberti at Rimini and Mantua, and those of Mantegna at Padua and Mantua. Indeed, it is likely that he spent time in Padua, Mantua and Ferrara; and at Ferrara he may have designed the doorway of the Palazzo Schifanoia which Ambrogio Barocci, who was also very active at Urbino and may have been connected with Bramante in other works, executed in 1474. Visits to cities of the Marche and of Umbria (Ancona, Pesaro, Loreto, Perugia, etc.) and to Venice can be conjectured, as well as to Florence, since his work in S. Maria presso S. Satiro, Milan, presupposes some knowledge of Brunelleschi. In any case, the cultures of Urbino, Padua and Mantua form the basis of his artistic education.

Lacking any documents earlier than 1477, critics have, with varying degrees of plausibility, attributed a number of works to the young Bramante. Among these are the architectural backgrounds which we have been discussing in some of the panels of the *Nicchia*
4–8 *di S. Bernardino* at Perugia (where the figure-painters included Perugino and Pinturicchio,

14 Piero della Francesca: Brera Altarpiece, or *Virgin and Child with Saints and Angels, adored by Federigo da Montefeltro*, formerly in S. Bernardino at Urbino: see Ill. 15 (Milan, Brera)

known to have been Bramante's friends later in Rome); the architectural setting in Federigo's
10 Studiolo (perhaps the occasion of his first visit to Florence, for consultations with the Florentine artists involved); the series of the Liberal
12, Arts in the library; and the *Reading* at Hampton
13 Court. Some say, hesitantly, that he may have had a part in the designing of the architectural background of Piero della Francesca's
14 altarpiece in the Brera, Milan, probably belonging to the years 1472–74. Another very uncertain
15 attribution is the church of S. Bernardino at Urbino, which was to be the mausoleum of the Montefeltro family. It is quite remarkable architecturally, and does contain motifs found in Bramante's later works; but it is almost certain that it was built, and its details designed, by Francesco di Giorgio.

A number of considerations, however, suggest that Bramante was active at Urbino, as architect and perspective painter, in the short period between Laurana's departure in 1472 and Francesco di Giorgio's definite appointment as chief architect; it is not impossible, indeed, that he should have collaborated occasionally

23

15 Urbino, S. Bernardino: drawing
by Peruzzi showing the interior
before 1536. The shallow eastern
apse, originally identical in size to
the side apses, was later lengthened.
On the altar is the Brera Altarpiece
by Piero della Francesca (Ill. 14).
(Florence, Uffizi, Arch. 245)

with the latter. During this period – certainly
before 1480 and perhaps around 1475 – the
Sacello dello Spirito Santo or Cappella del
Perdono at Urbino was built, and joined to it the
chapel dedicated to the pagan Muses. This was
an explicit cultural and literary humanistic
expression of the spirituality of an élite group in
whose universal religion the philosophers and
poets of pagan Antiquity met in profound agree-
ment with Christ, the saints and the Christian
philosophers. The Chapel of the Muses has
reached us in such a state that it is impossible to
have any critical views about it; but what is left
allows one to guess that it had many points of
contact with the Cappella del Perdono, which

has been preserved untouched. This chapel is
quite unlike any other part of the palace; it
cannot be Laurana's, nor does it seem to be
Francesco di Giorgio's. Both these very small
rooms show an effort to express a new, serious
heroic quality that suggests the Antique world
or Alberti (particularly in S. Andrea at Mantua),
or the background of Piero della Francesca's
Brera Altarpiece. One finds further affinities
if one looks at Alberti's copy of the Holy
Sepulchre in S. Pancrazio in Florence (also recalled by the Roman lettering on the entablature,
used at about the same time in the Studiolo, in
the library at Urbino, and in S. Bernardino); at
Masaccio's perspective Trinity; or at Donatello's

and Michelozzo's tabernacle of Orsanmichele in Florence. Classical or Early Christian precedents are S. Salvatore at Spoleto and the so-called 'Temple of Clitumnus', which perhaps also lie behind the centralized plan, with an apse framed by columns, of S. Bernardino at Urbino. In the Cappella del Perdono, however, the vividness of the polychrome marble, which was new to Urbino, was part of an effort to underline the sculptural unity of the parts and to enrich the entire space with more colour, atmosphere and light, transforming it into a precious jewel-case. But above all the careful, resourceful use of light gives an illusionistic effect of depth to what is, in fact, a very small space; this is achieved by the dramatic rhythm of the rectangular panels on the walls and by the 'heroic' spectacle at the end of the room of a tiny apse made of porphyry, opening beyond the angle columns.

Brunelleschi had already transformed architecture from the medieval 'built' space to a logically controlled framework of visual structures. Alberti carried this further, so that the 'design' virtually _was_ the building. Now it was tending to become 'painting', the equivalent of a representation which was no longer merely _drawn_, delineated, but painted and coloured; the spectator was affected not just intellectually but also through the senses and the emotions, by means of colour, light, perspective and atmosphere. Leonardo, significantly, was drawn to this work at Urbino in 1502, and left a quick sketch of it (MS 'L', f.73v).

We do not know whether Bramante, as has been plausibly suggested by Rotondi, was the architect of these two chapels and in particular of the Cappella del Perdono; it seems very likely that the decorative parts were actually carried out by the Lombard Ambrogio Barocci. Bramante may have planned them, just as he may have planned S. Bernardino (though this seems much less likely). Certainly the two chapels are linked by certain characteristics which to some extent can be seen in later works by Bramante. Their differences may be the result of the fact that Ambrogio Barocci and Francesco di Giorgio, who carried out the detailed work, had entirely opposing tastes. One must remember that at this time of his life Bramante was putting forward architectural ideas, and at the same time designing and painting buildings in perspective, buildings which other artists later took up and occasionally reinterpreted: this may have happened in the Studiolo and in the Room of the Liberal Arts, in the Cappella del Perdono and perhaps in S. Bernardino. It may seem rather a wild hypothesis until

16 Urbino, Palazzo Ducale: Tempio delle Muse or Cappella di Apollo

we consider Bramante's exceptional skill in architectural and perspective painting, which all the sources confirm and which even his earliest work had shown; this ability also presupposes a definite capacity to plan. The way in which work was done by many artists together, in an atmosphere of active participation and collaboration, particularly in Central and Northern Italy in the second half of the fifteenth century, may also help to explain it. In any case, it was at least partly work of this kind that Bramante must have done in Lombardy and later in Rome; sometimes merely producing architectural drawings in perspective for painters (as was certainly the case with the Prevedari engraving), or, probably in charge of a team of assistants, making paintings from his own drawings. In the field of architecture itself, he quite often left a great deal to his assistants, and in Rome, working with a well-organized team, he would leave others to deal with details and the actual execution of the work, What he really cared about was the realization of his spatial plan, his 'invention' of the whole.

Chapter two

Lombardy: first works

ACCORDING to Marcantonio Michiel, writing in about 1525, Bramante in 1477 was working on the frescoes of the façade of the Palazzo del Podestà in Bergamo, then part of the Venetian Republic, under the orders of Sebastiano Badoer, praetor, and Giovanni Moro, prefect of the city. Bramante was now about thirty-three years old, and this is his first certain work.

We do not know why, after leaving Urbino, where Francesco di Giorgio had been appointed chief architect, he settled in Lombardy. He seems not to have gone to the capital, Milan, until later (the earliest mention of him there is in the autumn of 1481). According to Vasari he 'made his way to Lombardy, where he went now to one city, and now to another, working as best he could, but not on things of great cost or much credit, having as yet neither name nor reputation. For this reason he determined at least to see some noteworthy work, and betook himself to Milan, in order to see the Duomo' (which was still under construction): 'having studied that building and having come to know the engineers, he so took courage, that he resolved to devote himself to architecture.'

When Bramante arrived there, Lombardy was one of the most powerful and politically active states in Italy; but it was still only marginally involved with the new Renaissance architecture. In the previous thirty years, a number of Florentines, isolated in the hostile Lombard milieu, had produced works of remarkable interest and had provided a basis for the development of the new ideas in a context that socially, economically and politically was very different from that of Florence in the early fifteenth century. According to some biographers, Brunelleschi himself had been to Milan in 1431; he certainly was there in 1435; and Alberti spent some time there later. Echoes

of Brunelleschi can be found for the first time in Lombardy in the church of Villa a Castiglione Olona, finished in 1441. However, the first real products of the new Renaissance architecture reached Milan only after 1450, when Francesco Sforza, who ruled until 1466, seized the dukedom of Lombardy and established new political, financial and cultural links with Florence. In 1451, on the recommendation of Piero de' Medici, the Florentine architect and sculptor Antonio Averlino, known as Filarete, who had worked in Rome and had some knowledge of Antiquity, came to Milan. He returned in 1461 and stayed until 1469, working on the tower of the Castello Sforzesco at Porta Giovia, and serving for a time as chief architect of the cathedral. Here he produced his *Trattato,* in which he described the famous 'ideal' city of Sforzinda, named in honour of the Sforza family and filled with strange buildings, and his huge plan for the Ospedale Maggiore, first drawn up in 1465, which clearly shows the relations which existed between political power and architecture in Milan at the time. But the hospital was only partly built, and Filarete's design was greatly distorted in the process. His plan for the cathedral of Bergamo was also only partially carried out. Michelozzo, a favourite of the Medici family, reached Milan between 1462 and 1468 in order to build the Milanese branch of the Medici Bank, given by the Sforza family to Cosimo il Vecchio (only the doorway now survives). But Michelozzo's design, of which a sketch appears in Filarete's treatise, seems to have been strongly conditioned by local taste and altered in the course of building. The same thing happened with the chapel for Pigello Portinari (director of the Milanese branch of the Medici Bank) in S. Eustorgio, begun about 1462: it was probably designed by Michelozzo, but

17 Milan, S. Maria presso S. Satiro: the crossing and 'false choir' seen from the nave (see p. 37)

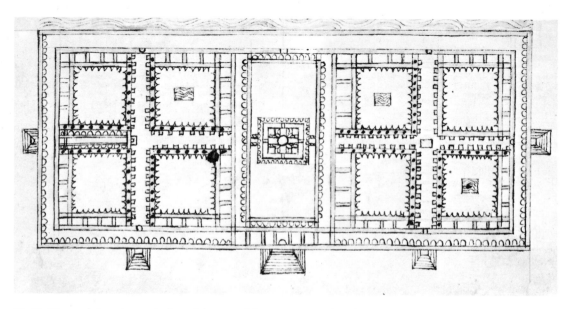

18, 19 Filarete: elevation and plan of the Ospedale Maggiore, Milan, from the *Trattato* (Florence, Biblioteca Nazionale Centrale, Codex Magliabechianus II.I.140, ff. 83v, 82v)

altered during construction to such an extent that it has also been attributed to Filarete. Other buildings with remarkably interesting plans, such as the church of S. Maria di Bresanoro, which seems to have been started in 1460, perhaps on a plan by Filarete, came to nothing or were again altered during construction. Another Florentine, Benedetto Ferrini, worked in Milan and in Pavia, but he had even less influence as an innovator than Filarete or Michelozzo.

In fact, until at least 1475–80 the now weary Lombard tradition – late Romanesque rather than distinctly Gothic – carried on by Giovanni Solari and then by his son Guiniforte held the field. This is clear in such major buildings as the Certosa at Pavia, Milan Cathedral, where work went on seemingly endlessly, and churches such as S. Pietro di Gessate (*c.* 1475) or S. Maria delle Grazie (begun in 1463 but completed only about 1490), the apse of which was later to be transformed by Bramante. It was the powerful defenders of local tradition, and their followers and colleagues, supported by conservative elements in the city, often against the prince's wishes, who gave fifteenth-century Milan its particular regional character.

Heir of the Solari family, since he was Guiniforte's son-in-law, was Giovanni Antonio Amadeo (1447–1522), sculptor, architect and engineer, who, especially after 1475–80, had a hand in nearly all the most important work in the dukedom. His Colleoni Chapel at Bergamo (planned, it would seem, shortly after 1470) is based on the Portinari Chapel in S. Eustorgio, but its exterior surfaces are given complex, over-abundant sculptural and polychrome decoration, rich in fanciful elements and motifs taken from various sources. The same characteristics appeared in nearly all Amadeo's works – for instance the façade of the Certosa at Pavia, which was built later – and created a style that was to dominate Lombardy in the last twenty years of the century and beyond. Amadeo also worked on buildings in which Bramante himself was to have a hand – such as the façade of S. Maria presso S. Satiro (not completed and later altered), the cathedral of Pavia, and the east end of S. Maria delle Grazie – giving them a Lombard flavour. However, Bramante was quite ready to collaborate with him and with other Lombard architects at the Sforza court, and to adapt himself, at least partly, to their taste. He may even have worked on the Colleoni Chapel and the nearby sacristy of S. Maria Maggiore at Bergamo, since so many of their decorative motifs turn up in his own early buildings. Besides, one of the elements of later fifteenth-century taste in Lombardy was the influence of Filarete, who, having been trained as a sculptor and being well able to adapt himself to local traditions, had produced ideas which, at least superficially, could easily be adopted by Lombard artists. Bramante must have made a careful study of Filarete's buildings and have read his *Trattato*, which contains volumetric and spatial schemes that were to appear later in his own work. A document of 1484 shows, in fact, that Bramante had made a drawing, probably an elevation, of Filarete's Ospedale Maggiore in Milan. This has led, perhaps mistakenly, to the suggestion that he drew the illustrations for the Marciana manuscript of the *Trattato* (Venice, Biblioteca Marciana, MS Lat. VIII, 2), dedicated to Matthias Corvinus and apparently executed in 1489.

Bramante's work in Bergamo in 1477 showed, however, that his links with Urbino were still close, although the frescoes on the Palazzo del Podestà have reached us in such poor condition that it is impossible to understand his intentions completely; only a few fragments remain, removed from their original wall. It is evident that he tried to shape and unify the front of the existing medieval buildings by painting on them a three-dimensional illusionistic architectural design with pillars and framed niches of

20 Milan, S. Eustorgio: Portinari Chapel, designed by Michelozzo (or Filarete?)

21 Bergamo, S. Maria Maggiore: Colleoni Chapel, by G. A. Amadeo

varying depth in which monumental figures of ancient philosophers, in the style of Melozzo, were placed. As if trying out the possibilities of this kind of representation, Bramante took the perspective tricks used at Urbino in interiors, and used them out of doors, on an urban scale. Painterly perspective was adapted as an *architectural* means of decorating the city in a humanistic way, to 'stage-manage', as it were, the urban setting. The same device was used later, possibly by Bramante himself, on the façade of Casa Fontana in Milan, and on the house-fronts in the piazza at Vigevano.

22

36
69

During his twenty-year period in Lombardy that followed his work in Bergamo, Bramante was frequently to make perspective drawings of buildings (both interiors and exteriors) which other painters inserted into their own compositions, with or without his permission. This kind of collaboration may have taken place in the frescoes of what is now the Casa Angelini in Bergamo (undated, but almost certainly a good deal later than 1477); or in Milan, where Bramante may have worked with the painter Donato Montorfano, first on the architectural backgrounds of the *Story of the Baptist* in

22, 23 Bergamo, Palazzo del Podestà: schematic reconstruction showing the position of Bramante's frescoes on the façade (below; from Förster), and fresco fragment showing the philosopher Chilon (Bergamo, Palazzo della Ragione)

S. Pietro di Gessate (c. 1480–85), and later in the Cappella Bolla of S. Maria delle Grazie (c. 1495) and the large *Crucifixion* (1495) which faces Leonardo's *Last Supper* in the refectory of the same convent. He may even have collaborated with Ambrogio Bergognone on the design for the architectural frescoes in the transept and main chapels of the Certosa at Pavia (1492–93 *et seq.*). Although the part he played in these works has not been documented, motifs quite clearly derived from Bramante and from Urbino appear in them. In this way he proved a potent influence on a wide range of artists in Lombardy, especially in their attitude to volume and space.

The early 1480s saw a decisive artistic renewal in Milan, coinciding with the rise of Ludovico il Moro to absolute power. Ludovico was unopposed ruler of the dukedom of Milan from 1480 to 1499 and made it one of the largest and richest cities of Europe (with a population of 300,000). He had been educated by the humanist Francesco Filelfo, and from 1471 he had been in touch with the new Renaissance ideas of Florence, Mantua, Padua and Venice; in 1476 he had lived in France, then at Pisa. His court became the meeting place for artists and men of culture from the whole of Italy; his policy, in which he was often supported by his brother Ascanio, Bishop of Pavia and later Vice-Chancellor of the Roman Church, needed art and, to an even greater extent, architecture as a means of political propaganda and as an affirmation of his riches and power. Of this campaign Bramante and Leonardo da Vinci – both from outside Lombardy – became the effective leaders.

We have already noted some features of the Lombard scene that would have interested Bramante – the surviving Romanesque-Gothic tradition, the work on the cathedral, where French and German Gothic masons were working along with Italians, and the occasional signs of Florentine influence. But above all, as Murray in particular has pointed out, an artist like Bramante must have been particularly attracted by the Late Antique buildings which still survived in the city.[11] Through artists and men of letters at the court of Urbino, perhaps through Alberti himself and Mantegna, he had been brought up in the cult of Antiquity, of an ancient world that was more dreamed about and longed for than actually known. Murray also suggests that Bramante's interest seems to recall imperial Milan in the days of Theodosius, Ambrose and Augustine: perhaps, after the advent of Ludovico il Moro, there may even have been a touch of political interest in this. But no firm distinction was

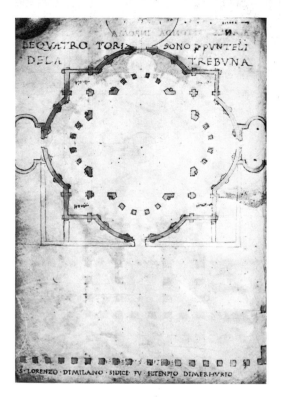

24 Milan, S. Lorenzo: plan, drawn by Giuliano da Sangallo (Siena, Biblioteca Comunale, Sangallo Sketchbook, f. 18v)

made between what was genuinely Classical and what was Late Roman or Hellenistic. Late Roman buildings such as S. Salvatore at Spoleto and the Temple of Clitumnus had been imitated at Urbino in the Cappella del Perdono and in S. Bernardino. Bramante's 'Classical' interest went even further: as far as Carolingian works of the time of Bishop Anspert (ninth century, but, as Cesariano shows, thought to be ancient). Churches such as S. Lorenzo in Milan, from the end of the fourth century, with its adjoining chapels, and the Carolingian S. Satiro (also studied by Leonardo) were to remain a fundamental part of Bramante's experience, even later and even in Rome. Even after he had acquired a first-hand knowledge of 'true' Roman Antiquities, he tended to see them and to interpret them above all in the spatial terms of the Late Antique.

Late Antique and Byzantine-Carolingian space, translated into Renaissance terms, is recalled by the image in the famous print 'cum hedifitijs et figuris', which, according to a document of 24 October 1481, the Milanese

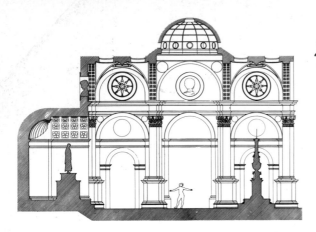

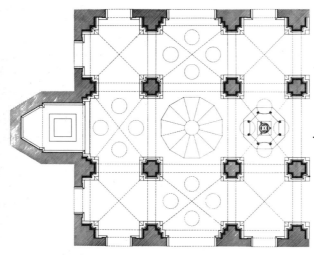

25 Reconstruction of the elevation and plan of the architecture in the engraving *Ruined Temple*, opposite (drawn by G. C. Miletti)

engraver Bernardo Prevedari, commissioned by 26 the painter Matteo Fedeli, agreed to 'fabbricare . . . secundum designum in papiro factum per magistrum Bramantem de Urbino'. This is Bramante's first documented work and the first definite evidence of his presence in Milan; although it is likely that he had been there, and probably working on the church of S. Maria presso S. Satiro, as early as 1478–79.

Prevedari's engraving, *Ruined Temple*, is a 25, perspective representation of a real architectural 26 scheme, each part set down in precise order, and with both plan and elevation exactly defined. It is probably the most advanced example of Renaissance architecture around 1480, a demonstration of Bramante's principles and of the direction in which he was moving at the start of his Milanese career. What is shown in this engraving is essentially a variant of the architectural scheme known as the cross inscribed in a square: a building with a central dome and four arms of equal length forming a cross is inscribed in a square perimeter (for the symbolic significance of this design, see p. 148; however, as Metternich points out,[12] the arm opposite the apse might be extended to form an aisled nave, producing a longitudinal building). This is the spatial theme that was to excite Bramante for the whole of his life, from his 154 time in Milan to that in Rome – to St Peter's, 166 S. Celso, and the church of Roccaverano. 167

In the 1521 commentary on Vitruvius by Cesariano, a pupil of Bramante, designs very similar to that in the engraving appear as illustrations exemplifying the types of Antique temples described by Vitruvius. In the *Ruined Temple*, however, we also find a pillar resembling a candelabrum surmounted by a cross. This makes one think that Bramante – probably as a theoretical exercise – wanted to show an Antique temple (the sculptured figures in the building seem to be pagan) which has partly fallen into ruin and has been adapted as a Christian church, as if to indicate, as in the Studiolo and the chapels at Urbino, the continuity and concord between the pagan and Christian worlds.

We know, however, that the inscribed cross design is not pagan but late Byzantine in origin. In Milan, as elsewhere in the West, it had been introduced around 868, in the chapel of S. Satiro (adjacent to Bramante's church of S. 28 Maria). In the fifteenth century, a building of this type, seen from the outside, had appeared on a silver plaque (now in the Louvre) attributed by some to Brunelleschi, and certainly known to Michelozzo and in particular to Filarete, who used it in some of the designs in his *Trattato*.

26 Bernardo Prevedari after Bramante: *Ruined Temple*, engraving (London, British Museum)

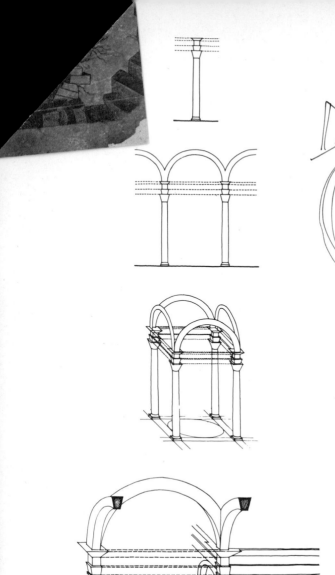

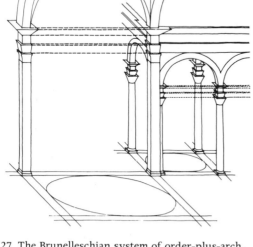

Bramante may have known some of the latter; and he may have remembered some medieval churches in the Marche whose plans were not unlike that of the building shown in the engraving. But he produced a very up-to-date version of them, using the vocabulary of Brunelleschi and Alberti.

In his revolutionary attempt to establish a 'new' and 'scientific' style for architecture, Brunelleschi had found in the Classical orders and in the semi-circular arch – understood as elements that could be standardized and pre-determined in form and proportion – the basic elements for the structure of every building. The *order-plus-arch* had to appear visually as 27 the basic structural element of each spatial entity or module (mostly based on the cube or on solid forms that could be reduced to it), the totality of which formed the building. When Brunelleschi was faced with the problem (which arose in S. Lorenzo and in S. Spirito, for instance) of linking two spatial entities that were sub-stantially similar but of different dimensions (such as the vaulted bays of the aisles and the large dome over the crossing), he reduced the problem to one of connecting in a strictly syntactical way, or as it were of interlocking, two similar order-plus-arch systems of different dimensions, linking them in such a way as to make the upper entablature of the smaller system (the arcade arches) correspond to the moulding at capital level of the larger (the crossing arches) – a solution perhaps suggested to him by medieval buildings like S. Miniato al Monte, which he believed to be Antique. This method of connecting two order-plus-arch systems of different dimensions, used by Brunel-leschi especially when he treated space in a three-dimensional perspective way, could also be used two-dimensionally to define a surface or a façade. It was thus used by Alberti, for instance, in the façades of S. Maria Novella in Florence and S. Andrea in Mantua. Alberti used it three-dimensionally, and less surely, in the internal structuring of S. Andrea, in an attempt to link the minor spaces of the chapels with those of the nave and cupola. This way of rationalizing, in perspective and proportion, a plan of Byzantine/medieval origin such as that of the inscribed cross, reducing it to a hier-archical and interconnected set of syntactically correlated spaces of varying sizes, is used in the building shown in the Prevedari engraving. 25 There are three order-plus-arch systems of different sizes, and these serve to articulate the three different types of space which appear in the design: that of the cupola and of the four arms of the cross; that of the four corner spaces;

27 The Brunelleschian system of order-plus-arch, shown in two dimensions, in three dimensions, and as a means of coordinating elements of differing sizes: in the lowest diagram, the entablature above the arches of the small arcade is also the entablature of the larger order.

and that of the voids which open into these spaces.

Brunelleschi's method of coordinating and controlling every space by its relation to the whole is here tested and taken as far as it will go, expanded into a 'universal' method, by which the building could be arranged three-dimensionally as a rhythmic, complex spatial *macchina* or 'mechanism' (and by applying the same formula to exteriors, a volumetric *macchina* too), in a way which was quite new in 1481, and entirely Bramante's own.

Seen in this way, the Prevedari engraving becomes an attempt to construct architecture in terms of painting, to make a predominantly visual image dynamically active in space. One must also see it in its historical context. The building shown in the Prevedari engraving represents a broadening of Renaissance experience, for it is the product of a complex series of historical influences. A Byzantine plan, already reinterpreted in the West by the Romanesque, is rationalized, and, through the Brunelleschian vision of the order and the arch, turned into a linked and logical grouping of spaces. It is an up-dating and a combination of two contrasting architectural philosophies: Brunelleschi's arcade of columns, seen as a series of separate, shaped members, and Alberti's arcade of piers, seen as a solid wall with openings. The wall is not denied or disguised, but is integrated into the framework of arches, so that the whole structure (in a way that recalls Romanesque and Gothic buildings) becomes as tense and springy as one of Pollaiuolo's nudes.[13] Thus what Alberti had suggested in his *De re aedificatoria*, but had never put into practice successfully (being preoccupied with the problem of absolute, abstract proportions which could be expressed only theoretically, in two dimensions), had come into being, although only in an interior. Here one sees the building conceived as a living body in which 'each limb belongs to the whole', in which each part is strictly linked to the other parts and related to the whole in an absolute identity, as Argan put it, 'between the plastic quality of the form and its structural function'. Bramante was to develop this later, and eventually, in Rome, to find fully successful means of expressing it.

Parallels with Urbino are not difficult to find. The relationship between buildings and figures recalls the panels of the *Nicchia di S. Bernardino* at Perugia. The use of a twelve-sided cupola without a drum is possibly derived from an illustration in Piero della Francesca's *De prospectiva pingendi* or the *Reading*, then at Urbino. But the insertion of oculi at the base of the cupola goes back to Early Christian and Byzantine examples. The Corinthian capital divided into two parts, so typical of Bramante, with a band of interlace placed between the foliage and the shaft, seems to allude to the Vitruvian legend of the origin of the Corinthian capital as a bunch of acanthus leaves growing out of a basket, but it also goes back directly to medieval examples like the capitals of the canopy above the high altar in S. Ambrogio in Milan. There is a hint of Gothic, and also of Piero della Francesca, in the pendant boss in the centre of the crossing, and of Ravenna (or of the Tempio Malatestiano at Rimini) in the decorated plinth below the pedestals; there is a hint of Ferrara in the character of certain figures, and in the taste for figurative ornament showing scenes in a continuous sequence (found also, however, in the chimney-piece 'della Jole' at Urbino), and of Padua in some decorative details, such as the busts of heroes set in medallions. Mantegna's example probably suggested the particular way of distributing the light dramatically and of using strong shadows to show up both the sculptural form of the structural elements and their function as dynamically active agents in the formation of space. But the multiplication of structures seen through other structures, and the energetic use of these secondary, decorative structures in continuous curvilinear forms varying in size and brought to life by the light, is entirely Bramante's. So is the hard, almost metallic way in which the forms stand out, rather as they do in his paintings. Renaissance architecture had never before fused so completely the methods used by the painter and the architect. Nothing so rich in memories and past experiences, and at the same time so new and personal, had yet appeared.

The Prevedari engraving, however, really belongs to no definite tradition or Renaissance 'school': Bramante was an isolated character, a wanderer uprooted from his original background. He had no master, he followed no tradition. In Milan he was an outsider, and basically he was to be so in Rome as well. Although he seemed able to respond to what the society he worked in might ask of him, although he seemed receptive to his colleagues' tastes, and even to collaboration with his helpers and with those who carried out his ideas, he was never really integrated into the world he lived in, but always faithful to himself – not so much to a single, limited ideal of expression as to his restless longing to know, to experiment, and to test the truth. His strength lay in this very detachment from tradition, in this optimistic openness

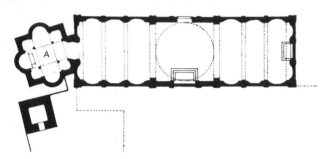

28 Milan, S. Maria presso S. Satiro: conjectural plan of the long, narrow chapel probably originally planned as an extension to the Carolingian S. Satiro (A, shown in its original state). The entrance was on Via del Falcone, at the top.

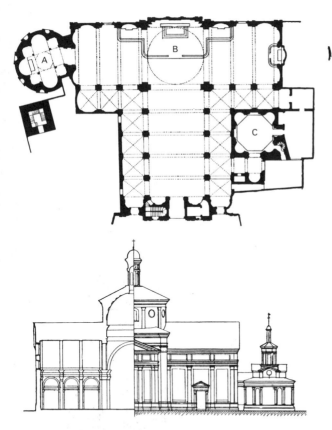

29, 30 Milan, S. Maria presso S. Satiro: plan of the church as built, and section and elevation of the transept arm as seen from Via del Falcone (top, in the plan). A S. Satiro, in its remodelled form (compare Ill. 28), B crossing in front of the 'false choir' (Ills. 17, 31), C sacristy (Ill. 33)

to all kinds of stimuli: it allowed him to recover and bring out the lost values of history, it gave him critical detachment, and the chance of changing himself, of adapting himself continually to all kinds of surroundings; it gave him the capacity to take a vast and varied range of experiences as far as they would go and to test their possibilities. This gave him an advantage over the other great architects of his day, at a time of transition and crisis, and in the particular historical conditions in which he found himself: over Francesco di Giorgio and even more over the man who was to be his most cultivated, most gifted rival in Rome, Giuliano da Sangallo.

To Bramante, then, the methods of the painter and the architect were interchangeable: essentially, architecture became 'painting', a visual fact, a representation complete in itself. He had achieved it on paper. It was time to test it against reality. The first building which he actually put up, in which for the first time he applied the principles of perspective illusionism to a large structure, was the eastern part of S. Maria presso S. Satiro.

In spite of a wealth of surviving documents, the early stages of the building of the church of S. Maria presso S. Satiro are not known with absolute certainty. Most probably what was wanted at the start was a large chapel or a small church beside the Carolingian chapel of S. Satiro, and opening on to Via del Falcone. The documents at first mention a chapel, already started before 1478, not a church; and the way in which it was built suggests the same thing. This chapel would correspond to the transept of the present church. It was only later, probably about 1480–81, that it was decided to enlarge the building, change its orientation, add the nave and aisles, and put the main entrance on the side opposite Via del Falcone, facing the Contrada di S. Maria Bertrade (now Via Torino). Bramante's name only appears for the first time on a document of December 1482, as a witness to the purchase of a piece of land necessary for this plan to be carried out; but it seems likely that he had already been working on it, possibly since 1480 (although his name is not included on a list of engineers working in Milan in May 1480), and that he may have planned not only the church in its final form but also the original chapel and, certainly, its details and decoration. It is significant that in plan this chapel (the present transept) follows Brunelleschi's Pazzi Chapel, though with different relationships between its parts: an oblong space with an opening in one of the long sides (here on Via del Falcone), consisting of a central cube,

17, 29– 34

28

29

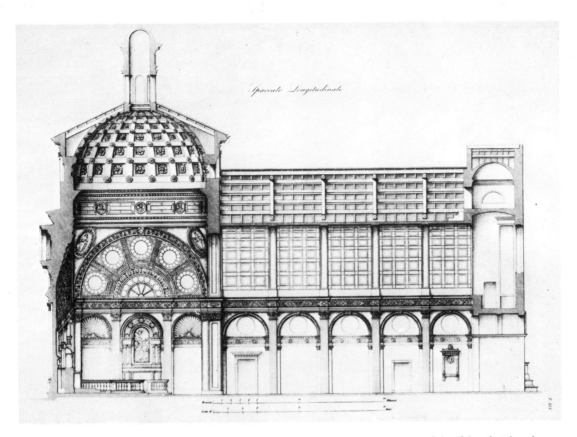

31 Milan, S. Maria presso S. Satiro: cross section, showing the shallow projection of the 'false choir' at the far left. Here the entablature and capitals are steeply raked down to create an effect of depth (see Ill. 17). Just left of centre is the transept aisle, leading to a doorway. (F. Cassina, *Le fabbriche più cospicue di Milano*, 1840–64)

covered by a dome on pendentives, flanked by two spaces covered by barrel vaults. Brunelleschi is also recalled in a very remarkable way by the use of pilasters 'bent' asymmetrically to turn the re-entrant corners: an unconventional solution which appears, as far as I know, only in the Pazzi Chapel and here, and shows not only knowledge of Brunelleschi's work but a profound understanding of it. Here too, as in the Prevedari engraving, there is an effort to update Brunelleschi in the light of Bramante's own more 'modern' experiences (for instance, by putting niches around the perimeter, as in S. Spirito) or in the light of Alberti's late work in Mantua (for instance, by using a heavy, Roman-style cupola and, on the walls, the Roman scheme of the arch framed by an order).

It would seem that when the time came for the church to be enlarged it was again Brunelleschi's example that suggested the plan of the whole. The site available, on the side opposite to Via 29 del Falcone, demanded a plan in the shape of the

letter T. But Bramante was obsessed by the idea of central planning, and must, as Chierici has pointed out,[14] have had Brunelleschi's S. Spirito in mind: a cruciform plan, with a cupola over the crossing, and aisles running completely round the church. If the shape of the site did not allow building on all sides of the existing structure, then it would have to be completed illusionistically. The nave as built, together with the aisles which continue along only one side of the transept, would be impossible to understand if it did not set itself up as the first stage of an illusionistic enlargement of the physical space into a further space beyond the transept – which in fact is not there at all but only seems to be. If the 'fourth arm' – that of the choir, which should have been the logical end of the vista – could not be built, it would be represented in 17, low relief to simulate a non-existent recession; 31 and if there was no room for aisles matching those built along one side of the transept, then 29, niches on the other side would suggest their 32

32 Milan, S. Maria presso S. Satiro: view of the transept from the nave. Niches on the altar wall, on the left, balance the bays of the aisle on the right.

33 Milan, S. Maria presso S. Satiro: detail of the sacristy

presence. The methods of perspective illusionism, applied not merely to the four walls of a room but to a complex building, could make the impossible seem real. As in the Prevedari engraving, and again in Brunelleschi's S. Lorenzo and S. Spirito, it recalls the method of coordinating parts and spaces through two systems of order-plus-arch of different dimensions fitted into each other; even if Brunelleschi's system is here modified by the example of Alberti, and expressed with a Roman gravity in its proportions. There is also, particularly in the perspective arrangement of the arm of the church beyond the cupola – the so-called 'false choir' – a hint of Piero della Francesca's Brera Altarpiece and possibly also of S. Andrea in Mantua. And, as in the Prevedari engraving, there are suggestions of Late Antique and Romanesque architecture, associated with ideas from Padua and from Mantegna, which treat perspective space (no longer expressed only through a linear 'rational' design) in a very special way. Light, colour and decoration come together to unite the various influences, and above all to fuse the real and the unreal, the space that is built and the space that is merely represented, into a single arresting image.

The sacristy of the church, a centrally planned, octagonal, well-lit building, fairly lofty in order to take its windows above the surrounding roofs, shows the influence of the Late Antique (such as the chapels which were attached to S. Lorenzo in Milan) and of Romanesque. It is enriched by complex, exuberant sculptural ornament in the Paduan manner executed in 1483 by Agostino de Fondutis, a Paduan follower of Mantegna, with, according to some, Bramante's direct participation.

Bramante's restoration of the old chapel of S. Satiro, completed, like the church, by about 1483, clearly shows the additional influence of Brunelleschi's unfinished S. Maria degli Angeli, especially in the cylindrical lower part, where the thick wall is cut into on the outside by niches, just as it is inside by the apses of the original medieval structure.

By the spring of 1483 the internal walls of the church must have been substantially finished. Decoration continued during the following years, probably interrupted by the plague of 1484–85. In September 1486, Giovanni Antonio Amadeo made a coloured marble façade on the instructions of Bramante ('fatiatam marmoream de illis coloribus quibus videtur magistro Donato de Urbino dicto Bramante'): the lower part and some fragments of this survive, behind the present late nineteenth-century façade, and suggest quite an original design.

34 Milan, S. Maria presso S. Satiro: view along the façade on Via del Falcone, with S. Satiro in the foreground. (Compare Ill. 30, and see p. 43.)

In about 1482 Leonardo da Vinci arrived at the Sforza court. (In the summer of 1481 he was still in Florence; in April 1483 he was certainly in Milan.) Bramante and he must soon have known each other, but it seems very unlikely that it was Leonardo who was responsible for the influence of Brunelleschi in Bramante's early work in Milan – an influence that is quite unmistakable although expressed in a wholly original way – even though the plan of S. Spirito and that of S. Maria degli Angeli were later to be sketched by Leonardo, and to appear, among many other architectural drawings, in MS 'B',

f.11v. The probable explanation is that Bramante visited Florence in the years before he came to Lombardy.

In the meantime, however, he did not give up perspective painting, used, as it had been in the Studiolo at Urbino, as a means of dealing architecturally with interior space. The frescoes from Casa Panigarola in Milan (fragments of which survive in the Brera) may belong to this period, 1480–85. Here, a room that is more or less square is visually transformed, merely by adding painted semi-circular niches decorated with pilasters and containing heroic martial figures:

10

35, 37– 39

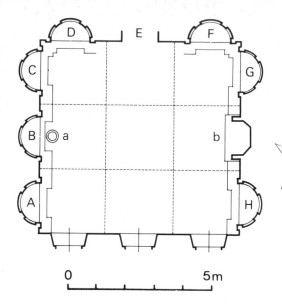

35 Milan, Casa Panigarola: diagram of the space represented illusionistically in the painted room. A *Youth holding a Mace* (Ill. 38), B *Man with a large Sword* (Ill. 39), C *Man at Arms,* D *Singer,* E *Heraclitus and Democritus,* above the door (Ill. 37), F *Man crowned with Laurels,* G *Youth with a Lance,* H *Youth wearing a Breastplate, a* basin, *b* fireplace

real men, contemporary figures, at once realistic and perhaps subtly ironic, dressed in a way that is both Antique and modern, as in one of the many courtly banquets in Milan under the Sforzas. Heraclitus and Democritus, on either 37 side of a globe – personifications, according to Marsilio Ficino, of tears and laughter – are painted above the entrance to the room, cleverly seeming to warn us that life is much more real, complex and contradictory than any artistic 'fiction', and recalling the sly gaiety that makes some of the sonnets Bramante composed during his time in Lombardy so alive.

The way the room's cross axes are emphasized by the presence, real or represented, of particular architectural elements is worth noting because it shows that to Bramante even a minor work of this kind was a chance to experiment with space. As a method of organizing a centrally planned space it had already appeared embryonically in the two arms of the transept of S. Maria presso S. Satiro, with their curved 31, niches and blank rectangular spaces with doors 32 in them, and it is found, too, in the painted façade of Casa Fontana in Milan, attributed to 36 Bramante and probably belonging to these years. There the axis of the entrance is particularly emphasized, not only by the porch, but by the painted figures of giants above, completely contradicting the scheme with superimposed orders which Alberti had worked out for the Palazzo Rucellai in Florence.

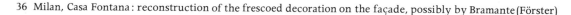

36 Milan, Casa Fontana : reconstruction of the frescoed decoration on the façade, possibly by Bramante (Förster)

37–39 Milan, Casa
Panigarola: frescoes formerly
decorating the painted room
(see Ill. 35). Above,
Heraclitus and Democritus;
below left, *Youth holding a
Mace*; below right, *Man
with a large Sword* (Milan,
Brera)

Chapter three

The creation of the 'organic' building

LEONARDO'S presence in Milan, and the fact that he was probably often in contact with Bramante at the Sforza court, explains at least to some extent why Bramante's work took such a great leap forward after 1488. After Urbino and contact with the school of Mantegna, he had been seeking an architecture that was essentially pictorial and theatrical; now, although he did not give up his 'illusionistic' vision – indeed, he made it more delicate and mature – or his interest in the visual and the spectacular, he saw the building as a *macchina,* or 'mechanism', a three-dimensional structure organically arranged in relation to the technical problems of building.

26   As the Prevedari engraving showed, he had already envisaged the interior space as being
17   organically structured; the interior of S. Maria presso S. Satiro, considered as a visual whole – partly built and partly only represented pictorially – also shows this, less richly and less inventively but perhaps more impressively. Bramante's effort to express the values of the interior through the arrangement of the volumes and surfaces of the exterior is seen, for instance,
30,   in the façade of S. Maria on Via del Falcone,
34   through the combination of two orders of differing dimensions: the lesser corresponds, ideally, to the interior order on which the vaults and arches of the cupola rest; the other, to the cube on which rests the hemispherical shell of the cupola itself. And this attempt to express the three-dimensional quality of the volume is emphasized by the way in which Bramante treated the corners, one that was to become quite usual in his work. The result was not successful, however, partly because of the site of the church, choked as it was in a network of surrounding streets, but mainly because of its own partly 'illusionistic' arrangement. The only way in

which Bramante could solve the problem of the exterior was by treating it not as an organic whole but as a series of separate features seen from these streets: the tall cylindrical cupola, which recalls that of the Portinari Chapel at 20 S. Eustorgio; the side on Via del Falcone (the only fully exposed side), which has the 'false choir' behind it; the isolated volume of the chapel of S. Satiro; and the tall narrow façade in front of the nave, which, as in S. Andrea at Mantua, had to occupy only the central part of the building and which seems to have been crowned by a sort of aedicule in the wall with twin openings, probably placed there to allow the cupola to be seen from the Contrada di S. Maria Bertrade (Via Torino).

    At that time, in the years before 1488–90, Leonardo was developing new methods of representing three-dimensional objects so as to convey the maximum information about them. These methods started from his interest in the study of anatomy, and his anatomical drawings tend to show the human body as a 'mechanism', a system of limbs organically related to one another both functionally and mechanically. Transferred to architecture, this method of representation is used in many of Leonardo's sketches involving perspective bird's eye views, 41– which, with the help of a plan or sometimes 43 combining plan, section and exterior, elucidate the structural organization of volume and space: in this way they not only give complex information about the building's three-dimensional form but, above all, help to produce an idea of architecture that rejects the traditional distinction between 'design' (on one plane) and 'structure' (in three dimensions). Leonardo went beyond the old forms of conventional representation, consisting of plan, elevation or perspective views at ground level. The very

40 Milan, S. Maria delle Grazie: crossing dome (below) and umbrella dome over the choir (see p. 56)

43

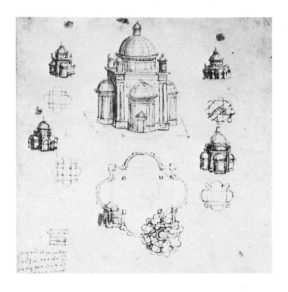

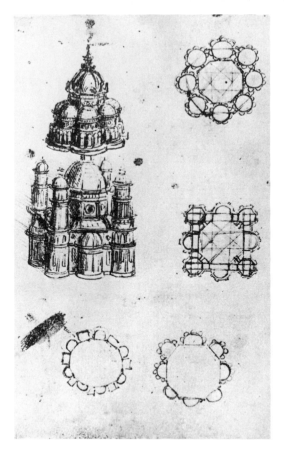

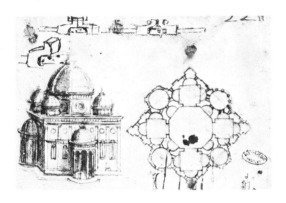

41–43 Leonardo da Vinci: sketches on the theme of centrally planned churches (Paris, Institut de France, MS 'B', ff. 3v, 22, 25v)

analogy between the building and the human body – taken up by all the theorists following Vitruvius – tended to make Leonardo and Bramante think of all works of architecture as organic three-dimensional bodies in which each limb was part of the complete spatio-structural organism.[15]

Leonardo's interest in architecture increased after 1487, when he worked on the *tiburio* of the cathedral in Milan. It is apparent, around 1490, in the many drawings in MS 'B' which, as Heydenreich has suggested, were probably done as explanatory illustrations for a treatise on architecture. Leonardo was above all concerned to investigate engineering problems, and to demonstrate, almost didactically, and with copious arguments, the possibility of using spatial or volumetric units in a variety of more or less elementary combinations, to form organic wholes, complex and articulated central-space

structures. By 1490, structures not unlike those of Bramante's St Peter's or S. Maria della Consolazione at Todi had appeared among Leonardo's sketches. The models which influenced him were the same as those which inspired Bramante: Brunelleschi's S. Spirito and S. Maria degli Angeli in Florence, S. Lorenzo and S. Satiro in Milan, S. Maria in Pertica at Pavia, etc.; although naturally Leonardo had stronger and more frequent memories of Florentine buildings, like the Baptistery, or the Rotunda of SS. Annunziata. As we have seen, the idea of the building as a complex, three-dimensional spatial mechanism had already been foreshadowed in the Prevedari engraving. It is quite likely that it was Bramante who brought Leonardo to this new way of conceiving architecture; and Leonardo in his turn may have persuaded Bramante to reconsider his position as a pure perspective painter rather than a real architect and

41–
44

149
154
170

24
28

25,
26

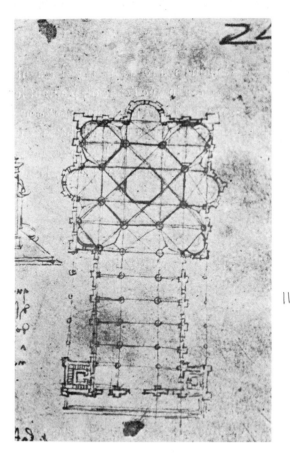

44 Leonardo da Vinci: design for a church with centrally planned east end and long nave (compare Ill. 46) (Paris, Institut de France, MS 'B', f. 24)

'engineer' – to look at the relationship between space, volume and construction in a new, truly three-dimensional way.

Contacts and exchanges between the two men, as A. M. Brizio in particular has shown, seem to have become especially close in 1487–88.[16] They probably began over the perennial problem which aroused passionate arguments in Milan, the *tiburio* or crossing tower of the cathedral. Both Leonardo and Bramante (and indeed many others between 1487 and 1490) had put forward proposals for it. Leonardo had been particularly interested in the engineering and technical problems, which he had been able to define, as he explained in a sketch in a letter to those responsible for the cathedral building, through a careful scientific investigation.[17] His proposed solution was for an octagon with a dome that had a double extrados: it is known through several of his sketches, and, although

there are hints of the Gothic in it, its model is substantially Brunelleschi's dome of Florence Cathedral and its essence is structural ingenuity. The solution proposed by Bramante, on the other hand, seems to have been unexpectedly for a square plan, possibly covered with a single large cross vault of slightly pointed section, of the kind illustrated by his pupil Cesariano in some drawings of Milan Cathedral inserted in his commentary on Vitruvius. Bramante also left (and there is no reason to deny his authorship) an *opinio* or report on the problems of the *tiburio* and on the projects proposed by various artists; it was probably written in 1490 and is the only theoretical piece of writing of his that has come down to us.[18] He maintains that the *tiburio* must satisfy four requirements: it must have *strength* or solidity and static efficiency, it must *conform* or adhere to the organic plan of the building, which had already been started, it must have *lightness* and it must have *beauty*. *Conformità*, a term and concept which he derived from Alberti, is the fundamental requirement from which the other three are really derived. For Bramante, it meant the need for making the structure not simply outwardly Gothic – if it was just a matter of 'ornament', he said, the problem would easily be solved – but Gothic in the sense that it obeyed the same laws of composition and proportion of the parts as those followed by the building's first architect, laws which he defines and analyses critically.

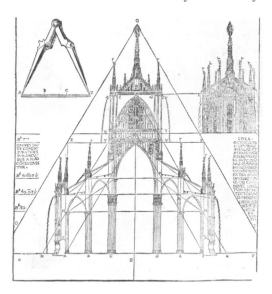

45 Milan Cathedral: theoretical section and detail of the *tiburio*, by Cesariano, perhaps reflecting Bramante's design for the *tiburio* (*Di . . . Vitruvio . . . de Architectura*, 1521)

Strength and *conformity* tend, therefore, to coincide with the unity of the spatio-structural organism, assured by fidelity to the *primo ordine,* the original laws of composition which produce the design, determining its construction, its geometry and its proportion. The close interdependence between *strength* and *conformity* is emphasized several times in the *opinio;* and with a humanistic faith in the unity of the real, in the secret *correspondentie* between the laws that regulate the cosmos, he also connects *lightness* and even *beauty* (which shows itself, above all, in numerical proportions like those of the medieval cathedral) closely with strength and conformity. Any judgment on the plans presented, working on the basis of these parameters, will not, therefore, be arbitrary, but, as Alberti wished it to be, made with 'certainty and reason'; and Bramante's proposal for a dome or cross vault on a square base was the best answer to the theoretical requirements. (Although he was now probably out of the running, he judged the various plans with impartiality, good sense and responsible realism.)

The schemes of Bramante and Leonardo, like those of the other competitors, were definitely turned down in June 1490 in favour of Amadeo's more traditional solution which had already been approved in 1489 but was now partly altered by Francesco di Giorgio, called to Milan with Luca Fancelli expressly for the purpose. Immediately, before the end of the month, Francesco di Giorgio and Leonardo left Milan together on horseback, lodged at the 'Saracino' Inn, and went on to Pavia *pro consultatione* on problems relating to the fabric of the cathedral there.

46– The story of Pavia Cathedral had begun only
53 two years before. After a first project, made, it would seem, by Cristoforo de Rocchi, *magister a lignamine* (who seems to have been inspired by S. Sophia in Constantinople, known roughly from drawings), and modified by Amadeo, the first stone was laid on 29 June 1488; but because of quarrels between Amadeo and de Rocchi, Bramante was called in in August of the same year to make a *certum designum seu planum* for the new building. Bramante, indeed, would appear to have been mainly responsible for the project: in the document settling this decision his name appears first, and in December 1488 we know that he went to Pavia again and stayed there for several days.[19] Later, Amadeo appears as the 'chief engineer' of the work, and still later others intervened, especially after 1495, partly altering the original plan. In 1490 the building must already have been started, following this original plan; and the brief intervention

of Leonardo, who must nevertheless have been concerned, and of Francesco di Giorgio, can have had very little effect. In its general conception, Pavia Cathedral makes use of no specific Leonardesque solutions, but it undoubtedly 41–
reflects the attitude expressed in his sketches. 44

In the years after 1495, when Bramante no longer appears in the documents, and after the death of Cristoforo de Rocchi, the new *magister a lignamine* Giovanni Pietro Fugazza made a large model of the church, which has survived. 48,
The design is by Amadeo, Gian Giacomo Dolce- 50
buono and Fugazza himself, but it incorporates the part which had already been built under Bramante's supervision. At least the plan of the 46,
whole, the crypt, the lower part of the apse and 50,
sacristies, substantially the same in the model 52,
and in the actual building, must go back to the 53
first scheme, which was mainly his; this is also very likely in other parts of the model which correspond to Bramante's ideas. Although at first sight it may seem surprising, here too – as we have already seen at S. Maria presso S. Satiro – the basic design must have been suggested by Brunelleschi's S. Spirito, to which the plan corresponds in its general geometry and in 47
particular points of detail, such as the series of apsed chapels. The sacristies, too, remind one not so much of Roman buildings as of the Rotunda of SS. Annunziata in Florence and perhaps, in elevation, of elements in S. Maria degli Angeli. The geometry of S. Spirito, however, has been modified, partly by treating the walls in Albertian terms, partly by incorporating ideas from Milan Cathedral, with the result that the centralized nature of the plan and the preeminence, in terms of space and volume, of the sanctuary are emphasized. One is reminded of Florence Cathedral or, even more, of the sanctuary of Loreto which Bramante must have known.

Thus we have a church with a 'composite' 46,
plan (of the sort that also intrigued Francesco di 48
Giorgio), made up of a large eastern part with an octagonal nucleus covered by a dome, and a western part with nave and aisles. The eastern part, as at S. Spirito, is based on a square, each 47
side of which is equal to the entire width of nave and aisles. Within the square, Brunelleschi's small dome resting on four piers is replaced by a large unequal-sided octagon. Logically and boldly tied in with the surround- 49–
ing structure, the octagon rests on what seem to 51
be eight separate piers, but which in effect are four massive supports at the diagonals, each consisting of three piers linked by arches to make 51
up, on plan, an isosceles triangle, which can be seen as a single member, hollowed out and articulated – a sort of trial run or preliminary

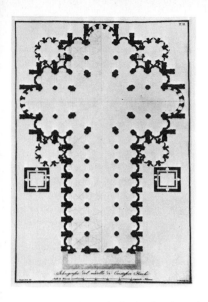
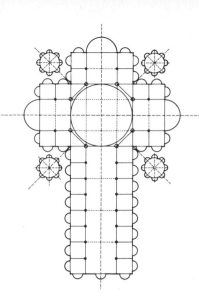
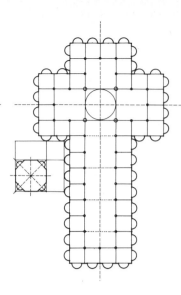

46, 47 Pavia Cathedral: plan based on the model (from Malaspina di Sannazaro), and geometrical analysis of that plan compared with Brunelleschi's S. Spirito in Florence

48 Pavia Cathedral: wooden model, made after Bramante's departure but reflecting his design in the plan and the lower part of the east end (Pavia, Museo del Castello)

sketch for the great piers of St Peter's. The
octagon, with its immense dome, brings a dynamic element into the heart of the building; an
element that challenges and destroys from within the regular arrangement of the Florentine
prototype, introduces a luminous space and
volume that overflows its geometrical limitations and spreads into nave, aisles, apses and
chapels with an irresistible centrifugal impulse.
As its energy gradually recedes, it models the
forms, throwing them into relief, but at the
same time merging them together and drowning
in what Baroni has called 'unreal northern
mistiness'. The completed work, therefore,
seems at first to embody 'Gothic' qualities, but
soon spatial values from the Late Antique world
also emerge, suggested by S. Lorenzo in Milan
and other examples of the kind.

Emotionally, one is immediately involved in
this 'spectacle' within the church; but the

154,
160
49,
51

24

Pavia Cathedral

49 Interior, looking from the choir to the nave

50 Interior of the model, looking towards the apse
which is shown in its original state (Pavia, Museo
del Castello)

51 Looking up in one of the tripartite piers that
support the dome

Brunelleschian method means that the building as a whole is well controlled. The use of at least three (or, in the original scheme, possibly four) systems of order-plus-arch, syntactically coordinated with one another, means that the spaces of varying size which form the whole are rigorously linked: the dome, the nave, the transepts and sanctuary, and the chapels. And the architectural order, which has again become a constructive bearing framework, is still, as far as the exterior is concerned, the basic element in a new structural arrangement of the building. Those who came after Bramante certainly made a good many changes in both the model and the building itself. However, both show that the traditional dichotomy between walls and architectural orders, between the physical construction and the *disegno,* between internal space and external volume, is here overcome through the concept of a spatio-structural organism, three-dimensional in a real, integral way, and seen as a hierarchical fabric of orders and structures that produce interior spaces and exterior volumes that are inter-related. It is a result very similar to some of the buildings drawn by Leonardo. Each constructive element in the building may quite naturally assume a 'Classical' form, and take on a value of its own which is visual as well as structural, contributing to the architectural value of the build-

ing and at the same time giving it a remarkable degree of boldness in matters of statics. The 'rationality' of each decision ('facere . . . aliquid certa cum ratione artis est', Alberti had said) guarantees that the various parts of the building are all in harmony; and finally it makes possible a rounded unity in the architectural organism – similar, as Alberti wished it to be, to that of an *animal,* of a living organism. This, according to the humanists' optimistic view of things, was an expression of *coincidentia,* the unified rationality of a harmonious cosmos.

In the last years of the fifteenth century, and the early years of the sixteenth, a significant number of churches – mostly with a central plan – which directly or indirectly recall Bramante, and some of which have actually been attributed to him, were built in the north of Italy; and a few were built in Central Italy as well, mostly through the activity of Lombards. Bramante may have had a hand in the planning of some of these – for instance, S. Maria de Canepanova in Pavia, S. Magno in Legnano, the Pozzobonella Chapel in Milan, and the Cappella dello SS. Sacramento in the parish church at Caravaggio. Other buildings with a character that on the whole recalls his works may have been derived from ideas of Bramante's. In every case, starting from elementary geometrical schemes, these buildings are made up of often complex relationships of space and structure which combine to produce a variety of plans; but they are always held together, by a planning method which (although in particular elements it sometimes gives way to effects of perspective and illusion) generally makes the building, both internally and externally, into a *macchina* – each separate feature an indispensable, organic part of the whole, indeed a structural, unifying element of it. The rigour of this method allows Bramante, as it had allowed Brunelleschi, to translate into new Renaissance terms models derived from history – from all periods of history. This is the method that, as in the case of Brunelleschi, produced the new 'invention'; or, one might call it, the 'composition' of new organisms. It is why Bramante, as Müntz put it, will go down in history as 'the greatest inventor of architectural ideas since Antiquity'.

And so it is that, at Pavia, as early as 1488, Bramante, more than any other architect at the time, appears at the deepest level as the real in-

52 Pavia Cathedral: lower part of the eastern walls (compare the model, Ill. 48)

53 Pavia Cathedral: detail of the crypt

heritor of Brunelleschi's innovative ideas. The architectural style of these early works of his may seem more like that of Alberti, but their basic organization recalls the teachings of Brunelleschi, the 'first founder' of Renaissance architecture. And yet Bramante was not merely copying him mechanically; nor, in any narrow sense, was he 'reviving' Brunelleschi, as he had been revived at about that time or a little earlier in Florence. He was trying out Brunelleschi's ideas and checking them critically in an effort to develop them further; checking not the outward forms and results obtained, but the rational ideas, the scientific objectivity, the universality of his methods. The confirmation, as we shall see, was to be S. Maria delle Grazie.

Bramante was now in the service of the house of Sforza, already well known and well thought of, although, in a biting sonnet, he jokes about his unhealthy financial state.[20] He is pretending to have a conversation with his tailor: 'Bramante,' says the tailor, 'you're asking me for clothes, and running up enormous bills. Do you think it means nothing when I send you a bill to pay?' 'Sir,' Bramante replies, 'I've got no money. Take a penny and then have me hanged.' 'What, don't you get paid by the Court? You're paid five ducats a month.' 'To tell you the truth, courts are like priests, they give you words and water and smoke. Anyone who asks for anything else is really up against it.' 'And what about Bergonzio and Marchesin [powerful men at the Sforza court], what are they up to? Aren't you in favour with them?' 'Everyone's deaf where money's concerned. But to get back to the stuff we were talking about: if you'll make me a new pair of hose, I'll throw away the boots I'm wearing now.'

But he enjoyed the patronage of Ascanio Sforza (who had commissioned the cathedral at Pavia) and of Ludovico Sforza himself, as well as that of several influential courtiers. At the court he was also in contact with humanists, poets and artists, in particular, it seems, with ie poets Antonio Cammelli and Gaspare Visconti; to Visconti he dedicated some poems, and Visconti wrote about him in his *De Paulo e Daria amanti* in 1495.

In the service of the Sforza family, Bramante worked as architect and painter (in a list of engineers working in Milan in the final years of the century he appears as 'ingegnerius et pinctor'). In fact, even after 1490, he seems not to have abandoned painting, though it was apparently almost always applied to buildings. The only painting on wood which is attributed to him, and that doubtfully (by Lomazzo much later, in 1590), is *Christ at the Column*, which used to be in the abbey of Chiaravalle and is now in the Brera; if it really is by Bramante, it probably dates from about 1490. Other paintings and frescoes, now lost, were attributed to him in the sixteenth century, such as a *Pietà* in the church of S. Pancrazio at Bergamo (which he may have painted as a young man) and a figure of the poet Ausonius and 'other coloured figures' on a façade in Piazza dei Mercanti in Milan. One fresco which does survive is that painted for 54 Ludovico il Moro, a mysterious picture of a mythological figure, possibly Argus, set in a complex architectural framework, on the door of the treasury in the Rocchetta of the Castello Sforzesco in Milan. This work is not documented, and some people – Roberto Longhi, for instance – deny that it is by Bramante, but it has characteristics that suggest it may be by him. If so, it must have been painted some time between 1490 and 1492–93, very likely with the help of his pupil Bramantino. Once again, it is a painting using perspective illusionism; but here this is no longer merely a method of increasing the space available and of giving the room greater apparent depth than it really has. Here part of the picture – the opening in which the figure stands – seems to recede into a mysterious compressed depth beyond the wall, while the rest – a conglomeration of heavy architectural elements (undoubtedly Bramantesque) supported with difficulty on two huge corbels – projects forward into the room. It can be read at the same time as a kind of escapism and as a sign of crisis: as if Bramante had given up trying to convince through rational means and was instead assaulting the spectator's emotions directly, forcibly. This is a side of Bramante's personality, often repressed but continually resurfacing, which was to assume fundamental importance in his later work in Rome.

Another activity, closely connected with architecture and perspective painting, must sometimes have occupied Bramante in Milan,

as it did later in Rome: arranging plays and celebrations at court, which we know Leonardo was also involved in at the time. On 15 May 1492, for instance, Bartolomeo Calco, Ludovico's secretary, wrote from Milan to the Duke (who had asked him to see that 'the day of the baptism be adorned with some worthy spectacle') that he had thought of 'sending for Bramante to get him to put some fantasy on show' and that Bramante had assured him that, in spite of the short time available, he would 'try to put on some show for the company'.[21] This 'show' must have been the 'offering which the people at the Eastern and Tonsa Gates' made on that occasion. Perhaps, as has been suggested, there were triumphal arches and other architectural fantasies of a theatrical kind. It seems likely, indeed, that with his ability in the use of perspective, Bramante may have been expert at painting scenery, even while he was still at Urbino; certainly there is always a theatrical element in his work. One engraving in particular, which may go back to a drawing of his and certainly recalls his ideas, seems to be a prototype for sixteenth-century stage designs from Peruzzi to Serlio. It can be dated to the years around 1500.

This activity, of which we know all too little, should not be considered entirely marginal and secondary. To Bramante it was a professional job, which was to go on occupying him later, for instance at Vigevano and after that in Rome. Once he had established that pictorial images and architectural images were substantially equivalent, it became a laboratory for him where he could experiment with problems and find solutions which could be embodied in real buildings.

After Pavia Cathedral, interest focuses on the project for rebuilding the Dominican church of S. Maria delle Grazie in Milan. Of this the centrally planned eastern part, intended as the mausoleum of the Sforza family, was actually built, the first stone being laid on 29 March 1492. But the project seems also to have involved the demolition and rebuilding of Solari's fifteenth-century nave, and certainly the construction of a new façade. A sketch by Leonardo, in MS 'I', f.70, shows roughly what the church would have looked like, and includes a design for the layout of the district around it.[22] Whether Bramante was in fact the architect of the eastern part of the church and of the rebuilt parts of the convent has not been proved by any reliable documents. According to old sources, Ludovico il Moro, who commissioned it, sought the opinion of several 'very skilful architects' (certainly Bramante, probably Amadeo and per-

132

40, 55– 59

haps, as has often been maintained, Leonardo). It is very likely that Bramante was responsible for the idea and the plan as a whole, and prob-

57, ably also for the design of at least most of the
58 incised decoration of the interior. The execution of this *sgraffito* and the final decorative touches,

59 especially on the exterior (except perhaps the lower part), must have been done mostly by Lombard artists such as Amadeo and De Fondutis, and have been largely beyond the architect's control; indeed, it is likely that important changes were made in the initial plan, especially in the development and arrangement of the exterior. Bramante may also have planned the sacristy and perhaps its cloister as well, but this is not documented, and is more doubtful.

As at Pavia, the plan involved the building of a church with a 'composite' scheme. But here, as Leonardo's sketch would seem to indicate, and as its function as a mausoleum

55, would also suggest, the east end had to be more
59 or less self-contained as an ideal centrally planned organism, particularly when seen from the outside. Once again, it was one of Brunelleschi's works that served as a model: the Sagrestia Vecchia of S. Lorenzo, the theme of which had already been used in Milan in the Portinari Chapel of S. Eustorgio. It seemed suitable to express the idea of a mausoleum in which, Förster has suggested, divine Grace, symbolized by the light, evoked the idea of victory over death, of the triumphant, beatific glorification of the Sforza dead.[23] Bramante emphasized the centralized nature of the plan by

57, using a single unifying motif of orders support-
58 ing concentric arches on the four inner walls – a device used by Brunelleschi on the end wall of the cube of the Sagrestia Vecchia (where the little altar space opens off), and which also appears in the Portinari Chapel. But here the motif, applied on all four sides and providing a sort of frame for the cubic space of the crossing (inspired by the Greek-cross plan of S. Sebastiano at Mantua and, to an even greater extent,

15 S. Bernardino at Urbino), made possible the
58 lateral expansion of the space into large semicircular apses on either side. The nave of Solari's

57 old church remained, but its impact was transformed, the centralized, brightly lit crossing assuming the role of dialectical antithesis to the dark space from which it grew. In order to appreciate Bramante's intentions in the new crossing, it is important to understand how he saw the function of this earlier part of the church.

55, On the one hand, the crossing appears to be a
56 centrally planned building, self-sufficient and complete in its strict proportions, based on the ratio of 1:2; on the other hand, the exact form

54 Milan, Castello Sforzesco: fresco of Argus (?) in the treasury of the Rocchetta

which it takes is determined by its relation to the nave, since it has to form the conclusion of the whole church. Indeed, the large central space, which seems quite still yet is vibrating 57, with its own quasi-Byzantine luminosity, is as it 58 were shot through by intersecting shafts of fluid energy. It is pierced, and dynamically brought to life by some kinetic impulse, some thrust from the depths, which begins at the entrance, moves forward and then explodes, spreads and spends itself in the crossing, straining the envelope that contains it and pushing back the side walls between the strong points of the structure and the orders, so that they 'generate' the apses. This thrusting impulse continues forward in depth, breaks through the

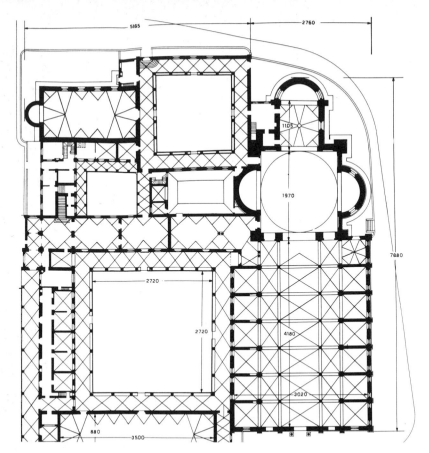

Milan, S. Maria delle Grazie

55, 56 Plan and longitudinal section. In the plan, the parts built by Ludovico il Moro are the east end of the church (right), the sacristy (top left) and the cloister that links them. (Pica and Portaluppi)

57 View of the crossing and choir from the nave

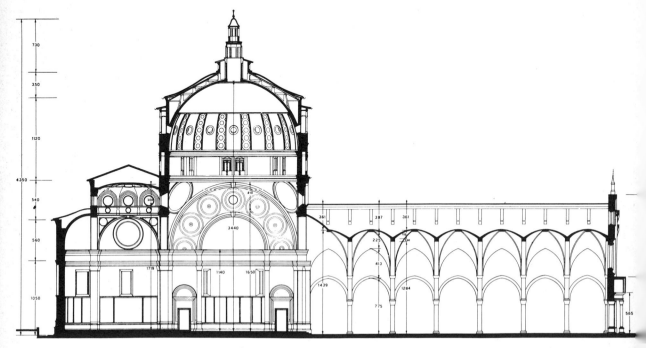

58 Milan, S. Maria delle Grazie:
looking towards the southern apse.
(The choir is to the right.)

wall in front, and pushes the eastern apse beyond the choir, to the very edge of the horizon.
The 'rational', crystalline arrangement of Brunelleschi's prototype is thus upset. The large
58 apses at the sides, raised to the gigantic scale of
the crossing, become part of the whole spatial
organization of the building: they are necessary
to give a feeling of space at the sides, and thus to
make the crossing appear to be centrally
40 planned. The large dome, pierced by oculi,
rests boldly on slender colonnettes set in twin
straight-headed openings in the drum, and
seems an ethereal, unstable and almost temporary covering of the void below.

The thrusting movement also alters the effect
of the choir, compared with that of the small
cubic eastern projection in the Brunelleschian
40 prototype. The umbrella dome over the choir,
which echoes the little dome of the altar space of
the Sagrestia Vecchia, here cannot serve as a
spatial conclusion: it is incongruous, a contradictory halt to the movement in depth which
flows from one end of the church to the other.

The lightly incised decoration which covers
every surface is not merely a delicate orna-
mental device. The lines of force established by
this decoration, the imagery, and the many
circles of varying size which are set into the
structure (as in the Prevedari engraving) to 26
animate and emphasize the surfaces, constitute
a quasi-structure in their own right, thus denying both Brunelleschi's abstract surface and
Alberti's simple constructional wall. These
lines of force continue the lines of the actual
building; above all, in an image governed by
light, they give the space a dense, vibrant
quality, and turn it into a kind of imaginative
vision, a pictorially emotive, suggestive struc-

ture. Light is indeed the fundamental element in this treatment of space: the clarity of Florentine space is replaced by something that recalls the vague, expansive space in the Byzantine S. Sophia. Sometimes the light moulds the surfaces, sometimes it sparks out in surprising silhouette effects, sometimes it quivers in tremulous reflections. It gives the forms an immaterial quality, yet at the same time a consistency that seems sometimes pictorial and sometimes sculptural, and thus it gives space a new quality, making it physical, almost tangible, and at the same time immaterial: it is a mass of air, a luminous, atmospheric fluid in motion which gives form to the wall surfaces and makes them recede into the depths, almost as in one of Leonardo's aerial perspectives. Nothing like it had been seen in fifteenth-century architecture, except perhaps in Pavia Cathedral and the Prevedari engraving.

49, 26

The problem of the relationship between structure and decoration, which was so important in Lombardy, is developed here within the larger problem of the relationship between appearance and reality; the problem, that is, of architecture as image, as 'painting' and therefore, as far as Bramante was concerned, as perspective, illusionistic spectacle. Decoration is no longer *lux superaddita pulchritudinis*, superimposed upon the building's walls, as it was for Alberti; nor, as it had so far been in Lombardy, an important yet superficial element in the whole building. It is an integral part of the perspective design of the whole, and that design is no longer considered as a manifestation of the absolute but as a means of representing a possible reality, an image of the physical world. Nor does the decoration, as it does in Lombard architecture, destroy the outlines of forms: it makes the definition of them less clear, less precise and unequivocal, so that the image may more effectively be turned into an illusory representation, and at the same time it guarantees the image's reality, its physical, concrete nature. Architecture considered as appearance, as represented reality rather than physical reality, is the basis of Bramante's work in S. Maria delle Grazie. But he no longer applies painting methods to architecture, as he had done in S. Maria presso S. Satiro. Here, as later in Rome, the illusion is based completely on the constructed building. Reality and illusion interpenetrate each other, so subtly and persuasively that there scarcely seems to be any illusion about it. And yet it is the one thing that shapes and gives significance to the result.

The internal hierarchy of spaces produces an external hierarchy of volumes, which, as in

59

Leonardo's designs, determines the expressive image. Very little that is truly Bramantesque is now visible on the exterior, with its often laboured piling up of parts and superficial combination of disparate elements. Yet the unified logic of the volumetric scheme as a whole is still clear, the ordered grouping of masses, reflecting the organization of the interior and culminating in the dome. As at Pavia Cathedral and in Leonardo's sketches, Bramante denies any distinction between two-dimensional *disegno* and structure. The exterior is no longer made up of surfaces to be defined (as Alberti would have defined them) through a *disegno*, a decoration superimposed upon them. Exterior and interior are born together; the building becomes a concrete *organism*, a three-dimensional spatio-structural 'mechanism' in which the problem of surfaces and façades ceases to exist. In other words, the building resolves itself in its own *primary* terms: interior *space* and exterior *volume*, the terms of an architecture in which the details, the individual elements, however delicately designed or personally expressed, necessarily diminish in importance and it is the totality which matters.

41– 43

48

59 Milan, S. Maria delle Grazie: view from the east

Chapter four

Final years in Lombardy: methods of work and interest in urban spaces

BETWEEN 1492 and 1494 Bramante was busy with a number of works in Milan, but even so it appears that he was away from the city several times.[24] In May 1492, two months after the first stone of S. Maria delle Grazie had been laid, a letter from the Duke's secretary, Bartolomeo Calco, to the Duke refers to searches being made outside Milan to find the absent Bramante. However, he must have been in Milan in September of that year. The account book of the *fabbrica* of S. Ambrogio, under the date 11 September, records that 'a change was made' in the cloister of the Canonica, on orders from Bramante, and on 19 September it is noted that Ludovico ordered Bramante to 'design and plan this Canonica as he thought fit, and he made the design'. Because of the strongly Brunelleschian character of this building, it has been suggested that in the summer of 1492 Bramante had been in Florence – perhaps, as Förster suggests, having quarrelled with his collaborators and the builders of the east end of S. Maria delle Grazie, who were not following his directions exactly. It may well have been first-hand knowledge of Brunelleschi's work which produced this apparent alteration in the project for the Canonica. At any rate, he was certainly in Milan during the autumn, for in October the chapter of S. Ambrogio commissioned from him a figure of the Virgin for the nearby church of S. Clemente (later demolished).

Bramante must have stayed in Milan at least until the end of June 1493 (Bartolomeo Calco mentions his presence in the city on 23 June). On 29 June 1493 he signed a report, which survives in his handwriting, on a problem concerning the fortifications of Crevola in Val d'Ossola (above Domodossola), the efficiency of which seems to have been endangered by the construction of a building by a local nobleman,

G. Battista del Ponte.[25] Ludovico was not entirely satisfied with Bramante's report, which was short and really rather evasive, and decided to send 'someone who knew more about the profession of war'. But towards the end of the year, perhaps earlier, Bramante was again away from Milan. On 11 December 1493, Giovanni Stefano Castiglioni, on Ludovico's behalf, mentions that Bramante was being looked for 'in Florence or in Tuscany' (he might be 'with Perugino, or someone else notable for pictures or sculpture'), and a letter from the Duke on 25 December to Stefano Caverna asks for news of him in Rome. On 16 February 1494 he was in the dukedom of Milan again and was receiving columns and blocks of marble for the Porta Ludovica of the Castello Sforzesco in Milan (probably designed by him and built c. 1492–96) and for Vigevano. Again, on 24 February 1494, Duke Ludovico gave Bramante, 'our architect', permission to take marble from the ducal supplies for work at Vigevano.

The work for Ludovico at Vigevano must have involved Bramante earlier, perhaps around 1492. It seems likely that he planned the piazza (built between 1492 and 1494, but considerably altered at the end of the seventeenth century), and also probably designed the decorations painted on the façades of the houses around it, which consisted of large triumphal arches in illusionistic perspective (see pp. 64–65). Of Ludovico's other buildings at Vigevano (in which Leonardo da Vinci was also involved) it is difficult to attribute any to the hand of Bramante, except perhaps the Palazzo delle Dame and possibly the whole arrangement of the tower and staircase leading up to the castle. His work as an architect at Vigevano is, however, mentioned by Cesariano and other sixteenth-century writers, and documents in the archives

60 Abbiategrasso, S. Maria Nascente: façade of the church, fitted into an existing cloister (see p. 66 and Ill. 71)

record him as a painter there too. Thus on 4 March 1495 Bianchino da Palude writes to the Duke, mentioning 'a new room which Bramante is having painted, near the street' and giving an account of the work which, probably under his direction, was being done in the castle of Vigevano, notably in the Duchess's bedroom and in her antechamber. In connection with these interior paintings and decorations (one should note he had 'had them painted' – that is, he did not paint them himself, at least not entirely) Bramante had to go to Pavia 'to copy some designs of planets from the clock in the library to decorate a certain ceiling in a room at Vigevano', as Giacomo da Pusterla, commander of the castle at Pavia, wrote to Ludovico in March 1495. Bramante also seems to have done other work at Vigevano which is now either lost ('a chapel of the Conception', for the friars of San Francesco, referred to in a letter to the Duke from Guglielmo da Camino on 13 July 1494) or no longer identifiable ('the design for the altar to hold the relics', mentioned in a letter to the Duke on 5 September 1496).

Between 1494 and 1496, Cesariano notes, Bramante also built a small bridge or covered passage across the moat of the Castello Sforzesco in Milan, apparently what is known as Ludovico il Moro's *ponticella*. As we have seen, the Porta Ludovica of the castle is probably also by him. In 1497, according to a date carved under an 60, arch, the façade of the church of S. Maria Nas-
71 cente at Abbiategrasso was built (see p. 66). The documents do not say for certain that Bramante designed it, but it is generally accepted as his. Finally, between 1497 and 1498 the account books of S. Ambrogio in Milan mention expenditure on the building of a chapel in the church (later largely remodelled); and Bramante's name appears several times in accounts connected
61, with the renovation of the monastic buildings of
72, S. Ambrogio, built at the expense of Ascanio
73 Sforza, a patron 'held in perpetual remembrance' by the Milanese convent. It seems that this building was to have been organized around four large cloisters (only two of which were built) and to have included a refectory, a library and a number of rooms on the ground and first floors. Bramante made a wooden model of it. It must have been quite far advanced by 1499 when, with the fall of Ludovico il Moro, work was interrupted. In the early sixteenth century it was taken up again by the same contractors, using Bramante's plan, but was only in part completed. It was Bramante's last work in Milan.

Bramante seems to have been away from Lombardy a number of other times between 1492 and 1498. In a sonnet addressed to his friend the poet Gaspare Visconti, he says that he has returned from a journey in which he went through Genoa, Savona, Nice, Alba, Asti, Acqui and Tortona before arriving at Pavia. Other verses of his are dated 'the first of September 1497 in Taracina'. And in a poem written before 1499 the poet Cammelli sends greetings to Bramante, who is away from Milan.

All these journeys – not all of them on professional business for the house of Sforza, since the Duke had him searched for – on the one hand show Bramante's restless character and possibly a feeling of impatience with the situation in Lombardy which had begun to affect him; but on the other hand they also explain the nature of his work after 1492, which in some ways was quite new. We should not forget that in these years, after the death of Lorenzo the Magnificent and then of Innocent VIII (1492), came the invasion of Charles VIII in 1494, Savonarola's revolution in Florence, the failure of the Medici Bank, and the collapse of the already precarious political balance in Italy. It was a time of crisis and insecurity, when old certainties were overthrown – in art as in other fields – leading, as at other such moments in history, to the search for new certainties, and to the psychological need for people to base their work upon principles thought to be more secure, universally valid, rationally based. The leading artists, and in particular the leading architects of the time – from Francesco di Giorgio to Giuliano da Sangallo – were not immune from this attitude. But it seems that, particularly in the years after 1492, Bramante felt the need to find certainty in a renewed examination of his predecessors: the work of Brunelleschi, the 'first founder' of Renaissance architecture; Roman architecture – not ideal and imagined but real, 'true', historical; and Vitruvius. He was still seeking for new rigour and control in his way of working, with a consequent stripping off of unnecessary ornament. Bramante's (lost) theoretical studies – on illusionism, on perspective, on 'practice' – mentioned by earlier writers may belong to this period, and it seems likely that the arrival of Giuliano da Sangallo and Luca Pacioli in Milan in October 1492, as well as his continuous and ever-increasing contacts with Leonardo, had some influence upon his new ideas. Giuliano da Sangallo brought the latest problems from Florence and more than anyone else at the time had a profound knowledge of real Roman architecture; Pacioli was an ardent advocate of the use of mathematical instruments in art and architecture, a spreader of Neoplatonic ideas

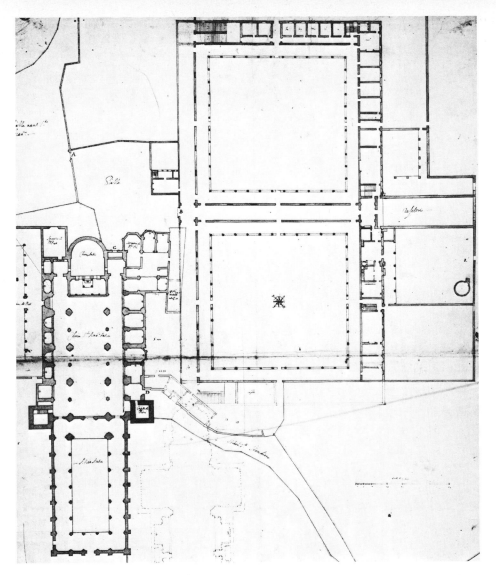

61 Milan, S. Ambrogio: plan. At the left is the church; to its left is one range of the cloister of the Canonica (Ill. 62); to its right are the Ionic (lower) and Doric (upper) cloisters (Ill. 72).

and at the same time a fanatic follower of Vitruvius.

In any case, it is in the years between 1492–94 and 1500 that Bramante's thought must have assumed the form that became characteristic of it: he became conscious of the need (emotional as well as intellectual) to seek and affirm in his work a complete and solid 'universality' whose actualization could only be at best problematic and ambiguous. It was a period that was crucial to his work, a period in which he learnt the rigorous methodology which was to appear particularly in the convent of S. Maria della Pace in Rome. This phase, extending into his later work and continually enriched by new experiences, opened the way for his mature manner under Julius II, the basis and conceptual premise of which it was to become.

The journeys which Bramante almost certainly made to Florence in 1492 and 1493, and to Rome, probably in 1493 and perhaps in 1497 too, must have been extremely important to him, for they got him away from the largely 'regional' problems which had faced him in his first ten years of work in Lombardy. His works of this period – from the Canonica of S. Am- 62 brogio to the *ponticella* of Ludovico il Moro and the other cloisters of S. Ambrogio – are full of 72 direct references to Brunelleschi: to a Brunelleschi no longer seen as the originator of ideal methodological models, as was the case in Bramante's early work in Lombardy, but a Brunelleschi tested and proved in practice. It seems as though Bramante saw in Brunelleschi a sort of architectural Dante (whom he greatly admired), and was trying to 'rinse in the Arno' the provincial dialect of his earlier works, acknowledging the primacy of Florence in the new architecture, as in the new literature.

As well as his rigorous methodology, after the recovery of *organic* architecture achieved at Pavia and at S. Maria delle Grazie, Bramante seemed to take a consistent interest in the theme of defined and delimited space – cloister, courtyard, piazza – which he suddenly saw to be of tremendous importance to the experience of towns as entities. The art of architecture was no longer to be restricted to single buildings. It was not just that, as in nearly all Brunelleschi's works, from the cupola of S. Maria del Fiore to the Ospedale degli Innocenti and S. Spirito, the individual building gained in value as a part of the city, but that the arrangement of his spaces was now full of implicit 'urban' allusions: a cloister or a courtyard was, ideally, a piazza, a
65, 'forum', of a city; and, conversely, a piazza like
66 the one at Vigevano was a courtyard, an open-air hall.

61– To appreciate this quality in the Canonica of
64 S. Ambrogio one must remember that only the range along the left side of the ancient church was built. Bramante probably intended a square courtyard with buildings on all four sides identical to the one actually built. In this design he was thus reinterpreting, on the basis of a further study of Brunelleschi, the schema of the courtyard of the palace at Urbino (itself derived from the arcaded façade of the Innocenti, also used in designs by Filarete with the walls of the upper storey divided by pilasters). But the courtyard at Urbino has a strong emphasis on the corners, and appears to consist of four walls conceived as separate units simply juxtaposed. Bramante, on the other hand, emphasizes the centre of each side, on the cross-
35 axis, as he had done in the painted room in
62 Casa Panigarola. In the Canonica the centre is marked by a triumphal arch, which breaks the continuous rhythm of the arcades, appearing as an ideal entrance to the open space. This theme
66– of 'triumphal arches' inserted in a portico with
69 columns recurs in the piazza at Vigevano and was probably derived from Alberti, who did in fact want the entrances to his 'forum' to be marked by triumphal arches. The courtyard of the Canonica would therefore take on the dig-

nity of an ideal space in a city 'in the Antique manner', an ideal, Vitruvian, square 'Greek forum'. The way in which the large arch is inserted is regulated by the rigorous use of two order-plus-arch systems of different sizes – the smaller on columns, the larger on pilasters – which had been Brunelleschi's solution at S. Lorenzo and S. Spirito, and which Bramante had already used previously (see p. 34). The corner, as in Brunelleschi's courtyards, is (or would have been) marked by a single isolated column, 64 instead of the complex solution with pilasters and half-columns which is found at Urbino. But this column, which is both a vestige of the idea that the corner must be 'marked' as the end-limit of each of the adjoining planes, and a sign of Bramante's desire to show their continuity, is of a special type: its form is that of a tree trunk, which may be an allusion to the Vitruvian theory of the wooden origin of the column (though a tree trunk was also part of Ludovico's coat of arms). However, Bramante did not wish the corner to be emphasized in any particular way and to impose itself as an interruption. The *ad trunconos* form, which is less clear-cut than that of a turned column, lessens its importance as a pivot feature between two walls. And to lessen its impact still further, the same tree trunk form is used for the columns next to the large central arch. The large arch in 61 its turn is given greater emphasis by the use of a giant order on a high pedestal (which gives it a specially dynamic quality, seen again later in the cloister of S. Maria della Pace in Rome), and 74 by the framing of the pilaster that supports the wide arch by a second 'ghost' pilaster set behind it. This second pilaster links the large projecting arch both laterally and in depth with the system of smaller arches on columns behind it. It was also meant to lead upwards to a second small order of pilasters which (as in the court- 62 yard at Urbino) were to frame the windows of the upper floor, their height (as in the doorway of S. Domenico at Urbino) in turn regulated by the height of the large central arch. Thus, in a solution that is a good deal more complex and articulated than that of the loggia of the Innocenti or the courtyard at Urbino, the spatial planes are arranged in layers which suggest an ideal depth. And the large central arch marking the end of the cross-axis takes on a special importance, and tends to dominate and characterize the space. In particular, its presence largely deprives the corners of their significance as caesuras, negates the idea of a space formed simply by four juxtaposed walls, and above all, stresses the three-dimensionality of the central void which now, by being allowed to penetrate

Milan, Canonica of S. Ambrogio

62 The brickwork clearly shows the traces of pilasters above the columns. (It would originally have been plastered, and is so now, but the modern plaster conceals the pilasters.)

63 Tree trunk column and pier flanking the central arch

64 A tree trunk column marks the corner. Another range was planned to extend from the large arch at the left.

63

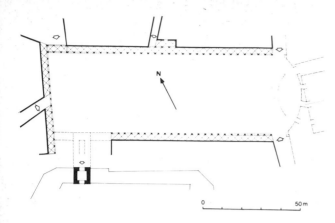

Vigevano, Piazza Ducale

65 Plan showing the original arrangement. The space in front of the castle (bottom left) was open, and filled by a monumental stairway. Note the entry of streets under the arcades on the west and north (see Ills. 67–69). (After Lotz)

66 View of the south and west sides, looking towards the castle tower. The arcade now runs continuously in front of the castle.

into the centre of each wall, tends to acquire a novel spatial value in itself, as if it, rather than the walls which define it, were the real protagonist of the entire plan. It marks the emergence of a new concept of the role of space in architecture, which Bramante was to develop in Rome, and eventually came to express fully.

His interest in open spaces seen specifically as urban spaces found expression in the Piazza Ducale at Vigevano.[26] As it appears today, the piazza is a fairly long rectangular space (about 48 by 134 m.), flanked by uniform arcades and closed on the east by the façade of the cathedral. Originally, as Wolfgang Lotz has shown, it was spatially very much richer. (It was altered, some two hundred years after its completion, by Bishop J. Caramuel von Lobkowitz.) The two main streets which lead into it from the north and west did so through two monumental arches which interrupted the continuous rhythm of the colonnades, though before 1493 their architectural elements were only represented illusionistically in paint. Entering through the arch on the north side (whose architectural scheme, taken from Alberti's S. Andrea in Mantua, foreshadows the arrangement of the upper courtyard in the Belvedere), one faced the great entrance tower of the castle, which recalls that of the Castello Sforzesco in Milan. This tower dominated the western part of the piazza above a monumental staircase that interrupted the arcaded buildings. The western side of the

square extended southward towards the tower by two extra arcaded bays. In the centre of this western side, the other painted arch was the ideal point from which to view the cathedral façade on the opposite side. In this way two main visual axes were established, crossing at right angles and marked by two pairs of architectural elements, real or painted: triumphal arch + tower, and triumphal arch + cathedral façade.

The idea of a piazza enclosed by uniform arcades was no doubt derived from the humanist wish to revive the Roman idea of the forum, which Alberti, following Vitruvius, had described in *De re aedificatoria*. The idea of triumphal arches – which we have already met in the Canonica – certainly came from Alberti, whose book Bramante undoubtedly knew well (Leonardo owned a copy of the edition printed in 1486). The idea of a great tower dominating the piazza and a church occupying one side of it is probably taken from the illustration of the piazza of Sforzinda in Filarete's *Treatise*. Through Filarete Bramante rediscovered and rationalized some significant features of the medieval piazza, an urban space which gathers together and sums up the civic organization of the city and expresses visually the values and relationships of power: the authority and justice of the prince; the power of the Church; the civil power (expressed at Vigevano by the insertion of the Palazzo del Comune on the north side,

67–69 Vigevano, Piazza Ducale: painted triumphal arches. The scheme of the north-western arch (top) with doubled pilasters, derived from Alberti, foreshadows the pattern of the upper Belvedere court (Ills. 108, 109). Above and left, the western arch, as it appears today, and redrawn to emphasize the use of orders of various sizes (compare Ill. 27).

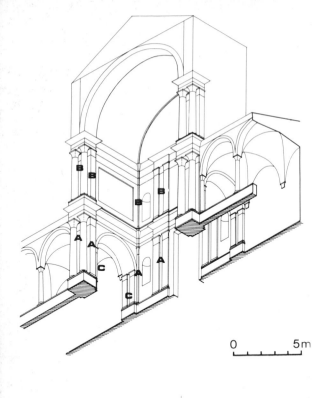

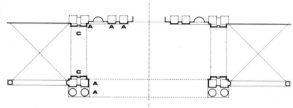

Abbiategrasso, S. Maria Nascente

70 Axonometric view and plan of the façade, showing the use of orders of various sizes, and of columns combined with pilasters. A is the tallest, C the shortest; C occurs only in pilaster form. In the corners, the pilasters are reduced to 'thread' form (compare Ill. 91).

71 Inner face of the left side of the façade, showing its integration with the existing cloister (Ill. 60), its orders of two different sizes (A and C in Ill. 70), and the placing of columns in front of pilasters. Note the use of different stones—coarsest for the shafts of columns and pilasters, finest for the mouldings.

where it is relatively unemphasized, thus conceding the subordination of local to princely power). What was typical of Bramante was his ability to exploit the existing features, and to translate them (in visual and architectural terms) into an 'ideal' urban scene, a crossing of visual axes. With a few restrained touches he has brought the square into line with an abstract, pre-established, perspective structure.

The idea of a triumphal arch inserted into a courtyard with continuous arcades so as to organize and give direction to the space occurs again *c.* 1497 in the façade of S. Maria Nascente at Abbiategrasso. Here the idea may allude to the dedication of the church – to the birth of Mary, which starts the process of the incarnation and redemption, so that she is *janua coeli,* the gate which opens to man and lets him triumphantly enter paradise, from which he had previously been excluded by original sin. But here too the presence of a large arch at the end of an open space surrounded by arcades gives it the feeling of an urban space. Bramante rejects Alberti's concept of the façade as a flat 'drawn' plane. He imagines it as a kind of gigantic portico, or rather an enormous porch; as a three-dimensional spatial structure, formed by the fitting together of several systems of 27, order-plus-arch. Cleverly linked syntactically 70 to the arches of the pre-existing irregular colonnade, the façade becomes an unexpected, complex union of energetic elements that dominate and vitalize the whole of the surrounding space with their presence. It becomes a theatrical image, like one of those fabulous pieces of temporary scenery used in triumphal entries, in which all the plastic and structural values of the parts give solidity to the structure and yet melt into the whole, in a pictorial, atmospheric way. The discreet, subtle colouring which comes from the use of different materials—which had already 71 appeared in the Canonica, and was to appear again in Rome – emphasizes Bramante's intention to turn architecture into painting. Alberti's 'heroic' monumentality has become 'landscape' monumentality, as Baroni suggests.

In the great arch at Abbiategrasso, the 'heroic' 60 arrangement of the whole and the use of certain elements in ways that had never been seen before in Bramante's work, such as the way the columns are placed in front of pilasters and superimposed in two tiers, are perhaps derived from first-hand experience of Roman architecture. Bramante may of course also have seen drawings from the Antique, perhaps by Giuliano da Sangallo or Francesco di Giorgio. But, as we have seen, it is not at all unlikely that he actually was in Rome in the early 1490s, perhaps on

business for Ascanio Sforza, who, as Vice-Chancellor of the Church, lived there. (This would be a reason for connecting him with the first projects for the Palazzo della Cancelleria, on which he may have worked later, as Vasari says, when he was living in Rome.)

77

61,
72

In any case his last work in Milan, the Doric cloister of the convent of S. Ambrogio (1497; final plan 1498), seems to show the almost brutal conjunction of two quite different experiences: that of Florence and that of Rome, that of Brunelleschi and that of Antiquity. The basic motif of the arcades in these cloisters shows remarkable compositional rigour, particularly in its proportions. The geometrical framework of the elevation of each bay is three squares, one above the other. The lowest square conditions the height of the columns, the middle square that part of the elevation between the abacus of the columns and the continuous entablature above the arcade, and the top square the whole of the upper floor, including the cornice. The top square is divided vertically into two by the motif of arches framed by pilasters. This motif, and more generally the division of the upper floor into two, seems to be taken from a Roman prototype, the so-called 'Crypta Balbi' in Rome, which Bramante must have known. (Though a drawing of this building also appears in Giuliano da Sangallo's *Libro,* and a similar scheme was used by Leonardo.) The splendid cornice also seems to suggest a knowledge of Roman models.

Bramante seems to have used an extremely rigorous method in designing this division. It was here, after the practice run of the Canonica, that he started on a period of research characterized by a strong determination to attain greater depth, by discipline, by a rejection of all merely pleasing decoration and by a decisive effort to simplify and to eliminate whatever was superfluous. This all suggests what was to come in the cloister of S. Maria della Pace in Rome. But it was also an enterprise which, by seeking to prove the universal validity of the method and first principles of Renaissance architecture, was already tending to expose the contradictions and inner conflicts of those principles. Fidelity to rigorous method, and to a clearly formulated programme, appears in the general plan of the Doric cloister, which was suggested by Filarete's schemes. It is based on an overall grid which is not even interrupted at the corners, where there are simply square piers whose sides are equal to the diameter of the columns. But another result of this stylistic logic is that the springy, dynamic Brunelleschian lower storey (whose pedestals precisely reflect the abstract grid of the plan) holds up the 'Roman' upper storey only with a

61

72

visible effort. The two storeys are contrasted by the use of motifs which are different not only in style but also in scale. The upper wall, with its persistent duplication of a motif that is in itself heavy and complex, fails to form a unity with the linear structure of the lower floor, where the wide, shadowy, empty spaces are only faintly touched by the luminous flash of the columns, slender, dynamic supports compared with the unusually wide space between them. The two storeys and the two motifs seem in fact to be deliberately presented as contrasts, as Bramante was to do at S. Maria della Pace, in the Belvedere and in the Tempietto of S. Pietro in Montorio. They appear as two ways of conceiving the architecture of humanism, two ways which coexist and have not yet been unified; and both, in spite of their difference in form, in principle and in method, claiming to be 'universal'.

74,
102,
134

In Rome, Bramante was to try to resolve these contradictions, and to go beyond the two contrasting manners (here, basically, that of Brunelleschi versus Alberti's 'Roman manner') to a new and more mature expression, without denying either of them — indeed reaffirming them and proving their *universal* validity. Bramante's final work in Milan is therefore closely linked to his first work in Rome: both were part of a continuous process that went beyond style, important though that was, and involved both his objectives and his methods of working. In the convent of S. Ambrogio, the pilastered front of the canons' entrance achieves a new synthesis, with a result that foreshadows Bramante's style in Rome, immediately before his final flowering, when he discovered the monuments of the ancient world.

73

73 Milan, S. Ambrogio: canons' entrance (Förster)

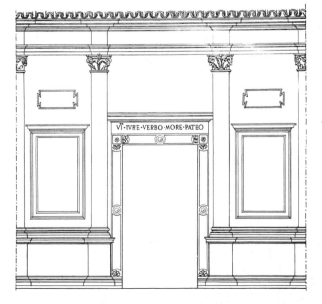

VI·IVRE·VERBO·MORE·PATEO

72 Milan, S. Ambrogio: elevational view of the Doric cloister

Chapter five

Bramante's first work in Rome: the cloister of S. Maria della Pace

BRAMANTE'S presence in Milan seems to be documented for the last time at the end of 1498. It is likely, however, that he remained in the dukedom of Lombardy until the eve of the political events which led to the flight of Ludovico il Moro and the occupation of Milan by the French on 6 September 1499. A notebook of Leonardo's of 1499 (MS 'M', f.53v) contains a well-known sketch of the drawbridge, 'which', Leonardo writes, 'donnjno showed me'; that is, Donato Bramante. This drawing reappears, as Pedretti has shown,[27] in the Codex Atlanticus (f.284r, *a*) with the date 1 April 1499. In July the French army, having passed Asti, was already seriously threatening Milan. Vasari, who generally seems well informed about Bramante's Roman period, possibly from first-hand witnesses, writes:

Having therefore departed from Milan, he betook himself, just before the holy year of 1500, to Rome, where he was recognized by some friends, both from his own country and from Lombardy, and received a commission to paint, over the Porta Santa of S. Giovanni Laterano, which is opened for the Jubilee, the coat of arms of Pope Alexander VI, to be executed in fresco, with angels and other figures acting as supporters.

(This fresco, destroyed when the Lateran basilica was remodelled in the seventeenth century, is recorded in a sketch by Borromini in the Albertina in Vienna.)

At the beginning he served as under-architect to Pope Alexander VI for the fountain of Trastevere, and likewise for that which was made on the Piazza di S. Pietro.

(The fountain in front of St Peter's, erected at the beginning of the year 1500, was later dismantled, and some of its elements were re-used for the present right-hand fountain in Bernini's piazza.)

He also took part, along with other excellent architects, when his reputation had increased, in the planning of a great part of the Palace of S. Giorgio . . . near the Campo di Fiore . . . carried out by one Antonio Montecavallo. Bramante was consulted with regard to the enlargement of S. Jacopo degli Spagnuoli, on the Piazza Navona, and likewise in the deliberations for the building of S. Maria de Anima, which was

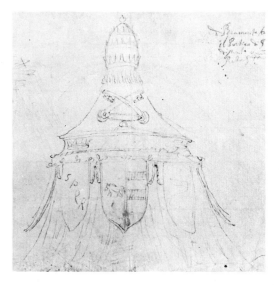

75 Rome, S. Giovanni in Laterano: fresco by Bramante showing the arms of Pope Alexander VI, formerly over the Porta Santa (drawn by Borromini before its destruction during his alterations to the basilica in the seventeenth century. Vienna, Albertina, Arch. 388)

74 Rome, S. Maria della Pace: detail of the cloister. Ionic pilasters, set high on pedestals, are placed against piers which are intended to read as two Tuscan pilasters in profile (see pp. 79–80).

76 Rome, Piazza of St Peter's: fountain made up of elements from Bramante's destroyed fountain (see Ill. 121)

77 Rome, Palazzo della Cancelleria: façade, possibly associated with Bramante. The arrangement with paired pilasters and rustication resembles the present façade of the palace of Cardinal Corneto. (Engraving by Ferrerio, 1655)

afterwards carried out by a German architect. From his design, also, was the Palace of Cardinal Adriano da Corneto in the Borgo Nuovo, which was built slowly, 78, and then finally remained unfinished by reason of the 79 flight of the Cardinal . . .

So Bramante was working on all these projects in the early years of the sixteenth century; however, there are no documents or firm evidence to confirm it. It is only in the case of the palace of Adriano Castellesi di Corneto (later the Palazzo Giraud-Torlonia, in the present Via della Conciliazione) that Vasari says explicitly that a building was designed by Bramante. The general plan of this palace and the detailing of some of the parts, such as the courtyard, the staircase and possibly the lower part of the façade (later, it seems, altered), may well go back to Bramante's design, which at some later stage was abandoned, since, as Vasari says, work on the building continued for a long time. The original scheme (as it appears in a plan in the 'Coner Codex' in Sir John Soane's Museum, 78 London) is of great importance, for it seems to show an attempt to create a model 'house for a private citizen', based on Vitruvius's 'house of the ancients', its proportions strictly governed by a module which is the height of the pilasters in the courtyard. With its simple arches on piers, derived from the study of ancient Roman 79 buildings, the courtyard is remarkably innovative, and may have been the model for a number of houses later in the sixteenth century.

The other works mentioned by Vasari are referred to in terms which may only mean that Bramante served as consultant or collaborator, and it is difficult to know the actual extent of

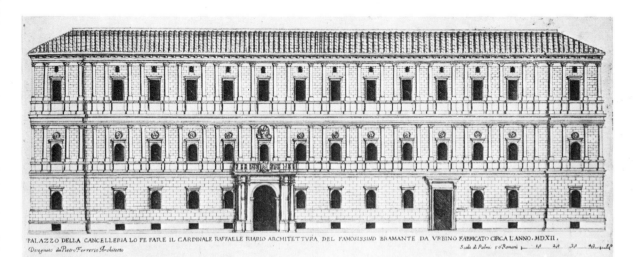

PALAZZO DELLA CANCELLERIA LO FE FARE IL CARDINALE RAFFAELE RIARIO ARCHITETTVRA DEL FAMOSISSIMO BRAMANTE DA VRBINO FABRICATO CIRCA L'ANNO · MDXII .
Disegnato da Pietro Ferrerio Architetto

his involvement, particularly in the case of the fountain of St Peter's. During the pontificate of Alexander VI Bramante may not have been particularly anxious to get commissions, preferring to devote himself to thought and to the study of ancient buildings. Although it seems likely that he had already been to Rome, he now had a chance to look more intensively, and at greater leisure. Vasari in fact says:

Bramante had brought some money from Lombardy, and he earned some more in Rome by executing certain works; and this he spent with the greatest economy, since he wished to be able to live independently, and at the same time, without having to work, to be free to take measurements, at his ease, of all the ancient buildings in Rome. And having put his hand to this, he set out, alone with his thoughts; and within no great space of time he had measured all the buildings in the city of Rome and in the Campagna without; and he went as far as Naples, and wherever he knew that there were antiquities. He measured all that was at Tivoli and in the Villa of Hadrian, and . . . made great use of it.

A rare pamphlet entitled *Antiquarie prospettiche romane*, signed with the pseudonym 'Prospectivo Milanese depictore', dedicated to Leonardo da Vinci (with whom the author shows he was friendly in Milan), and printed in 1499–1500, may show Bramante's keen interest in the Antique at this time.[28]

This renewed serious and profound study of Roman architecture was of fundamental importance for the achievement of Bramante's new mature or 'grand' manner. As Vasari seems to suggest, it may have been through his study of the Antique that Bramante met Oliviero Carafa, Cardinal of Naples, a very rich and influential prelate at the Roman court, passionately fond of literature, art and Antiquities, who represented the interests of the King of Naples and the Spanish party in Rome. Various historical factors may explain why, particularly in his early years in Rome, Bramante obtained numerous introductions to influential Spaniards, who commissioned or administered at least some of the works Vasari attributes to him (the fountain of S. Maria in Trastevere and S. Giacomo degli Spagnuoli). In any case, as Vasari says, Carafa commissioned the first work by Bramante in Rome that is undoubtedly his and has survived, the convent and cloister of S. Maria della Pace. For this, on 17 August 1500, the mason Bartolomeo Lante (or Lande or Laude), son of Francesco da Fiesole, agreed 'to make and perfect eight square piers . . . with capitals in the Ionic order . . . according to the form of the design by

74,
80–
91

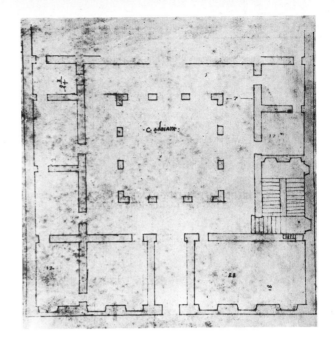

78, 79 Rome, palace of Cardinal Adriano Castellesi di Corneto (Palazzo Giraud-Torlonia): plan, from the 'Coner Codex' (London, Sir John Soane's Museum), and proportional system of the courtyard. A ceiling level of *piano nobile*.

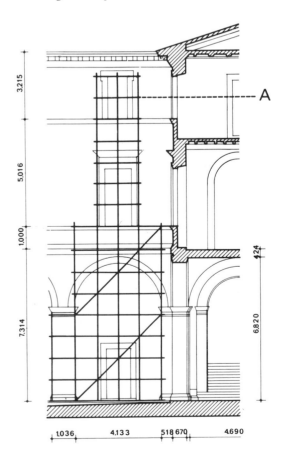

73

master Bramante . . . '. Building went on until the end of 1504, the year inscribed in the very
74 beautiful lettering on the Ionic entablature, which recalls the famous inscriptions in the courtyard at Urbino and on the Cancelleria.

The work at S. Maria della Pace is highly typical of the end of Bramante's period of trial and experiment which had begun during his last years in Lombardy and was the mainspring of his later, mature work in Rome. It is useful to try to reconstruct analytically the planning process involved in it, in order to clarify the complex problems confronting him at this turning-point of his art.[29]

In S. Maria della Pace, having taken note of the physical limitations of the site, Bramante must have been concerned above all to work out a system of proportion for the whole which could regulate the position and dimension of each part in both plan and elevation. The site was roughly square, the best of all possible shapes, according to Renaissance planning theory going back to Brunelleschi, for it could be translated into whole numbers upon which the spaces could be based. From various possible ways of laying out the plan of the cloister, he
81 chose one based on the line of the street which ran behind the church, the Vicolo della Volpe. All the walls were to be parallel or at right angles to this line. Its length, divided into four equal parts, provided the basic module according to which the area could be subdivided into squares. But the site is irregular, especially on the entrance side, and here the network had to be interrupted, and linked to the adjoining buildings in a rather haphazard and untidy way. Even so, most of the available space is covered by the modular grid. By subdividing
83, the basic squares again, Bramante obtained
84 further modules for use later in the design. Setting aside the row of squares on the side opposite to the church as the site of the refectory and other convent rooms, Bramante arrived at a large square of about 26 Roman *braccia* – the sum of the smaller squares – which was to form the courtyard. If one adds the refectory wing, the resulting rectangle has the proportions of 3:4. The siting of the supports in the cloister was a natural result of the basic geometrical decision. The outer row of smaller squares dictates the bays of the cloister walk, to be covered by groin vaults, and the subdivision of the central space gives the position of the piers of the arcade (sixteen in number, the 'most perfect' number, according to Vitruvius, like the columns of the Tempietto of S. Pietro in Montorio); subdivide it again, and one has the positions of the piers and columns of the upper

storey. The same squared module also serves to fix the heights. One complete side of the court- 82, yard, including the end bays, has the propor- 85 tions of a rectangle with the ratio of 1:2 (or an 'octave'). Each wall of the courtyard forms a rectangle with a ratio of 3:4, a 'one and a third times' proportion, of 'a quarter plus a third', recommended by the theorists, which we have already encountered on the plan. The height of the whole is now subdivided into two storeys in the ratio of 1:2, as Bramante had already done in the cloisters of S. Ambrogio. The height of the courtyard, too, was based very exactly on the theoretical rule, suggested by Vitruvius and used by Alberti and later by Serlio, that the second order should be equal in height to the main order less a quarter.

Having thus settled the proportional, 'musical', scheme for the whole, which guaranteed that the parts would be strictly coordinated to one another and to the whole in three-dimensional space, it was then necessary to realize the abstract geometrical schema in an actual building. We have seen how in Milan Bramante had already been interested in 'space in itself', in the shape of a void thought of as having a three-dimensional quality of its own: emptiness not conditioned by the shape of the walls around it, but, on the contrary, conditioning them. In the Canonica of S. Ambrogio, this still 62 tentative vision found expression in the triumphal arches used to emphasize the cross-axes. In the much smaller space of the cloister of S. Maria della Pace, Bramante tried to do the same thing by simpler means. He made the cross-axes of the centrally planned cloister coincide with the fundamental perspective axes and, most unusually, marked them by four solids, not voids, by placing a pier in the centre of each side. 80, The perspective of the axes seems therefore to 82 materialize in the form of these piers, whose importance is emphasized by the fact that on the upper storey they bear the client's coat-of- 89 arms. The eye, led along the perspective cross-axes, is drawn to the central piers but is halted when it reaches them; indeed, they send it back to the interior of the open space, to 'emptiness'. It is this open space that becomes the real protagonist of the architecture, greatly diminishing the stress upon the wall as the enclosing element that is provided by the angular piers. By a process that was already noticeable in his last works in Lombardy, and was to find its highest expression in St Peter's, Bramante's interest thus tended to move away from the enclosing walls and the elements that express 'enclosure' to voids, space which is exciting in and for itself.

80 Rome, cloister of S. Maria della Pace: view from the entrance corner towards the church

The idea of stressing the perspective by means of a solid had been introduced by Brunelleschi (particularly in S. Spirito), and Bramante himself had also applied it in Milan. It turned out to be exactly the right way to express the Renaissance vision of how perspective could be used in planning. But here, in the cloister, the position on the axes of solid piers instead of empty spaces – contrary to Alberti's explicit 'rule' – meant that the entrance to the courtyard, which traditionally and logically should have provided the best viewpoint, did not fit into

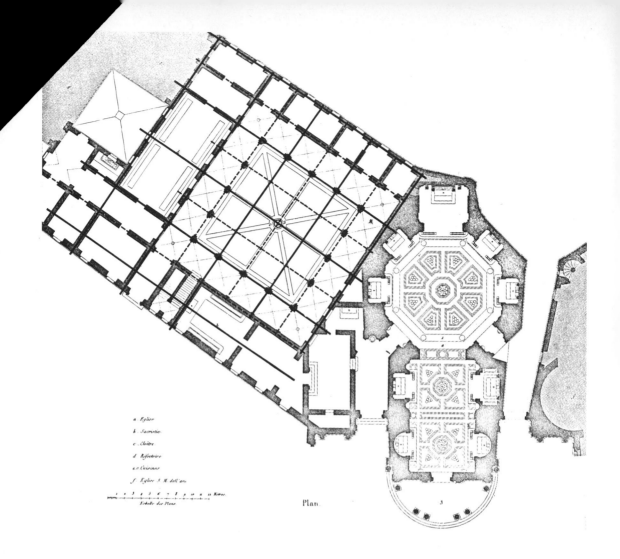

a Eglise
b Sacristie
c Cloître
d Refectoire
e.e Cuisines
f Eglise S. M. dell'ari.

1 2 3 4 5 6 7 8 9 10 11 12 Metres.
Echelle des Plans.

Plan.

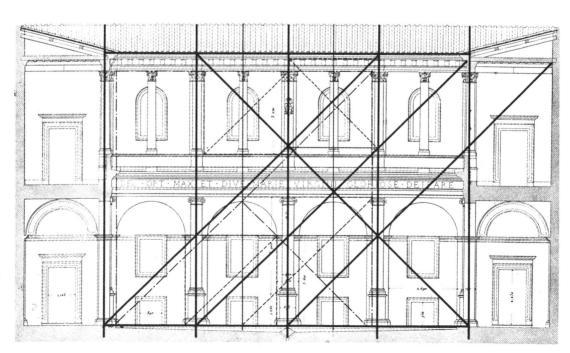

OPT · MAX · ET · DIVÆ · MARIÆ · VIRGINI · GLORIOSÆ · DEL · ARE

Rome, S. Maria della Pace

81 Plan of the church and convent, showing the
basic grid used for the conventual buildings. The
line along the Vicolo della Volpe at the top provides
the starting point: it is divided into four equal
parts, of which one corresponds to the refectory
and the other three to the cloister. The latter are
then subdivided (see Ills. 83, 84). The entrance is at
the bottom left. (Based on a plate by Letarouilly)

82 Elevation of one side of the courtyard (compare
Ill. 85). The overall proportion is 3:4; the ratio
between upper and lower storeys is 1:2. Once
these proportions are fixed, together with the
placing of the piers (Ill. 84), everything is
determined by the proportional system. Solid black
lines define the centre of members, dotted ones the
surface of projecting mouldings. A line drawn
diagonally through three bays, for instance, inter-
sects the verticals at (1) capital level of the Tuscan
order of the lower storey, (2) entablature level of
the main Ionic order, and (3) base level of the upper
Composite order. The dotted lines can be
interpreted in a similar way. (Based on a plate by
Letarouilly)

83 Here the line of the cloister arcade is marked in
heavy black. A-A and B-B are the cross-axes,
dividing the space into quarters. C-C and D-D
divide these into quarters, and E-E and F-F into
quarters yet again. These last divisions fix the
position of the piers and columns of the upper
storey (Ill. 80).

84 The cloister with its walks occupies nine squares
of the basic grid (Ill. 81). Each of these is subdivided
into four. The outer squares now form the cloister
walk (shaded in the section below), with the piers
of the arcade corresponding to the dividing lines.
The rest is void. (The dotted lines show the further
subdivision which governs the upper storey, as in
Ill. 83.) The main cross-axes (A-A and B-B) are
'closed' by piers, and the entrance is banished to
a corner (arrow).

85 Schematic section of the cloister, with the
covered area shown by shading. The elevation as a
whole has a proportion of 1:2, the central open
space a proportion of 3:4. The height is derived
from the same module that governs the plan, and
is subdivided into two storeys with a proportion of
1:2.

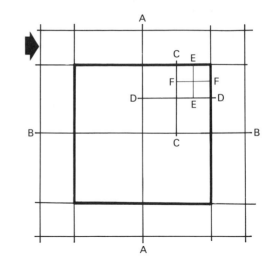

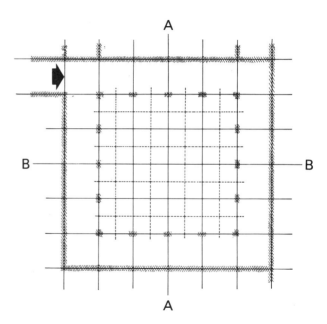

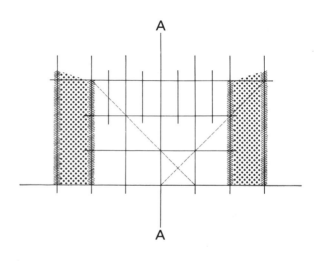

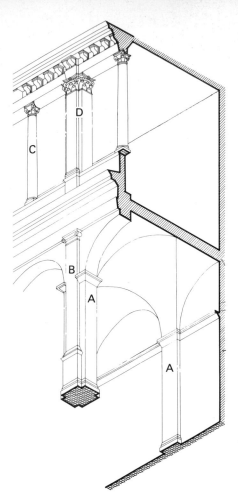

86 Rome, cloister of S. Maria della Pace: Bramante's use of orders. A Tuscan, B Ionic, C Corinthian, D Composite

way in which the whole was proportioned, the actual cloister tended to appear as a self-contained organism, an abstraction, unrelated to its position in time and space, with no life of its own in the context of the real city, although it reflected 'urban' ideas. The same situation, on a different scale and for different reasons, was to recur to some extent in S. Pietro in Montorio and in St Peter's.

To Bramante, a cloister meant essentially an open space surrounded by colonnades or loggias, just like a palace courtyard or a piazza. In Milan, in the cloisters of S. Ambrogio, he had planned an arcade on columns of the kind used by Brunelleschi, and this allowed the bearing elements, ideally rectangular on the plan, to coincide exactly with the modular grid (see p. 69). The system of arches on columns was nevertheless a hybrid of two different building systems with different historical origins: Alberti had declared in his *De re aedificatoria* that to bring them together was 'irrational' and 'against nature'. Besides, such a system, used on the ground floor to support an upper storey, also contradicted the ordinary law of statics, that a weaker structure should be supported by a stronger one. The Romans had two characteristic solutions when it came to designing a portico or a loggia: to combine the order with an arcade, or to use a straight entablature. The 'logical' thing to do at S. Maria della Pace would therefore have been this: either to superimpose two orders supporting arches, or to superimpose two orders with straight entablature. But the first solution would have made it hard to proportion the second order in relation to the functional height needed and to the proportional system of the whole; and the second solution would have involved difficulties in construction, especially on the ground floor, and would have made the use of vaulted roofs illogical. Bramante decided to superimpose the two different systems (as he was later to do in the courtyard of the Rocca at Viterbo), using an elevational system with arches framed by an order on the ground floor and a straight entablature on the upper storey. Everything would thus be made to seem logical and rational. The only difficulty was to reconcile the pedestals on the ground floor, which were necessarily no longer rectangular in form and not even square in plan, with the modular grid of squares established for the whole.

Meanwhile, he had to decide what kind of architectural orders to use in the cloister. For Bramante, who knew the rules established by Vitruvius and again by Alberti, Filarete, and Francesco di Giorgio, this was no trivial choice,

61, 72

122, 80, 86

the perspective scheme at all: wherever it was placed, the entrance would contradict the whole fifteenth-century vision of what perspective could do. Bramante found it impossible to solve this problem in a consistent way. His only option was to minimize the entrance as a part of the cloister's 'void' space: to put it in a corner, tucked into one of the four cloister walks so that it almost disappears, a non-participant in his perspective game. The result is that there is no prescribed point from which to look at the cloister, and that the central space 'in itself' takes over. But in this way perspective – conceived as a means of connecting all the parts of the building and even the street outside, the surrounding houses, and the whole city, in a visual relationship – was limited to a single part, the cloister. It no longer served to connect, but to isolate. In spite of the rigorous a decision depending on nothing but the individual taste or judgment of the client or architect. It had to be taken according to standards of structural logic and in conformity with the profoundest laws of nature; it had also to agree, symbolically and anthropomorphically, with the specific purpose for which the building was being built. So in this building dedicated to Mary, the Mother of Peace, seen not so much as Virgin (which the Corinthian order would have suited) but as Mother of the People, the most appropriate order was the 'maternal' Ionic. But the cloister was two-storeyed. The usual succession, which was 'logical' according to statics, of Doric, Ionic, Corinthian, etc., was impossible: an Ionic with entablature, confined to the second floor, smaller than the Doric on the ground floor, would not have had the emphasis needed in this particular case; in a building, that is, dedicated to the Mother of Peace. So difficulties were arising contradicting the method and 'rational' rules put forward by the theorists. Was this method, were these rules, not then universally valid? Bramante tried to show that *his* method – the method of classical architecture – *was* universally valid, capable of solving all the problems in every situation and under any conditions. Ingenuity could provide a satisfactory solution; all four 86 basic orders would appear in the cloister. This bizarre solution showed Bramante's taste for *capriccio*, for intellectual games.[30] The game consisted in getting into difficulties by setting oneself apparently insoluble problems in order to enjoy solving them – solving them lucidly, and if possible with a touch of wit. Basically this was not so much a taste for paradox as a profound sense of the subtle ambivalence of things, and at the same time a wish to affirm man's rational dominion over them.

Should the ground storey of the cloister of S. Maria della Pace, according to the Classical succession of orders exemplified in the Colosseum, be Doric (or Tuscan)? The scheme of the arch framed by an order could solve the problem. All that was needed was for the profile of the pier from which the arch springs to be considered as an 'order' (Bramante had already done this occasionally in Milan): i.e. a Tuscan 74 pilaster resting on the ground, with the proportions and forms of a Classical pilaster. The pilaster of the Ionic order framing the arch would be placed at a higher level, on a pedestal, thus acquiring the necessary emphasis. The impost mouldings of the arch, suitably modified, could easily be assimilated to a generically 'Tuscan' capital and given the appearance, in profile, of the top of a pilaster. In this way the

87 Rome, cloister of S. Maria della Pace: view from the entrance along the north-eastern cloister walk. The Ionic pilasters are concealed, and the only order visible is 'Tuscan'.

meaning of the single elements becomes ambiguous: against all the rules, a series of Classical mouldings is at the same time both cornice and capital.

This advice solved the problem of coordinating the piers of the arcade with the inner walls 87 of the portico. For various practical reasons it was impossible, here, to apply the external order simply and mechanically to the inner face of the pier and then on to the opposite wall of the portico, as had been done in ancient Roman buildings such as the Colosseum. On the back of the pier Bramante used not the Ionic pilaster but the Tuscan one which formed the pilaster supporting the arch and projected it on to the inner wall of the portico to carry the quadripartite groin-vault of the roof. This solution fully solved the problem of introducing a Tuscan order at ground level and of emphasizing the Ionic, also placed on the ground storey but on a pedestal. In fact, since, as we have seen, the entrance was placed at the end of one of the cloister walks, anyone entering saw first the Tuscan order and only later, after turning to the open space, the 'maternal' Ionic of the cloister. In this way Bramante replaced the usual superimposition of orders in space by a new sequence of orders which reveals itself to a moving observer in *time*, finding there its connection and its unity.

But there was more to it than that. At this point Bramante remembered that the capitals of the Tuscan pilasters, placed on the sides and backs of the cruciform piers and against the back walls, were in origin the cornices of the imposts of the arches. In order to coordinate the various members and therefore the whole space of each walk he felt he must link, linearly, all the 'capitals' of the pilasters against the outer walls. He therefore extended their mouldings along the wall, which is slightly recessed behind them. But if this connecting cornice had the form already presented as a Tuscan 'capital', the 'capitals' and the Tuscan pilasters would not have a separate identity. Bramante solved the problem with another piece of artifice: in the continuous connecting cornice he suppressed the moulding which corresponds to the echinus of the capital, thereby restoring it to the status of cornice. Thus with a series of devices he felt he had solved the problem and shown the universal validity of the method; and with the blessing of the ancients, of Vitruvius and of

88 Rome, cloister of S. Maria della Pace: the capitals of the Tuscan pilasters set against the outer wall are distinguished from the cornice only by an echinus moulding.

Alberti at that. This intellectual and sophisticated treatment takes us forward to Mannerist attitudes: individual elements one by one change their function and although they keep their own features they are used with a different meaning. That is, the forms of the Classical world become ambiguous in relation to their original and 'natural' uses. Each element tends to lose its autonomy and to acquire meanings unlike those it originally had through its relation to the other elements and to the observer.

Other problems appeared when Bramante came to the details of the upper storey, whose relationship with the whole was strictly defined by the initial proportional scheme. To set a colonnade with an entablature on the piers beneath would have been the simplest and most logical solution. Visually, however, there would have been a great difference between the two storeys. Moreover, since the height was determined by the overall proportional scheme, the proportion of the columns themselves was also determined, and they would have seemed too slender in comparison with the very wide intercolumniation. Finally, the 'solid' on the axis of each façade would have seemed too weak if it had been marked merely by a small

89 Rome, cloister of S. Maria della Pace: detail of the upper storey showing the alternation of Corinthian columns and Composite piers. The Composite capitals are deeper. The coat-of-arms of Oliviero Carafa, Cardinal of Naples, who commissioned the work, appears at the left: it marks the central axis of the cloister.

column. Different logical arrangements were thus in conflict with one another, and the theory was in danger of finding contradictions within itself. All that could be done, if one was pursuing the path of reason, was to solve the difficulties with compromises, expedients and ingenious devices. On the upper floor, above each ground-level pier Bramante placed not a column but a smaller pier. It had to conform to the canonical proportions of an architectural order; and, so that it would seem the right proportion both in itself and in relation to the lower piers, it had to have a composite section, one side of it assuming the role of a pilaster. This pilaster, in order to match the lower order, is given a pedestal. The space between the piers, visually too wide, is divided by a column, which also serves structurally to hold up the heavy entablature. All this follows the prearranged proportional plan, which anticipated such subdivisions of the basic geometrical figures in both plan and elevation. But to what order were the piers and columns of the upper storey to belong? Bramante had already used Tuscan and Ionic in the floor below. It seemed logical and possible to continue with the Classical vocabulary on the upper storey. So the com-

posite pier is given the Composite order, which also has the effect of making it visually more noticeable than the adjacent columns; and the columns are made Corinthian. Thus the four main orders are all represented in the cloister, dominated by the Ionic. But the result is extremely ambiguous; indeed, seen according to Classical rules, it comes close to paradox. Next to each other, under the same entablature, Corinthian supports alternate with Composite, contrary to every principle. According to Antique syntax, the lateral parts of the composite pier, placed to correspond with the Corinthian column, must be considered the projection and translation into mural terms of the Corinthian column. They should therefore have Corinthian capitals as well. But this would have a remarkable result: the same pier would be made up of pilasters of different orders, with one Composite and one Corinthian capital side by side, almost running into one another. Bramante dared not do this: he made a Composite pilaster correspond to a Corinthian column, and made no effort to hide the difference in form between them. But the result, looked at in the light of the 'rules', can hardly fail to be disquieting all the same.

Furthermore, the Corinthian capitals of the very slender columns are shorter than those of the piers. This, too, is deliberate – the result of a choice which is logical, rational and conscious. The diameter of the lower part of the column, whose height is determined by the overall proportion, is smaller than the width of the pilaster: according to the rules, its capital should be in proportion, even if, as a result, two adjacent supports have capitals of different depths, which is against the rules. This is not outlandish or extravagant, as some of the solutions noted earlier had been; nor is it even a case of finding a merely formal expedient, something which could satisfy the eye. It is a case of rigorous reasoning, in which all aspects of the problem are involved, even if they belong to different 'logical' categories, and all are allowed to coexist and to act together. The result is like the demonstration of a theorem. In the process of planning, subjective judgment, intuition and personal sensitivity are not ruled out; they are used as needed, depending on the circumstances and on the method used; they become a tool in work that seeks to be seen as a mathematical *science,* which uses foolproof means of establishing spatial units.

Once the proportions of the whole and of the lower part of the cloister had been settled, a serious problem must have arisen for Bramante when he came to the corner piers. A proportional scheme can be expressed by imaginary lines and points, but a building consists of walls and columns, of physical elements which, as Alberti would have put it, 'have a place which they occupy'. In the cloister, for the grid of the plan to be made up entirely and only of squares, the supports, particularly those at the corners, all had to be the same size. This was why Brunelleschi, and Bramante himself at an earlier stage in Milan, in the Canonica and the cloisters of S. Ambrogio, when faced with the difficulty of reconciling the abstractions of mathematics with the physical reality of material, had identified the space which the structure took up on the plan with a point, and had used only columns in the corners (or piers of the same bulk). In other words, if you want to emphasize the importance of the corners, as is done in the courtyard of Urbino, say, by using a stout pier, and at the same time to maintain the position of the other supports and the proportions of the space between the columns constant, it is impossible to keep the modular grid of squares spread over the whole area as planned. In theory, to make the modular plan work out, the total bulk of the corner piers must be comprised in a square whose sides are equal to the front width of the other piers, while the interval between the piers is kept constant, even at the corners, and their centres continue to align. But considering the rectangular plan of the standard pier in the cloister, this is impossible. If the centres of the supports are to be aligned

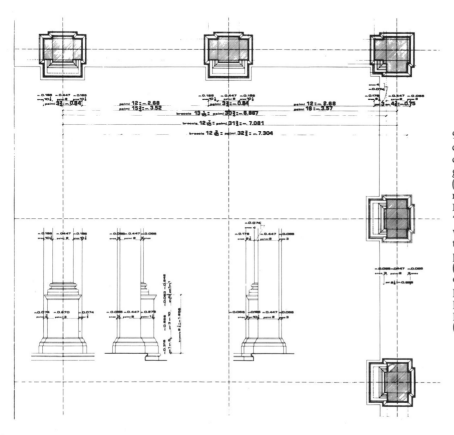

90 Rome, cloister of S. Maria della Pace: analysis of the corner treatment on the ground floor. The corner pier (shown in elevation at the right) is compressed and its Ionic pilaster reduced to 'thread' form (see Ill. 91), while its Tuscan pilasters at the back are wider. By comparison, on the other piers (shown in front and side elevation at the left), the pedestals of the Ionic pilasters project abnormally far — perhaps due to an afterthought (see p. 85 and Ill. 80).

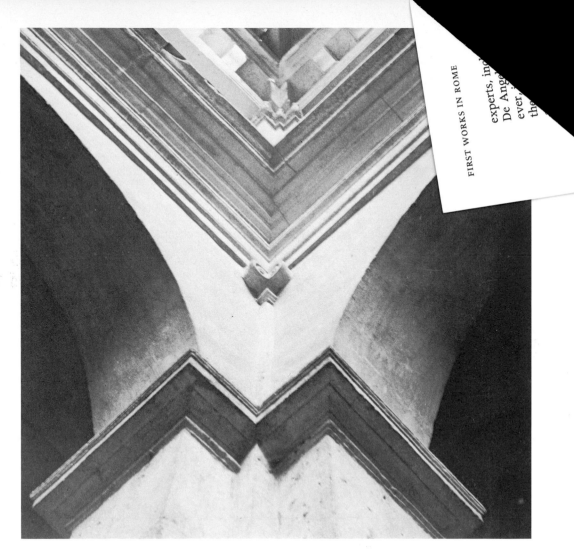

91 Rome, cloister of S. Maria della Pace: in the corner, the Ionic pilaster appears only in 'thread' form, and is cut across by the impost mouldings or 'capitals' of the Tuscan pilasters on either side (compare Ill. 74). In the upper storey, the regular spacing of the corbels is interrupted and they are distorted where they meet in the corner (see Ill. 89).

even in the corners, the corner piers have to be so much more compressed than the normal pier that it becomes impossible to treat the Ionic pilaster on pedestal in the usual way. Bramante, while keeping the intercolumniation unchanged, made the size of the corner piers as small as possible by reducing the Ionic pilaster on a pedestal to what has been called 'thread' form. It is made no wider than it is deep, and the base and capital are reduced to fragments, hardly recognizable 'abstractions' of the elements on the other pilasters. (The 'thread' pilaster had already appeared in the work of Brunelleschi, and Bramante had introduced it in the inner corner of the façade of Abbiate-

grasso.) Disturbing consequences then appear in the arrangement of the other elements. In the topmost entablature, projecting above the piers and columns of the upper floor, the corbels are displaced and contracted; on the ground floor, the impost mouldings of the arches (which, as we have seen, perform the function of capitals) become confused with the 'thread' Ionic pilaster in the corner, which projects rather less, and so the continuity is broken: the impost moulding has the advantage, visually, over the Ionic pilaster. In the corners the system deriving from the order on its pedestal weakens abruptly.

This solution to the problem of the corner may not appear very satisfactory, and many

...uding Adolfo Venturi, Bonelli and ...ns d'Ossat, have criticized it.[31] How-...t is quite in line with the organization of ...whole and with its characteristically Bram-...antesque logic; and it was no accident that he repeated it later in the courtyard of the Palazzo dei Tribunali. Above all, the abrupt contraction of the corner piers means that their role of closing the walls which define the open space is negated (the intention here is the opposite of what it was in the courtyard at Urbino). This agrees very well with the emphasis on the axes by means of a solid. It is as if the structural system embodied in the orders gradually diminishes in importance in each façade: start-ing from the middle, it becomes progressively weaker towards the corners, until it almost sug-gests the image of a square with chamfered corners. In this way Bramante emphasizes the centrality of the courtyard, which would be ideally realized in a circle. Above all, he em-phasizes the empty space in the courtyard as an artistic object *in itself*. As we have seen, this re-sulted inevitably from his proportional scheme. Two contiguous, uniform and perpendicular walls, each with its own perspective organiza-tion in three dimensions, intersect; and these walls form the spatial limits of the cloister. Logical and verifiable rules are put to the proof in concrete terms and vindicated. But at the same time something else emerges: the private impulse to control and conquer *space in itself,* though so far not visually realized with com-plete success.

Other details show Bramante's attempts both to analyse his problems systematically and to solve them consistently. Take, for instance, the 90 Tuscan pilasters on the inner side of the corner piers. In order to maintain the square plan of the vaulting bays of the portico even in the corners, these pilasters are a good deal wider (together with the supporting arch of the cross vaults) than on the standard piers. Again the result is disturbing: the Tuscan pilasters of the corner piers, with their varying sizes and proportions, are included in a series of equal-sized pilasters. This solution strikes one as all the more un-conventional since it seems to be inserted in a rigorously arranged context, the strictness of which is further emphasized by the insertion of another 'thread' pilaster (Tuscan this time) at the corners of the outer walls.

Other remarkable details in the cloister of S. Maria della Pace are of value in showing us Bramante's planning method and attitude. These are minor details, second thoughts, 'retouch-ings', springing from intuition, not from the meticulous application of his method – since we

can presume that the essential elements of the cloister were by now complete. They are last-minute changes made with the final, complete visual effect in mind, like those that a painter might make to a picture. For instance, the pilasters on the front of the upper piers (but not 80 the lateral pilasters) are marked by pedestals to show vertical continuity with the Ionic pilas-ters on pedestals below them; and square pro-jecting blocks (now vanished, but visible in the nineteenth-century drawings of Letarouilly), resting upon the Ionic entablature, seem to have corresponded with the Corinthian columns placed above the crowns of the arches.[32] Simi-larly, the topmost entablature breaks forward 80, above the pilasters on the front of the piers of 89 the upper storey (involving the use, above them, of double corbels, a stylistic anomaly), to em-phasize the vertical continuity of the main elements in the cloister walls. This entablature is of a peculiar type and closely resembles the Bramantesque one on the Palazzo della Cancel- 77 leria and on other Roman buildings derived from it. Like the Romans at the Colosseum, and Alberti at the Palazzo Rucellai, Bramante definitely felt that this entablature was not merely the entablature of the order of the upper storey, but also the culmination, the visual con-clusion, of the whole building. So in order to accentuate its importance, he enriched it, giving it more depth of light and shade, by inserting corbels at the level where the frieze would nor-mally be. However, although, as we have seen, on the one hand this entablature had to break forward in step with the pedestals, on the other it could not be allowed to lose its function of 'closing' the whole, of providing a full stop and a final conclusion. Its terminal line therefore must not be broken or 'open'; it must be con-tinuous and uniform, in order to form a definite conclusion to the entire wall. The problem is expressed with ruthless clarity, but the solu-tion could be found only through a piece of artifice. As he was later to do in the Belvedere, 10 Bramante did not hesitate to make the archi-trave and frieze break forward, while keeping the uppermost cornice, supported by the corbels of the frieze, uninterrupted – with the result that the paired corbels project into thin air.

Another thing: on the ground floor, the Ionic pilaster on its pedestal appears to be the privileged order, as it should be in a building dedicated to the Madonna. But the pier above it – the Composite one on the upper storey – has, visually, a prominence which is ambiguous but undeniable. True, the pilaster on the front is properly related to the Ionic below it, but the pier as a whole is a good deal wider, thus visually compromising the structural logic. This was another reason why Bramante gave only the Composite pilaster a pedestal and broke forward the entablature over it alone. But this was not enough for him. It was necessary to accentuate even more the importance of the piers on the ground floor over those on the upper storey, and it was impossible to do this without using another trick. Bramante makes the pedestals of the Ionic pilasters, against all the rules, jut forward further than the pilasters at the sides. It was clearly an illusionistic expedient. But yet again an anomaly appears, something which seems odd but which Bramante wanted: the pedestal of the corner pier juts forward much less than the others, in fact it keeps to the norm. This weakens the corner pier still further in comparison with the other piers; it emphasizes the whole effect of the continuity of the four walls without any pauses in the corner. This was decidedly the effect of the three-dimensional quality of *space in itself* which Bramante was seeking. The corner solution confirms the fact that this jutting forward of the pedestals of the other piers on the ground storey was a 'retouching', when the arrangement of the whole building and of the elements in it had already been settled. It also shows Bramante's 'painterly' outlook, his way of seeking particular visual effects from the point of view of the observer, by making empirical changes to a theoretically absolute process based on 'scientific' facts and unshakeable norms.

The cloister of S. Maria della Pace shows Bramante's efforts to apply a rigorous method very consistently in the first building which is definitely his in Rome. At the same time, he clearly intended to forge a new style which really expressed this method. The obstacle to this stylistic renewal may still have been a paralysing uncertainty about what he was trying to say.

We have reached the year 1500. In Rome, Alexander VI had not yet acquired the prestige which he needed if he was really to set himself up as the leader of Italian national aspirations. His policy was to found a monarchical state, but on the one hand his ambitions for his family meant that his objectives and methods were too personal; and on the other, strong feudal resistance made the realization of his programme doubtful and limited the scale of what he could do. The political crisis was not yet over. It was a time of confusion, of fear, of uncertainty. Culturally, Rome had not yet taken over from Florence as the centre of the arts. The spiritual and political prestige of the papacy had not yet

been consolidated by great cultural advances, nor, above all, had the Papacy and its rule yet succeeded in identifying itself wholly with the ancient Roman Empire. Nicholas V had initiated this process and Julius II, with the myth of the *renovatio Romae,* was to bring it to completion. But in 1500 we are still in a period of transition. Bramante, too, was not yet in the front rank of those in the Pope's service. He came as an émigré, bringing cultural habits, like those of Urbino or Milan, which might still have seemed provincial and which had developed in narrower circumstances than those which were to characterize the time of Julius II.

Bramante's uncertainty about the content of his work, and his relative isolation after a few months in Rome, reveal themselves in the uncertainty of his style, and in the fact that it was impossible for him to express himself through really effective visual symbols in a social, economic and cultural context that had not reached maturity. His forms seem to have no special depth or breadth of meaning: they are not pregnant with ideas which could really revolutionize the way in which things were expressed. His work took on the character, in many ways the *experimental* character, of an intellectual and cultural exercise somehow detached from his problems – problems which were not merely personal but collective, social, political. He had not yet found a style that was really consistent with his method. He had the methodological means to control the arrangement of space; but not what he needed to turn it successfully into expressive imagery. Even so, he was trying to select and sublimate his forms, and was tending towards simplification, towards the definite 'synthesizing' of means and expression which were the necessary preliminary for any renewal. While his references to the Antique are still indirect – present, but somehow diluted, implied rather than stated – and he is still using light in a way learnt from Urbino and from Mantegna, his architectural language has become restrained and schematized, subtly intellectualizing, and without any explicit personal character. The individual elements do not add up to an effective whole. But his work at S. Maria della Pace (the convent as well as the cloister) has a special fascination which springs from the sheer intellectual discipline of his method, and from his efforts to purify and synthesize. It is also infused by an air of youthful renewal, something sharp and fresh that was not to reappear in Bramante's work, which the lack of balance in the expression could not spoil – indeed, it may even have increased it.

Chapter six

Bramante's 'grand manner':
the Belvedere
and the rebirth of the
'Classical villa'

WORK at S. Maria della Pace went on until 1504. On 31 October 1503, Julius II, whom Bramante had probably known when he was Cardinal Della Rovere, had been elected Pope. Bramante, who was then sixty, seems to have been taken into his service at once to give the Vatican buildings (and incidentally, as it was to prove, himself too) a new lease of life. Perhaps, as Ackerman maintains, Bramante made at least a tentative project for the whole Belvedere complex as early as the first year of the new pontificate, 1504.[33] He had certainly done so before the spring and summer of 1505. The Belvedere is still linked to Bramante's work at S. Maria della Pace by a certain stylistic subtlety, and it is only in the first design for St Peter's, the so-called 'Parchment Plan', datable to the middle of 1505, that his 'mature manner' appears with complete assurance and success.

An inscription in the crypt of the Tempietto of S. Pietro in Montorio, however, and an account of its restoration in 1628 refer to its foundation in 1502 by Ferdinand and Isabella of Spain: 'sacellum Apostolor[um] Princi[pi] [. . .] poss[uerunt] an[no] sal[utis] kri[sti]ane MDII'. The Spanish Cardinal Carvajal was in charge of the work. The Tempietto would therefore stand in Bramante's *oeuvre* between the cloister of S. Maria della Pace and the Belvedere and St Peter's. But such an early date seems surprising in view of the mature character of this highly significant building (see below, Chapter 7). Indeed, in 1944 De Angelis d'Ossat, followed by other experts, suggested dating it 1505–06; and I myself, for a number of historical and stylistic reasons, believe that 1502 may only be the date when Bramante was given the commission and work began on the crypt; whereas the upper part could have been delayed for several years, until after St Peter's and

perhaps as late as 1508–09. In fact, several other important works, such as the Palazzo Caprini (later the house of Raphael) and the Nymphaeum of Genazzano, probably by Bramante, cannot be dated with any certainty, and buildings less mature in style – such as the west front of the present courtyard of San Damaso, the courtyard of the Rocca at Viterbo, and (if the initial design really was Bramante's) the church of the Consolazione at Todi – seem to alternate with others in which a new maturity has been successfully achieved. The problem is complicated by the active participation of assistants and colleagues in some of his works (men who might be a good deal younger, and were certainly less 'mature' and open-minded than Bramante); and above all by Bramante's own changeable character, by his readiness to modify and experiment with different styles and 'manners' in every work he produced.

The question when the Tempietto of S. Pietro in Montorio was planned may seem trivial, but in fact it is of fundamental importance in deciding when Bramante passed from the phase of systematized planning and practical experiment (which began, as we have seen, in his last years in Lombardy and ended with S. Maria della Pace) to his new 'grand' or 'mature' manner in Rome. Did this 'mature manner' begin with the Tempietto (and, according to some, with the Palazzo Caprini and the Nymphaeum of Genazzano) during the reign of Alexander VI, shortly after Bramante's arrival in Rome? Or was it fully revealed only in St Peter's, in the early years of the pontificate of Julius II, and in the new political and cultural climate which he brought with him? And was this 'mature' phase homogeneous, or at least consistent in its direction? Or, on the contrary, did 'mature' works alternate with others that are stylistically more timid and backward-looking, so that the 'mature' works take on the character of experiments?

It would seem that in those works where Bramante was most experimental and, perhaps, had most time and a chance to think deeply and to become involved, his 'mature manner' expressed itself in the form of a building considered as an autonomous architectural object. In other works, the building's architectural autonomy is so to speak renounced, and its interest lies chiefly in its place in the whole urban setting, so that purely stylistic problems become much less crucial. It would be a mistake to see too strong a contrast between these two views of architecture, but the Tempietto in 1502 might well signal the beginning of his mature manner. One has to conclude that this manner, which is fully expressed in the designs for St Peter's and later in the choir of S. Maria del Popolo, in the Palazzo dei Tribunali, in the churches of S. Biagio and S. Celso, in the Palazzo Caprini, in the 'Holy House' at Loreto, and in the *tegurio* of St Peter's, always existed side by side with revivals of his earlier style, in which tension slackens.

149,
173,
176,
179,
166,
181,
175

But as far as the development of architectural style in the sixteenth century is concerned, and, more generally, the whole transition from Renaissance to Baroque, up to the eighteenth century and beyond, Bramante's new mature manner was of fundamental importance. In it he drew together the results of all the experiments and wide-ranging research conducted throughout his life, and he also reached a peak of expressiveness in his use of spaces and volumes, both architectural and urbanistic. Even those works (by no means all minor) in which his style seems not to reach full maturity are also on the whole fully expressive of Bramante's 'grand' Julius II manner; in particular because of the way in which space, wholly urban space, is always fully realized in the planning. In them he tried out new spatial ideas, innovations in the grammar and syntax of architecture, and problems of theory and method. True, they are not always executed with a commensurate attention to detail. It is as if Bramante stopped short before the investigation was complete, neglecting – through lack of interest, or of expressive tension, or through pressure of time – to give either the whole or the parts their definitive forms.

The two groups of works, which overlap in time, seem complementary, and it is arbitrary and artificial to contrast them. However, one can say that in the first group (the works in a fully mature manner) the main problem, apart from that of style, is to organize the interior space and exterior volume; whereas in the second group the most important factor is Bramante's interest in the total plan, i.e. the building in its urban setting. These two groups of works will therefore be dealt with separately, starting with the second; for, as has already been said, the first seems to sum up Bramante's essential achievement and virtually includes what is most valuable in the other, so that the second seems almost to foreshadow the first.

The most complete example of the first group is St Peter's, of the second the Belvedere complex in the Vatican – though the latter must, by virtue of its mastery of the stylistic vocabulary, also be counted as a highly representative work of Bramante's new 'Julius II' manner. But the main distinction remains valid. The crucial problem in the former is that of the organic integration of volume and interior space, in the latter that of open space on a large scale, of urban space. Along with these two great public commissions can be grouped others which have to do with the same problems, works which tackle and solve particular questions, which offer alternative solutions and provide opportunities for trying them out in practice.

Although, as we have seen, some of the buildings which show Bramante's stylistic 'revolution', such as the Tempietto of S. Pietro in Montorio, may possibly have been planned at the end of Alexander VI's pontificate, that 'revolution' found its historical justification above all in the new political and cultural climate that appeared in Rome under Julius II, from 1504 onwards.

When Julius II became pope, Rome was in a serious situation economically. The government of Alexander VI and Cesare Borgia, the slackening of the state's authority, the internal struggles, and the armed bands which roamed the streets had all brought hunger to the city. Corn had nearly doubled in price. Financially, the situation in the Papal State was disastrous. Some banks had closed; the value of silver went down, compared with that of gold; money was devalued. Taxes, paid in devalued coinage and collected through a confused system, were insufficient to replenish the Papal Treasury, which Alexander VI had plundered so lavishly that in 1504 it contained less than half of what was needed to meet administrative costs. The city's health was in a serious condition too. From the end of 1503 until the autumn of 1505 the plague was raging; so fiercely, in fact, that the members of the Curia and even Julius II left Rome and retired to their villas in the country. Malaria was also prevalent in the low-lying areas of the city, and even Julius II caught it. The neglect of aqueducts (of the ancient aqueducts only the Acqua Vergine, which fed the Trevi Fountain, was still functioning) meant that people had to use water from the Tiber, which brought further disease.

The weakening of the central authority under Alexander VI had encouraged crime in the crowded areas of Rome, particularly in the outlying districts, in the port areas of Ripa and Ripetta, and in the countryside. Justice was not administered and public order was undermined. Hunger, and the outrages of the noble families, occasionally provoked uprisings among the people. With its houses concentrated for the most part in the loop of the Tiber, Rome still looked medieval (although several popes from Nicholas V to Sixtus IV had promoted building in the second half of the fifteenth century); but, unlike other medieval Italian cities, it had not been built to a pattern growing out of the communal, 'civic' organization of its people. The great aristocratic families were entrenched in strategic positions, and divided the city up into separate, quarrelsome districts and clearly defined zones of influence. Even the Borgo, with St Peter's and the papal residence in the Vatican, was an isolated area encircled by a wall. Another isolated district was Trastevere.

Julius II took immediate note of this disastrous state of affairs as soon as he became pope, and acted decisively.[34] His programme was a model of clarity and he promoted it with limitless ambition, great political ability, and willpower prepared to use every means available. He not only dreamed of creating a national, authoritarian monarchy under the Papacy, but aimed at a *renovatio imperii* in which the pope would also be emperor, just as Augustus, Tiberius and Trajan had been emperors and *pontifices maximi*. Julius II would be the new Julius Caesar. His very name announced an explicit purpose that bypassed medieval tradition and went back to Antiquity. While still a cardinal, Giuliano della Rovere had put an ancient, famous image of the imperial eagle in a place of honour in the porch of the church of SS. Apostoli, and now he meant to found a new empire that would be at once Antique and Christian. The small 'rational' state – the 'bourgeois city-state', which, as Garin puts it, 'lives in plurality and through plurality' – was now an ideal that had been superseded.[35] Praise of the civic virtues of republican Rome, which in the early days of humanism had entailed the condemnation of the imperial Rome of the Caesars (for instance by Leonardo Bruni), was now abandoned; and instead there arose a will

to power, which envisaged a 'universal' authority, no longer a merely local or regional one; an authority that would recreate the ancient Empire and rule over both the temporal and the spiritual worlds.

Julius spent his entire pontificate trying to put this programme into practice. His weapons were absolute personal commitment, willingness to stake everything on bluff, and readiness to act quickly and without scruple. But before anything else he had to improve the internal condition of Rome; in the first place, its economic and financial situation. As early as 1504, to stop the devaluation of the coinage, he ordered new revalued coins (*giulii*) to be minted. At the same time, in spite of strikes and popular uprisings, he demanded that taxes in the new currency should be collected ruthlessly. He then stabilized the price of bread by setting up public bakeries in July 1504; he brought in rationing; he hired ships to bring grain in cheaply from Sicily and France; he created a special official, the Prefect of Annona, to be directly responsible for the victualling of Rome; he expelled 'useless mouths' from the city and prohibited immigration.

Personally, Julius made himself a reputation for avarice; he cut down non-essential spending, and used every possible means of increasing revenue. Above all, the reform of tax collecting and the 'providential' death of several extremely rich cardinals whose goods were immediately confiscated meant that as early as 1505 the Papal Treasury was in a fairly healthy state (300,000 ducats in 1505, and about 500,000 in 1506). Peter's Pence provided a remarkable amount of money and war was not the last source of revenue. But it was his association with high finance that assured the Pope of relative economic stability. Agostino Chigi, the greatest banker and merchant of the time, whose agents and activities were in touch with the markets of the whole of Europe and the East, was not only linked to Julius by marriage but was also his financial adviser, his confidant, and his ally. And still more political power and stability, though they might not satisfy his energetic, autocratic ways, were assured as early as 1505 with the appointment of new cardinals, all chosen from among his friends.

Like all dictators of his type, Julius needed to assure internal order, hide inefficiency and poverty, and provide buildings to show off the power he was presumed to have. All these were essential parts of the political game (or tragedy). Architecture and town planning – the 'decorum' of Rome – had an outstandingly important political function. The humanistic ideal of the

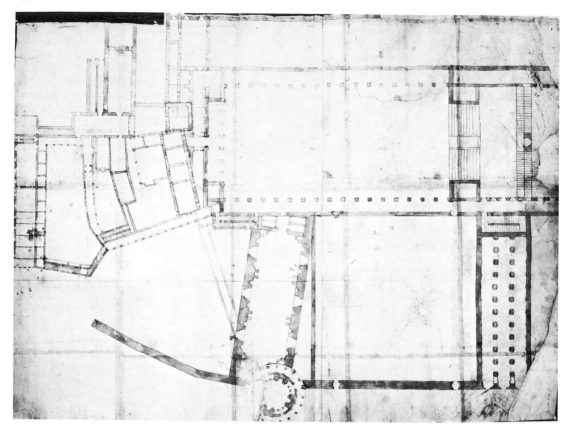

93 Rome, Vatican: project for the lower Belvedere court and the rebuilding of the Vatican Palace, by Antonio di Pellegrino da Firenze, after Bramante? (Florence, Uffizi, Arch. 287)

artist, no longer a *faber*, but an intellectual, integrated into the system, helped to strengthen the new economic, political and also cultural prestige of Julius's authority. And it was an authority which was being exercised over a much wider field than before, on a scale larger than that of the Florentine world or the court of Urbino or even that of Ludovico il Moro. A 'grand manner' of living and of conducting politics had to be reflected by a 'grand manner' in the look of the city and its architecture.

Bramante found that the architectural values of Brunelleschi or even of Alberti were no longer adequate. He would have to go not to the Quattrocento 'modern' tradition but directly to the ancients. As has often been pointed out, the building programme, the *instauratio Romae*, which Julius II had undertaken, was linked implicitly, and in several cases explicitly also, with the one proposed and begun by Nicholas V half way through the fifteenth century, and

taken up again by Sixtus IV Della Rovere, Julius's uncle. The reasons which Nicholas had for dedicating himself 'so fervently to building' are explained in his own famous 'testament' (1455), which has come down to us through Giannozzo Manetti.[36] Above all it was 'to assure the greatest prestige to the Roman Church and so that the Apostolic See [might] enjoy greater regard among all Christian peoples'. With the grandeur 'of buildings which [were] in a sense perpetual and testimonies that [were] almost eternal' the 'greatest and highest authority' of the Church could be affirmed and maintained. In addition, defensive works were needed to assure the Papacy of safety within the city; and in particular within 'worthy and safe dwellings . . . of the leader, the members and the whole Curia . . . against external enemies and those internal enemies who wish to overturn the established order'. Julius II's motives were to some extent the same. In addition, building satisfied his personal ambition and desire for glory and his longing to copy what the ancient Roman emperors had done. But it was also a direct instrument of propaganda, serving no longer a merely spiritual authority, but a specific temporal political programme. For this reason, the thought of imperial Roman achievements acted as a more powerful stimulus, and was more openly acknowledged, than it had been in the case of Nicholas V and Sixtus IV. And to emphasize the change of purpose in Rome under Julius II, the *aediles* Domenico Massimo and Girolamo Pichi in 1512 put up a stone to commemorate Julius's buildings in the city, which said that they had been built not for the defence but for the 'ornamentation of the city: 'urbem Romam . . . pro maiestate imperii ornavit'.[37]

The appearance of Rome and of its new buildings was intended to give the impression that the age of the Roman emperors, and their majesty and their power, had returned. The

Roman emperors' palaces – the Palatine, the Domus Aurea, Hadrian's Villa – were very definitely in the minds of Nicholas and Julius and their architects (Bramante in particular) when they were planning the rebuilding of the Vatican, the centre and starting point of the *instauratio Romae*. Those Antique palaces had been elaborate dwellings which gave splendid free expression to the demands of both ceremony and comfortable living: outside the restrictions of the walled city, with plenty of space around them, they were monumental complexes, almost towns in themselves, with rich and varied functions. Something similar – a combination of buildings, courtyards, gardens, fountains and a theatre – had been envisaged by Nicholas V. In his scheme, which he had begun but which was then given up by his immediate successors, he had intended to demolish and rebuild the old Vatican basilica. This scheme was taken up again in its entirety by Julius II. The whole Vatican area was to

94 Rome, Vatican: reconstruction showing the Belvedere courtyard (right) in conjunction with Bramante's first design for St Peter's (the Parchment Plan, Ill. 154). Though inaccurate in a number of details, this gives a good general idea of Bramante's two major projects in the Vatican. (Letarouilly)

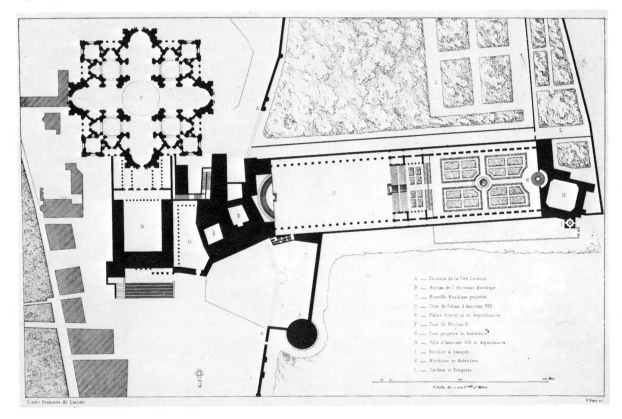

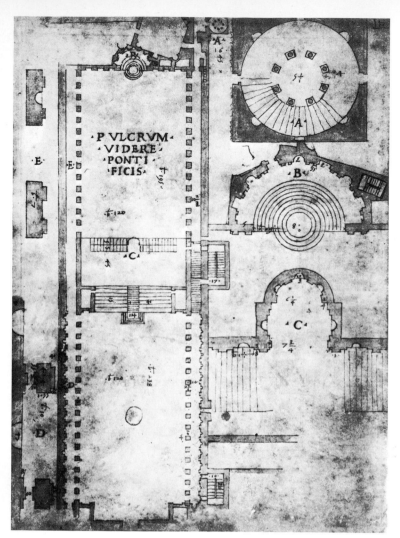

PVLCRVM· VIDERE· PONTIFICIS·

form the imperial palace of the new Julius Caesar, *imperator* and *pontifex maximus,* an explicit celebration of the pope-emperor. The old building was to be extended towards the 94 existing villa of Innocent VIII through the new complex of the Belvedere; St Peter's was to be demolished and rebuilt; the front of the old palace facing the city (later the loggia of the 121 courtyard of S. Damaso) was to be made regular; the system of defence was to be revised; and – at least in a proposal from Bramante, who perhaps wanted to demolish and rebuild not only the basilica but the whole of the old Vatican Palace, and who, according to Vasari, 'made a very large plan to restore and rebuild the 152, palace of the pope' – a large piazza was to be 153 made in front of and around the new basilica. As in other imperial residences at Constantinople, Aachen, etc., the new church was to be

a gigantic palatine chapel; the *martyrium* of the first *vicarius Christi,* the imperial mausoleum of the popes and at the same time the first church of Christendom. Papal palace and new basilica would constitute an earthly Jerusalem symbolizing the heavenly Jerusalem. The Belvedere, like a Classical imperial villa, would be available for recreation, culture and rest.

The new façade of the palace towards the city was to be a new *septizonium* or a new *Tabularium,* built upon the Vatican Hill. The whole complex, like an imperial acropolis, a sacred fortress, was to appear as a single ideal unity. New straight streets along the Tiber 120 would link it with the city. The old Ponte Trionfale, rebuilt, would provide access to the sacred area, seat and symbol of the greatest religious and political power on earth.

The plan for rebuilding may not have been

conceived all at once, with a precise and organic programme from the start. Originally it may have been even larger and more radical. We do not know how much of its special form must be attributed to Julius II, and how much to Bramante's daring ideas. Certainly different parts of it were started at different times. But from the very first year of Julius II's pontificate until his death in 1513, his enthusiasm for building, though it might be slowed down, never stopped, nor could it bear to compromise with practical obstacles. For these eight or ten years, while the plan was under way, unaffected by any thought that it could not be completed in the short span of a single pontificate, the work was coordinated by a single vision. Its realization was to involve Julius's successors for at least another hundred years.

98–101   Work began in 1505, on the Belvedere courtyard. The plan was to enlarge the Papal Palace northwards, by connecting it with the Belvedere, a villa built by Innocent VIII, then standing on its own about three hundred yards away. This villa was to be enlarged southwards by a courtyard which would be used as an *antiquarium,* a gallery of Antique statues. The villa's link with the palace, overcoming the difference in level between the two sites and bridging a hollow or valley between them, was to be accomplished quite easily by means of long horizontal walks, consisting of parallel passages with loggias, forming, as it were,

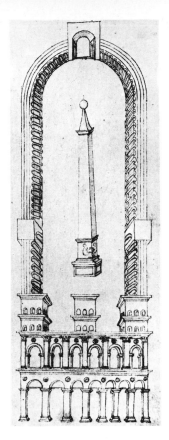

97 Filarete: drawing of the Circus of Caracalla or Maxentius in Rome (Florence, Biblioteca Nazionale Centrale, Codex Magliabechianus II.I.140)

96 Giuliano da Sangallo: plan of projected palace for the King of Naples, 1488 (Rome, Vatican Library, Cod. Barb. Lat. 4424, f. 41v)

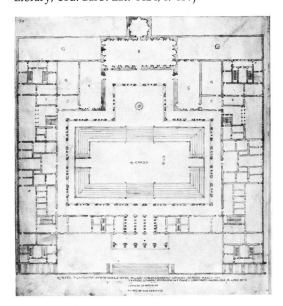

covered streets. In the space between these passages, which would be laid out in terraces, there was to be an open-air theatre with tiers of seats, in the Classical manner, and gardens with orange trees, pines and bay trees planted in beds, with fountains playing. Altogether, then, it was a building with many functions: for leisure, relaxation and shows, for culture and rest, for the moderate physical exercise of walking in the fresh air, as the ancients had done; a place for the humanist *otium* of the Pope and his court. Several entrances from the inside and the outside would ensure easy circulation throughout, and a number of staircases would link the various levels, some of which would be in the form of ramps suitable for horses. More-   117 over, as the new Belvedere was also an extension of the Vatican's defensive system, it had to be part of a fortified *enceinte,* at least on the eastern side. For this reason the perimeter wall on this side had to be mostly solid, allowing the country and city to be seen only occasionally through small galleries. As Ackerman emphasizes in his exemplary monograph on the Belvedere, the

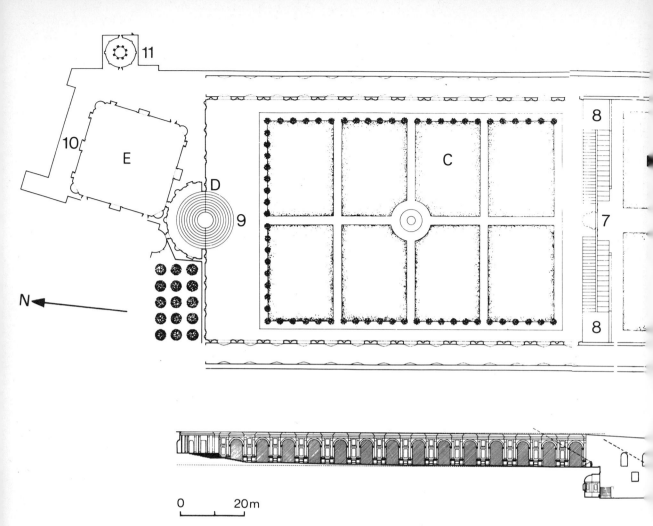

Rome, Belvedere: reconstructions of Bramante's original design

98–101 Plan, longitudinal section, axonometric view (after Ackerman) and transverse section. A lower court, B intermediate court, C upper court, D exedra, E statuary court or garden; 1 Borgia Tower and papal apartments, 2 fountain, 3 entrance from Porta Julia, 4 theatre area, 5 theatre seating, 6 towers, 7 nymphaeum, 8 ramps, 9 concave-convex stair, 10 villa of Innocent VIII, 11 spiral ramp-staircase. In the longitudinal section, sight-lines from various points are indicated; at the far right, the upper viewpoint is from the Stanze, the lower one from the Borgia Apartments.

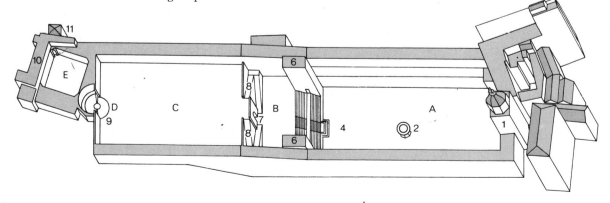

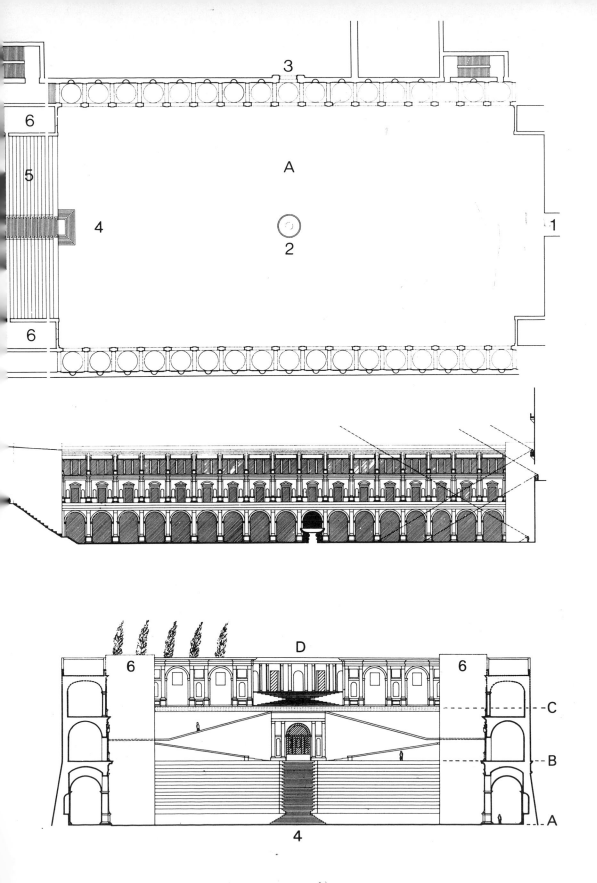

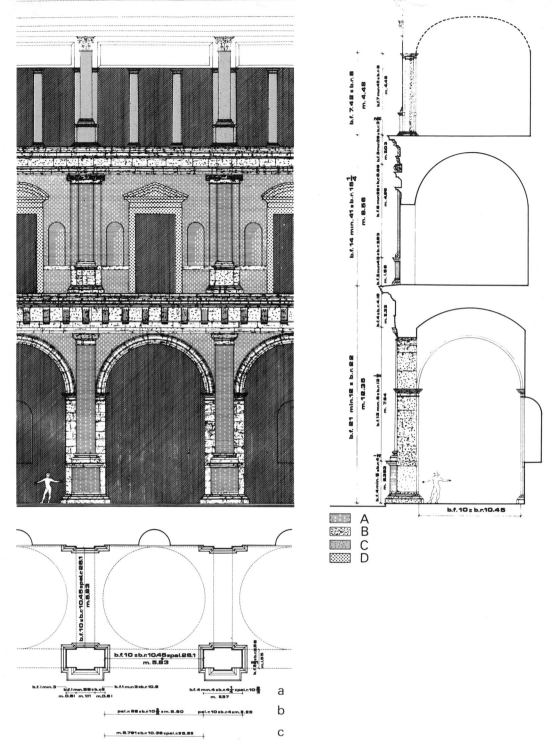

102 Rome, Belvedere: reconstruction of the design of the side walls of the lower court, in elevation, section and plan. The design recalls an inlaid door at Urbino (Ill. 9). Several materials were used: A brick, B travertine, C peperino (tufa), D plaster or travertine? The dimensions given at the bottom are based on the 'Coner Codex' (a), Peruzzi (b), and modern measurement (c). (Drawn by R. Lauri)

origin of the plan, which is more literary than visual, lies in the imperial villas and palaces of Classical Rome.[38]

In the administrative and ceremonial centre of the new city, the Pope and Bramante wanted to recreate a fragment of ancient Rome – perhaps the Circus of Nero, or the Naumachia, which was said to have been on the site of the Vatican. Lacking surviving concrete evidence, and with a still insufficiently precise idea of ancient architecture, they applied their fertile imaginations to those descriptions of famous buildings by ancient writers: Tacitus and Suetonius on the Domus Aurea of Nero (its position in a valley between two hills might appear similar to that of the Belvedere); and especially Pliny the Younger on his two villas, 'in Tuscis' and at Laurentum. Ackerman notes what surprising analogies can be found between the Belvedere and, in particular, the description of Pliny's villa in Tuscany. The analogy extends even to details, and it is quite likely that Pliny's text, which was in Julius's private library, served as a guide for the planning of the Belvedere. Certainly early visitors to the Belvedere wrote of it in Plinian terms.

The task facing Bramante was largely new. For the first time since Antiquity a permanent open-air theatre was to be built, a museum to exhibit and preserve ancient statues, and a garden which, contrary to tradition, was to be an integral part of the architecture of the whole. The old had also to be coordinated with the new, and probably the Belvedere scheme had to be envisaged as part of a larger plan to extend the Vatican buildings, with halls for audiences and meetings, and with rooms and services of all kinds for the various offices and the needs of the Vatican court. (A project by Bramante for the whole Vatican extension might, according to C. L. Frommel, be represented in Uffizi Arch. 287, once attributed to Peruzzi but possibly by Antonio di Pellegrino da Firenze, a colleague of Bramante's.[39]) The size and topography of the enormous site were in themselves a source of difficulty, but also a stimulus to invention. For Bramante, the fundamental problem posed by Julius's 'triumphalistic' intentions was one of planning on a scale that had no precedents, mastering an area about a hundred metres wide and three hundred long.

A complex of buildings in some ways comparable to the Belvedere courtyard had already

93

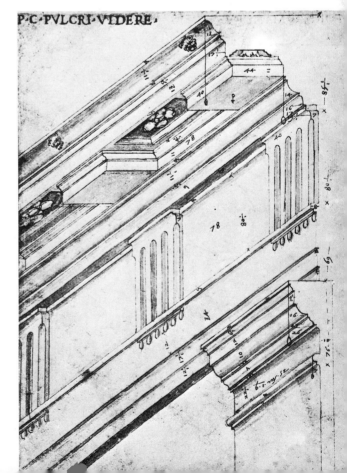

103, 104 Rome, Belvedere: details of the Ionic and Doric orders of the lower court (London, Sir John Soane's Museum, 'Coner Codex', ff. 69v, 61v)

en built in Rome, when the Palazzo Venezia was connected with the Palazzetto Venezia. Here again, a palace with a symbolic significance was associated with a *viridarium* surrounded by arcades and opening on to the countryside through archways; but the scale was much more modest than that of the Belvedere and the link between the two buildings was not worked out visually. Fairly large complexes had been built in the fifteenth century. But in some cases, as at Urbino, the fact that the whole was a collection of parts meant that the large dimensions had no effect in terms of spatial unity. And in others, as in Filarete's plan for the Ospedale Maggiore in Milan, or in Bramante's own cloisters at S. Ambrogio, symmetrical and perspective effects had been used to achieve a unified whole, but the breaking up of spaces and walls through the mechanical repetition of small divisions had avoided the problem of suiting the scale of individual elements to the scale of the area. From his Milanese period onward Bramante had shown that he was aware of the problem and had tried to solve it – in the Canonica, at Vigevano, at Abbiategrasso – by inserting into a façade elements on a larger scale, which, as we have seen, would interrupt the miniature uniform rhythm of the smaller part and be on the same scale as the enclosed empty space. With a certain awareness of the problems of large dimensions, and drawing more freely upon Antique examples, Giuliano da Sangallo had planned a large palace, or rather a gigantic villa, for King Ferdinand of Naples in 1488, and with similar intentions had made designs for a palace for Ludovico il Moro in 1492, designs which Bramante must certainly have seen in Milan. Although the surfaces are treated with an almost Mannerist complexity, the scale of the elements is still inadequate and belongs to the fifteenth century; yet Giuliano seemed to be trying to achieve largeness of scale in an architectural way – for instance, by occasionally using giant elements, by arranging the courtyard in stepped levels, by articulating the outer wall, by breaking up the traditional block into a number of masses, and by transposing the perspective effects along the main axis. Indeed, these designs, though unlike it in detail, are a kind of ideal precursor of Bramante's work in the Belvedere.

But in the Belvedere the dimensions are even larger and the intention was not to break up or disguise the enormous size but on the contrary to draw attention to it. Because of the site and the demands of the general programme, the building had to be long, rather like a stadium or a circus, in fact a long 'hippodrome', flanked by long blocks of buildings, just as Pliny described his villa in Tuscany. To show up its enormous size, one dimension, the depth, had to be emphasized more than the others. At the most distant spot, which was secluded and quiet, Bramante put the *antiquarium* for Antique statues: it was next to Innocent VIII's villa and built around a small octagonal courtyard with alternately long and short sides, just like the *zotheca* which Pliny described, beyond the hemicycle of the 'hippodrome'. This hippodrome is represented by the huge open courtyard of the Belvedere, flanked at the sides by long corridors like the ancient *ambulationes, gestationes* or *cryptoportici* and making a rectangle whose sides are in the ratio of 1:3 (the same proportions, according to ancient writers and Alberti, as those of the Circus Maximus in Rome). The most important element of the Belvedere complex, then, the central feature of this 'Antique villa', was to be 'void': the open space – the *xystus* of the 'hippodrome' – between the *gestationes,* the corridors.

Only the ancients had built on a scale comparable to that of the Belvedere. For Bramante, the study of ancient buildings now meant, as Ackerman puts it, 'learning the vocabulary of largeness'. The 'stadium' on the Palatine (whose own vaguely similar topography may have influenced the Belvedere), possibly Domitian's Villa at Albano, set on terraces, and with a hippodrome and a theatre, the villa of the Quintili, the villa of the Sette Bassi, and certainly Hadrian's Villa, must all have confirmed what Bramante felt about the Plinian associations of the villa-hippodrome. They must have appeared as concrete examples, supporting and complementing Pliny's description. The so-called Circus of Caracalla (actually of Maxentius) on the Appian Way had been drawn and described by Filarete as a typical example of an ancient theatre: with its towers (Pliny had mentioned *turres* in his description of his villa at Laurentium), the hemicycle at the end, and the position of its entrances, it may have suggested to Bramante the way of laying out a 'hippodrome' according to the ancients. But Pliny's *xystus* – the open space of the Belvedere, with dimensions in a ratio of 1:4 – must have been, as Pliny himself suggests, very unusual ('in plurimas species distinctus'). The unevenness of the site and the example of ancient villas set on a number of levels would have suggested arranging the open space in terraces. The lower area, which was closer to the Vatican Palace, was to be used for shows and the steps forming the seats of the audience had to look out over it, as they did in ancient theatres; but there also

18,
19
61,
72

62,
68,
70

96

98

97

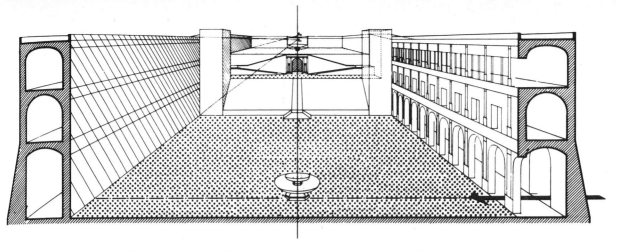

105 Schematic view of the lower, intermediate and upper courts as seen from the ideal viewpoint in the papal apartments (compare Ill. 99). On the right is the entrance from Porta Julia. The vanishing points of the lower and upper courtyard walls are indicated on the left; they are different, making the end wall appear farther away than it is.

Rome, Belvedere

106 The courtyard under construction *c.*1558–61, seen from the Papal Palace. In addition to the familiar elements, Giovanni Antonio Dosio's drawing shows the fountain and trees in the upper court. The east (right) side is complete, the west side scarcely begun. (Florence, Uffizi, Arch. 2559)

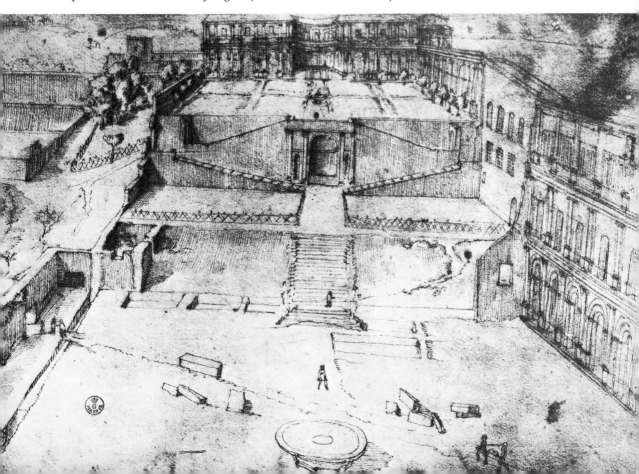

had to be a large entrance piazza from the old palace and from outside; like an ancient forum (the connection between *forum* and *circus* is mentioned by Vitruvius and confirmed by Alberti) flanked by porticos on several levels, from which 'gladiatorial games' could be watched (bull-fights, tournaments, etc.). So, following Alberti's directions, Bramante made this large courtyard-theatre-forum in a ratio of 1:2, as the Romans had made their forums. The intermediate area, proportioned apparently according to the golden section, was to contain the audience's seats, an intermediate terrace and the converging and ascending ramps to the upper courtyard, which was also a rectangle using the golden section, and was laid out as a garden closed at the end by a large terminal hemicycle (as in Pliny's Tuscan villa). Because of the differing heights, the corridors which flanked the space on the side of the Vatican Palace had to be on three levels – Doric, Ionic, and Corinthian, as in ancient buildings – but to end in the upper courtyard on a single level.

99, 101

But in order to coordinate the various elements of the space and the walls around it a unified perspective has to be achieved so that the end result is a unified image of the whole – which for Bramante meant a sort of spatial spectacle (*spettacolo*). The open space is to be given its own value, though the expression of that value is necessarily architectural. What is being presented is not simply a palace, nor a courtyard organized traditionally as a composition of structures around a fixed point from which the observer is invited, calmly and at rest, to contemplate the surfaces which define it. It is a *spettacolo,* a stage set, actually built and extended into depth, an artificial 'constructed landscape', such as the Romans had made, a rationalization of what was there already, the 'natural' *spettacolo*. It was as if 'petrified nature' was to become architecture. Taking to its limit a historical process which in Italy went back at least as far as the fourteenth century, architecture, the human environment, had to translate itself wholly, at least when seen from a certain point, into completely visual terms.

Architecture has thus become predominantly an image to be looked at; it has been translated into painting. Bramante *pittore,* although he was now employing architectural means and not painterly means as he had done at Urbino or at S. Satiro, has taken precedence again over Bramante *architetto*. As Ackerman acutely points out, he fixed the best viewing point of his gigantic 'stage set' outside it altogether. He placed it exactly where the Pope, without leaving his apartment, could see the whole ensemble

99, 105

from the windows of the Stanze or the Borgia Apartments; in particular, perhaps, from the window of the Stanza della Segnatura, Julius's private study, which in 1508, possibly on instructions from Bramante himself, was to be transformed by Raphael into an ideal space, dissolved on three sides into paintings, and on the fourth through the window, extended into the perspective *spettacolo* of the Belvedere: a private performance for Julius II only (and for his close associates). The other views, within the courtyard, were for the common people. But they were not the people for whom it had all been created. At most, when they arrived in the lower courtyard, they were to be overwhelmed and bewildered by the size of the open space and the surrounding buildings (over 28 m. high); walking about in the courtyard, seeing the unusual, 'archaeological', Doric order with triglyphs of the lower arcade, climbing the steps of the 'Antique' theatre, looking at the converging ramps and the nymphaeum cut into the lower courtyard, and the wide hemicycle beyond, they were to think that the age of the Caesars had returned and that Julius was the new *pontifex-imperator*.

168

102

104

114

Always conscious of the preferred viewpoint, which lay above the complex, Bramante organized the scene as a visual movement from lower to higher, from south to north, a movement that expands, leaps upward and becomes more concentrated as it recedes in depth. The horizontal plane, the stable basis of all traditional perspective building, is decisively altered: the space is rearranged on various levels, that achieve their effect through a coordinated dislocation in depth, articulated and linked together by gigantic staircases. Contrary to fifteenth-century tradition (but perhaps with vivid memories of ideas put forward by Leonardo) these staircases appear as images of 'movement', their sloping planes contrasting clearly with the right-angled buildings at the sides of the courtyard and with the horizontal ground. They are placed with a specifically artistic purpose: there is a dynamic quality implicit in them, like a break or sudden jerk. Once again the inspiration came from Antiquity. The Temple of Fortune at Praeneste (Palestrina) is often cited, but there may be other models, such as the Horti Acillani on the Pincio and the imperial villa at Albano. In the monuments of Antiquity Bramante sought above all a solution to his own problems and the confirmation of his own vision.

99, 106

But the final image of the Belvedere complex owes little to Antiquity. For the vast space to make an immediate impact, it was essential to emphasize the central axis: so a series of elements (which are in themselves expressive and interesting) is concentrated in the centre of the courtyard, rising progressively; one leads easily to the next, leading the eye into the distance as though the masses were themselves in motion and rebounding off one another, though still held together by perspective. The walls which flank the courtyard at the sides appear (from the ideal spectator's viewpoint) merely like wings in a theatre: flat, even, neutral surfaces, with a quiet, regular rhythm, lacking any three-dimensional emphasis that could distract the spectator from the centre of interest. Their visual function is merely to frame the scene, and, gradually diminishing in the distance from three to two and then to one storey, to stress the changes of level and to accentuate the visual thrust towards the end. The great extension in depth of the lower courtyard, closest to the ideal viewpoint, serves to distance the most important part of the composition to the point where its impact will be greatest. The upper level's distance from the viewpoint also means that it appears compressed, in a forceful and rapid ascent, accentuating the dramatic quality of an image whose fundamental artistic premise is a change in level.

At the north end of the lower courtyard, two towers flank the stairs. They are probably meant to recall the *diaetae* or the *turres* described by Pliny; they serve structurally to reinforce the long discontinuous side walls, they act as retaining walls, and they improve the acoustics of the open-air theatre; and they also help to make a visual break in the seemingly endless length of the courtyard, to mask the different heights of the side corridors and their difference in architectural treatment, and to eliminate the need for orders adapted to the inclined plane of the theatre seats. Above all they provide a narrowing-in that is necessary to the definition of the image; as visual supporting elements, points for the release of new energy after the important contraction at the intermediate level, and for its successive liberation and expansion towards the exedra at the end of the upper courtyard. The way they project, covering part of the side walls, makes the hidden space behind them mysterious. Their predominantly visual function, and the perspectival and illusionistic basis for the whole design, is shown by the surprising fact (noted by Ackerman) that the walls of the intermediate court concealed by the towers were given no architectonic treatment in Bramante's scheme.

Interest is concentrated on the void, on the open space itself. Between the towers, a crowded sequence of carefully worked out elements, getting gradually farther away and higher, guides the eye along the central axis from the lower courtyard to the climax at the end, the exedra in the upper courtyard. These elements are the large fountain at the centre of the lower level, the staircase between the theatre seats, the large double staircase forming a series of triangles in elevation with the nymphaeum in the centre, the fountain of the upper level, and finally the hemicycle with its convex and concave steps.

The design is a continuous succession of interpenetrating spaces, differentiated and characterized by varied elements and by varied treatments of the surrounding façades. Visual unity is no longer ensured by the completeness of these façades, as it was in the fifteenth century, but only by the expressive form of the contained space. Here the major elements, crowded together along the visual axis, echo one another in a series of insistent though freely treated leitmotifs, as they move gracefully and surely forward. The curve of the lower fountain, for instance, points to the apse of the nymphaeum, is re-echoed by the smaller fountain of the upper courtyard, and reappears amplified, as does the small apse of the nymphaeum itself, in the large hemicycle at the end.

This dynamic quality of the design is concentrated and epitomized in the central unfolding movement of the large triangular-fronted staircase, led up to by the sloping plane of the theatre seats. Here the lower ramps are only slightly inclined and rise slowly, diverging symmetrically from the axis. But the two upper ones are much steeper; they converge on the axis, climbing rapidly, galvanizing the whole design and preparing one for the leap on to the higher level. Again, the horizontal plane of the lower level is echoed on a smaller scale in the short, intermediate terrace, and it reappears, transformed into a garden, on the upper level. The triumphal arch motif of the nymphaeum façade foreshadows the wall treatment on the higher level. The long staircase in the middle of the theatre seats has squared steps, but seen in elevation the lower part contracts, then expands, a feature that looks forward to the contraction and expansion of the curved staircase in the hemicycle at the end. The niches on the first storey of the lower level reappear on the front and interior of the nymphaeum, in the back wall of the upper level and in the hemicycle. The unity of the design is assured by this continuous interweaving of forms that subtly correspond to one another, and pursue one another along the central axis in depth.

105

99,
106

101,
105

95,
99

101

101

101

99,
101

Rome, Belvedere: the upper court

107 The court as it appears today. Bramante intended a single-storey arcade, open at the sides, and a single-storey exedra with concave-convex stair (see Ills. 98–101). The north (end) wall had already been heightened in the sixteenth century (Ill. 106); the west wall (left) was built later, copying the design of Bramante's east wall.

108, 109 Triumphal arch motifs of the north (end) wall, as designed (London, Sir John Soane's Museum, 'Coner Codex', f. 41) and as built

110, 111 Elevation, plan and detail of the east wall, showing the progressive rise in level to the north and the corresponding reduction in height of the pedestals and slight upward slope of the entablature. In the detail (right) the northernmost and southernmost columns and pedestals are compared, demonstrating the change in ground-level and proportion. A base line, B horizon line used for instrumental measurement

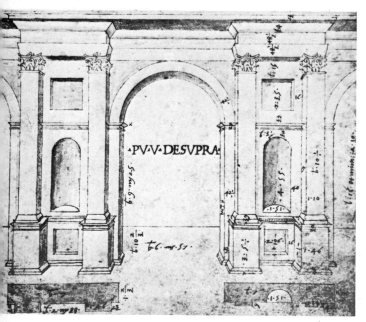

PV·V·DESVPRA

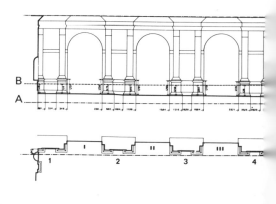

But it is a design made by a painter, worked out in essentially pictorial terms of colour, atmosphere and light, just as in Milan. The whole composition faces south, which is, according to Alberti (*De re aedificatoria,* Bk V, chap. XVII), the best possible position for visibility. The 'movement' of the architectural elements in space is enhanced by the movement of the sun throughout the day, and becomes a *spettacolo* that varies according to the eternal rhythm of the universe. The presence of plants and water (as in Pliny's 'hippodrome' and the ancient Roman villas) – the trees casting vague waving shadows and the fountains splashing – and the use of varied materials (travertine, brick, stucco, tufa) give an appearance of unity to the image which at the time had no precedent. The materials are not contrasted with one another by colour, as they were in the fifteenth century, but blended in a careful arrangement of tones ranging from brownish-red to yellowish-white. Seen from a distance, from the Pope's window, filtered through layers of air, as Leonardo would have noted, the Belvedere complex would really have been like the image of an ancient imperial city, reconstructed by

Bramante, and seemingly represented in a kind of three-dimensional painting.

But Bramante, as an architect, meant the Belvedere courtyard to be more than an 'objective' representation of what was actually there. It was to be a *spettacolo,* a theatrical fiction that was to deceive the spectator: once again, he was aiming at a perspectival, illusionistic representation.[40] The deception had to be so subtle that it was imperceptible. The Romans could manipulate vast spaces architecturally; but the area of the Belvedere courtyard was more than vast – it was gigantic. Julius II's architect, competing with the ancients, surpassing them, while using their own architectural language of grandeur, had to demonstrate that the Pope was capable of dominating even larger areas. Everyone who looked out of the Pope's window must realize that Julius was the most powerful of all the Roman emperors: he could sponsor the creation of works on a scale that had no precedent, even among the most splendid buildings of the ancients. The Belvedere, already immense, must seem larger still. Bearing in mind the perfect view from the ideal viewpoint, Bramante had to consider the treat-

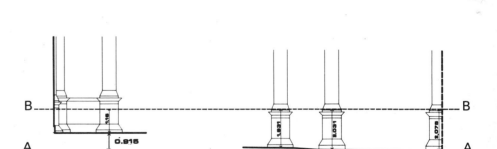

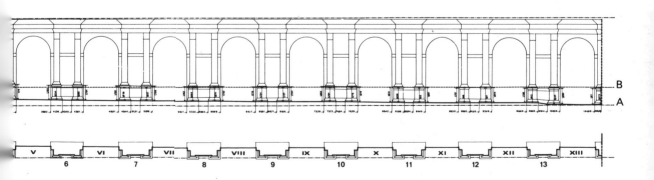

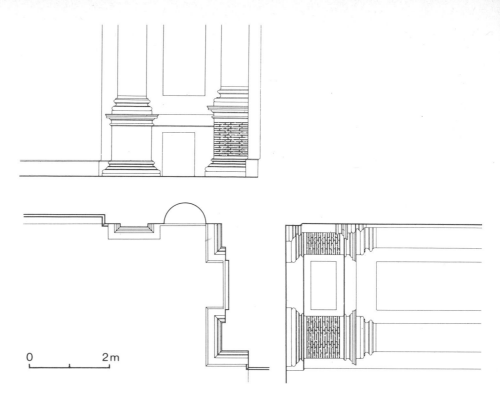

112, 113 Rome, Belvedere: the north-east corner of the upper court. The pedestals on the east wall (right) are taller and project farther than those on the north wall, causing an awkward and unorthodox junction.

ment of each element. Thus, in a number of cases, in the formal arrangement of individual parts he used subtle tricks to obtain particular illusionistic effects.

It was especially the upper level, the *spettacolo* beyond the towers, that was to appear deeper than in reality, and thus deceive the spectator. While keeping the same spacing as in the arcading of the lower level, Bramante changed the basic motif and adopted a system of alternating bays, with pairs of pilasters alternately enclosing arches and niches (a motif taken from Alberti, which Bramante had already used in the painted decoration of the piazza at Vigevano). This reinforcement of the vertical elements gives an illusion of greater depth. Then, just as on a stage, he made the ground in the upper courtyard slope up fairly steeply towards the end wall. He then placed the pedestals of the Corinthian pilasters on this sloping line, gradually reducing the pilasters' height and gently raising their base-line. At the same time, he made the top of the entablature slope slightly upwards towards the end. The slope and the differences in height, which are a fact and can easily be checked with a surveyor's instrument, are hardly perceptible to the spectator looking at the composition as a whole. However, they show that Bramante stage-managed the proportions of all the elements on the sides in order to make the whole wall seem longer. The end wall, to the left and right of the

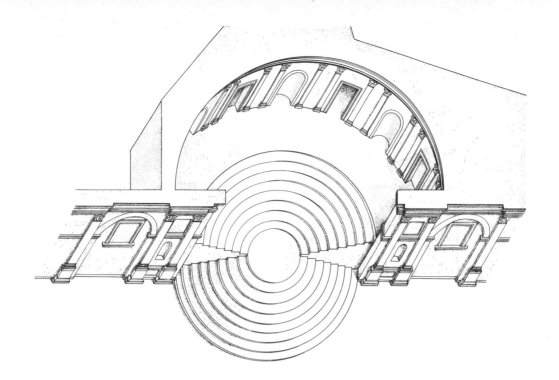

hemicycle, is treated similarly to the sides; but it must obviously seem further away than they. To achieve this visual distancing, Bramante subtly differentiated the formula of side and end walls: he accentuated the projection of the pairs of pilasters, thereby accentuating the shadows, he opened up the arcades into shady porticos, whereas on the end wall they are filled in (the sides are now filled in as well, altering the original effect), and he set the Corinthian pilasters on the side walls on higher pedestals, making the pedestals on the end wall seem farther away because they are smaller. His illusionistic scheme forced him into great boldness: in the corners, on the two adjacent walls, facing each other and quite close together, he placed pilasters that are similar but have different proportions and stand on pedestals of different heights, surmounted by the same entablature. He had been pushed into a solution that was syntactically wrong; but its ingenuity and intelligence equalled its boldness, and it did not worry him. From the Pope's window, the effect of spatial expansion was achieved and the 'incorrect' solution at the corners, from such a distance, was almost invisible. (Besides, the corners would be partly screened by trees and scarcely noticeable even close to.) But at the same time, this disregard for the rules of proportion did dangerously loosen those rigorous syntactical bonds which should have held the various parts together. One of the fundamental

112
113

114 Rome, Belvedere: reconstruction of Bramante's design for the exedra (Ackerman)

principles of the architecture of humanism had been contradicted for the sake of an illusionistic visual effect.

Something similar happened in the detailing of the hemicycle at the end. This in its turn had to be illusionistically 'distanced' even further than the already 'distanced' end wall from which it opened out. The problem here was complicated by the decision to put in another large staircase, the circular convex-concave one. This was not only necessary to reach the raised level of the statues standing round the hemicycle: it also had to appear as a fundamental element of the hemicycle itself and of the entire spatial plan. Bramante discarded the most obvious and academically 'correct' solutions. On the wall of the exedra he appears to carry on the pilastrade of the flanking walls, still keeping the upper line of the entablature constant; but he did not hesitate to use somewhat smaller pilasters. Once again the syntactical break between two adjacent motifs is quite definite, but concealed with masterly visual artifice. The result is again to make the smaller motif – in the exedra – seem farther away. With strictly architectonic methods and without using any pictorial expedients, without distorting the perspective elements in any way, the illusionism

114

101

he had used at Urbino and Milan now produces more mature results, subtly deceptive and 'universal'. The traditional relationships between *appearance* and *reality* are interpreted in a new way. Architecture is realized in a concrete way as structure and functional space; and at the same time it resolves itself into a picture, a visual artistic image analogous to that produced by the painter or the sculptor.

This new method of using (and above all of thinking about) architecture rejected in practice some of the fundamental architectural principles of the age of humanism. As we saw at S. Maria della Pace, Bramante believed in these principles and even wished to test them and to prove their absolute 'universality', their validity in all circumstances. (Was this not already a symptom of doubt?) And yet we see him in the Belvedere subtly questioning the principle of the syntactical coordination of the parts which assures their organic integrity, like a human body – that three-dimensional unity which he himself had so completely mastered in Milan. He is also challenging, in effect, the absolute metaphysical value of proportion which, according to Renaissance theorists, made architecture a reflection of the structural laws of a harmonious universe. Bramante, in fact, did initially arrange the proportions of the whole and of the individual parts according to precise, musical, numerical and geometrical relationships; but then, in practice, he denied the absolute value of these proportions, not just by changing them slightly in order to achieve particular visual effects, but also, as we have seen, by using the elements enclosing space in such a way as to make it seem to have different dimensions from those of real measurable space, established proportionally. And also in the final detailing of the parts – for instance, in the lower 102, section of both the upper and lower courtyard 108 walls – the proportions which presumably had originally been established according to orthodox theory (based on simple relationships and on the strict mathematical, modular, Vitruvian proportion of single elements) were later distorted by small 'corrections' in the 'theoretical' measurements, in order to achieve particular illusionistic effects.

What we have here, in fact, is a further stage in Bramante's dynamic process of development, following on the rigorous logic of S. Maria della Pace. As almost always with Bramante, it was not a settled conclusion but part of a continuing search, a search which he no doubt believed was getting him closer to the true, great and glorious manner of the ancients. Indeed, it had probably been suggested by some advice, often repeated but hitherto disregarded, misunderstood or not acted upon, from the venerated Vitruvius himself: 'When . . . the computed number of the symmetries has been established . . . then the architect's skill must be brought in to improve the nature of the place for the use and appearance of the building, and therefore, by adding and subtracting, he will introduce those corrections into the general symmetry, increased in some places and reduced in others, which will make the building seem to have no faults and allow the eye to rest upon it with complete satisfaction . . . since sight does not always seem to give a true idea of things, but often makes the mind move away from the right standards.'

Bramante actually seems to be practising exactly what Vitruvius preached, for the first time in the Renaissance. His intuition as an architect and his sensibility as a painter led him to modify the absolute standard represented by the musical proportions; though admittedly, with his feeling for perspective in the service of illusionism and his idiosyncratic idea of space, he went further than Vitruvius. To him proportion in architecture was a way of actualizing an abstract, universal value, and he certainly did not give up this idea. But at the same time he was bringing it down from the realm of the ideal, the absolute, the divine, to which Alberti had raised it, and making it real, subject to the variability and relativity of mundane things. In metaphysical terms, he was treating it not as *noumenon* but as *phenomenon*. And in the process the elements of individual choice, personal intuition and architectural sensibility called into question the supposedly objective and 'scientific' quality of his work. Contradictions of principle appeared. Questions arose about the whole theory and practice of architecture, engendering doubts that were soon to explode into the crisis of Mannerism.

As at S. Maria della Pace and again later, the process of testing principles through the consistent, complete application of a logical method, assessing it and modifying it where necessary, meant that occasionally insoluble problems and contradictions turned up in the process of planning. But it was the very effort of solving them by ingenuity that produced new plans and new stylistic motifs, which were often complex and dynamic. In the bold combination of different orders on different scales, or in the introduction of unusual features, Bramante's solutions were already almost Mannerist. An example is the treatment of the top storey of the lower courtyard. Each decision was the considered result of a series of interrelated critical con-

115 Rome, Belvedere: the Porta Julia, surrounded by massive rustication inspired by ancient Rome (compare Ills. 180, 182, 183). For the inscription, instead of Roman letters Bramante originally proposed to use hieroglyphics.

116 Rome, Vatican: cupola of the Borgia Tower, drawn by Peruzzi before 1523 (Florence, Uffizi, Arch. 134)

their universality: it was pointless to use motifs already tried and proved.

As Vasari acutely remarks, Bramante not only imitated the ancients 'with new inventions', but also added 'very great beauty and elaboration to the art'. The plan of each building and the definition of each element meant research and careful testing. Other parts of the Belvedere reveal this same impulse. The Porta Julia, which leads like a modern triumphal arch 115 from outside into the 'forum' of the lower courtyard, gave Bramante the chance to create an unusual *opera rustica* using rusticated blocks of stone. It went far beyond the tradition of the fifteenth-century Florentine palaces, going back to ancient Roman architecture and introducing new stylistic ideas which were fundamental for developments in the sixteenth century.

Even the great commemorative inscription 115 on the outside wall of the Belvedere, facing east, was originally, according to Vasari, to have been fantastically composed not of Roman letters but 'some letters after the manner of ancient hieroglyphics [in fact rebuses] representing the name of the Pope and his own, in order to show his ingenuity.' Other innovations appeared in the wooden cupola which was added to the 116 Borgia Tower in the old Vatican Palace in 1509 (and destroyed by fire in 1523). It is almost certainly by Bramante, and not, as has been assumed, by Giuliano da Sangallo. Its design includes a new type of drum, pierced on all sides by arches framed by ingeniously articulated orders below an entablature, and a large, curious lantern topped by the acorn of the Della Rovere family.[41] It is also the first instance of a cupola on a non-religious building. In size it was comparable to the dome of the Gesù. The statuary court or garden, completed in 1506 98 (the nucleus of the Vatican Museum) also gave Bramante the opportunity to create an entirely new type of space – although Francesco di Giorgio had roughly outlined something similar in his treatise. Here the interest is focused on the space in itself, and not on the walls around it. To this end the surfaces are kept unbroken, the corners chamfered and blurred by means of niches, and the traditional arcade and indeed any definite architectural element on the walls are omitted. All this enhances the importance of the Antique statues, which appeared brightly lit in the niches.

Next to this courtyard Bramante built a spiral ramp-staircase which exemplifies some 92 of his most characteristic concerns. Spatially 11 its basic idea is simple: a hollow cylinder containing a spiral supported on columns with architrave. The spiral is a rigorous mathematical

siderations that grew out of the concept of the whole, but it was conditioned above all by a desire to explore and to experiment.

Thus the new 'archaeological' study of Antiquity (which had a place, too, in Julius II's political programme) might lead Bramante to use Antique stylistic elements, such as the 104 Doric order with triglyphs on the ground storey of the lower courtyard; but at the same time he might reject as suspect other motifs with an equally good Classical pedigree if he had not tried them out for himself. For instance, given the programme, it would have been easy in 102 designing the elevation of the lower courtyard to use the scheme of three superimposed orders enclosing arches, like that of the Colosseum or the Theatre of Marcellus. But Bramante chose the harder path: he used a much freer and more complex scheme, which had appeared many 9 years earlier on a marquetry door in the palace at Urbino. He wanted to test principles, to assert

form, suggestive in itself of upward movement and of continuous ascent, and therefore eminently suitable for a staircase. Spiral staircases had been built by Francesco di Giorgio in Urbino and designed by Leonardo in Milan. Spiral staircases on columns had sometimes been used in the Middle Ages, and their architectural authority was confirmed by at least one Antique example – the so-called 'Portico of Pompey', which was drawn a number of times during the Renaissance, and, according to Palladio, was the source of Bramante's idea. But a spiral staircase is also a symbol. It is an image of motion – active and dynamic. It is, like all staircases, a connecting link; it implies movement from one point to another, and thus it gives visible form to another dimension, time. A difficult object, therefore, for static contemplation.

Bramante had not chosen the spiral form accidentally: as we have seen, movement is the key theme in the Belvedere complex. Here once again he makes the structure into a *spettacolo*, in this case of dynamic ascent expressed in visual terms. The whole staircase is designed to be seen from below by an observer who has just entered from outside. The only vanishing point in the whole image is high up, in axis with the empty well of the staircase between the columns, whose shafts, gradually diminishing in diameter as they rise and converge, join together visually from one level to the next, leading towards this topmost vanishing point. The staircase becomes an 'artistic' object, like a *sotto in su* perspective actually built. It was the only way of translating an essentially dynamic structure into a perspective unity – imprisoning movement, as it were, in a fixed optical frame, as in a painting. A whole tradition of perspective illusionism, from Masaccio to Mantegna, Urbino and S. Satiro, came together in this staircase in the Belvedere, enriched by everything implied and contained in the new political and cultural atmosphere of Julius II's Rome. From the realm of nature, from the endless expanse of the countryside (which used to come right up to this staircase), it leads upstairs up to the statuary court, to the garden forbidden to all except the emperor-humanist popes. The magic world of perspective – almost as in a stage set made real – both separates and connects the world of nature and the world of art, leading from the domain of ordinary mortals to the place where exalted converse is held with the ancients: the museum. Here no profane step is allowed, only an élite of 'superior' men, capable of contemplating beauty, in the enchanted castle which Julius boasted as the manifesta-

tion and the symbol of his dream of a humanistic *renovatio imperii*.

As he had done in the lower courtyard of the Belvedere, Bramante put the emphasis on empty space, as defined by the columns. He accentuated the solidity, the physical and sculptural coherence of these columns, in order to emphasize them as much as possible in space, and he gave them no logical connection with the inner wall beyond the ramp, so that the eye cannot measure the short distance between this wall and the columns, and it is reduced, in the shadows, to a mere neutral, enclosing element, a 'distanced' atmospheric background. The absence of horizontals, the reduction of the whole to a helix rolled round the creative force represented by columns (sculptural objects that glimmer round the central space at varying heights, perspective vectors aimed like arrows at the vanishing point above), and the oblique thrust of the architrave above the supports, all give the image a feeling of dynamism, of vibrant instability. It is characteristic of Bramante that he still achieves this by reducing architecture to 'scenic' representation: the image, drawn upwards in perspective, finds a new visual integrity that emphasizes the all-embracing unity instead of the single element. And the Renaissance ideal, here even more than in other works by Bramante, is given emotive colouring by suggestions from the Late Antique.

Insoluble problems, however, turned up in the final arrangement of the staircase. The spiral is an open form, which can be indefinitely extended in space, and this is wholly contrary to the Renaissance vision. Bramante could not – or would not – find a workable architectural solution for the top of the staircase. All he knew was that light must enter mostly from above, and fall on the columns so that the eye should be drawn to the vanishing point of the image. Because of its nature and function – it had to be accessible even to horsemen – the staircase was probably meant to be roofless. Bramante finally left it unfinished, just as he had done on other occasions when difficulties arose in his work, perhaps because of the intrinsic impossibility of finding any coherent solution. The failure of the image at the top almost seems to symbolize the failure of Renaissance Classicism.

Bramante was faced with other problems when he turned to the individual elements. He had decided that the staircase was to be supported by columns. But as the columns would appear on several levels, it would be 'illogical' to use a single order. The ancients taught, and study of statics confirmed, that buildings of

92

several storeys (such as the Colosseum) had to be
made up of different superimposed orders:
Doric, Ionic, Corinthian, etc., gradually moving
from the heavier, stronger orders to the lighter
and more slender. If this principle was universal and 'logical' in every multi-storeyed
building, then, Bramante thought, it must be so
in every situation; even if the columns occur
in a spiral staircase. His decision led to a number of problems which could only be solved by
artifice. As there is no break in the continuity
of the spiral, every time the order changes there
are two columns of two different orders, differ-
ently proportioned, next to each other and supporting a continuous entablature. This was
entirely contrary to the rules, and Bramante was
forced to conceal it in an ingenious way by
placing the meeting points above the entrance
door. Anyone coming in and looking from the
single perfect viewpoint at the foot of the stairs
finds the *sotto in su* perspective perfect; but if
he looks the other way, or worse still, goes up
the stairs, the conflict with the rules will appear
jarringly. Moreover, since the height of the
columns must remain constant in relation to
the spiral ramp, and since their thickness is
governed by the static load which they support,
it was impossible to maintain the canonical proportions of the various orders and their inter-
relationship with each other.

Once again Bramante was visualizing the
whole, and for its sake he invented rules of his
own to connect the superimposed columns. In
fact he designed them almost like sections of a
single structure, separated by the spiralling
ribbon of the entablature, and he exaggerated
the thickness of the lower columns so that the
more slender columns higher up would by contrast seem further away, illusionistically exag-
gerating the height of the staircase. But the
individual columns, deprived of their correct
relationships, are paradoxically distorted almost to the point of caricature, their tectonic
qualities being expressionistically stressed in
'dialectical' antithesis to the elasticity, the
dynamic tension, of the spiral.

There was yet another problem, that of connecting columns, which are conceived for
horizontal structures, to the oblique line of the
spiral. Bramante's solution was practical, and
not successful when seen close to, as one goes up
the staircase; but from the ideal vantage point
below, the ambiguous relationship between the
columns and the sloping structure is virtually
invisible, concealed by the projection of the
capitals.

The most difficult problem conceptually was
that of placing a continuous entablature on

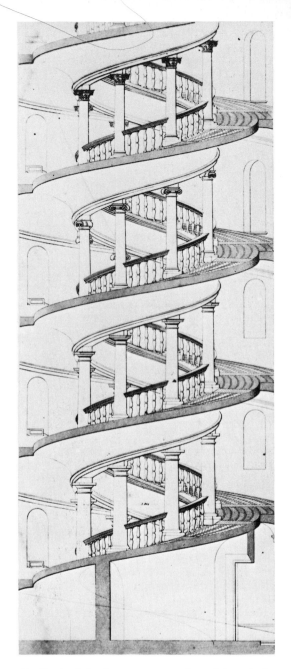

117 Rome, Belvedere: cut-away view of the spiral
staircase (Letarouilly)

columns of different orders. According to the rules, each order should have its own entablature, differentiated in form and proportion. But here it was unthinkable that the spiral facing of the ramp should keep changing in size to correspond with the columns below; besides, its dimensions were really too large to qualify as a conventional entablature in relation to the height of the columns, and its upper cornice could not project very far or it would hide the shafts of the columns. Bramante must have decided that he could not follow the rules without contradicting his own vision and getting a paradoxical result. Another piece of artifice was needed here. He designed the helix-shaped facing in such a way that only from a distance could it remind one of a Classical entablature: above the columns there is a small, simple architrave; at the top (directly beneath the next level of columns) a thin cornice; in the middle a very wide surface that was meant to recall the Classical frieze. The facing of the spiral has, ambiguously, become an 'entablature', especially if seen foreshortened, from below; but it is clearly not a 'true' Classical entablature: it is still a 'facing', with cornices tacked on to it, a mural border following the curve and moulded by geometrical and structural requirements.

This was a contradiction of the principles and rules, a proof that they were not universal. And yet Bramante, a 'most remarkable architect', as Palladio called him à propos this very building, solved his problems with lucid, critical awareness and a great deal of visual sensitivity – or 'artifice' and 'the most ingenious' devices, in the words of Serlio and Vasari. Indeed, he was so open-minded and so subtly intellectual that in comparison with the Belvedere spiral the later helix-shaped staircases of the sixteenth century and the Baroque age, which all derive from it, seem formal academic exercises. And the superimposition of different orders in a spiral staircase – a paradoxical idea, the experimental result of a ruthless intention to put principles to the test – was never tried again by anyone.

In the project for the Belvedere complex and its various parts, what finally appears, then, is the result of clear, analytical choices, guided on the one hand by a perspective and illusionistic vision (springing ultimately from Bramante's own personal instincts and influenced by emotive qualities and historical associations), and on the other hand by a precise, determined methodological discipline that sought to be 'objective': a 'scientific' and authoritative method of affirming and testing theories and principles. It is ambiguous, many-sided and

can be read in many ways. And although the image of the whole appears completely effective from the ideal viewpoint, its 'universality' is called into question by the existence of partial views which show up Bramante's compromises, tricks and expedients. The very rigorousness of the planning created insoluble problems, led to paradoxical solutions and, while putting forward claims to universal validity, simultaneously nullified them. 'Objectivity' and 'personal choice' are interwoven in the planning process and together achieve a result which is visually successful only, or mainly, as a total image, from a single predetermined position.

A consciously literary and humanistic revival of the 'Classical villa', in a sense different from that which applies to the Belvedere, is seen in these years in the so-called Nymphaeum of Genazzano, not far from Palestrina, now in ruins. There is no documentary evidence for Bramante's authorship, but C. L. Frommel has made a convincing and wholly acceptable case for it.[42] When it was built is not certain, but it would seem to have been not later than 1517 (when Raphael was designing and beginning to build the Villa Madama in Rome, perhaps with the plan of this 'nymphaeum' partly in mind). It may belong to the years 1501–02 and have been built for the Borgia pope, Alexander VI, or, as seems much more likely, to the years 1507–11 and have been commissioned by Cardinal Pompeo Colonna, who, according to Paolo Giovio, 'loved hunting and shooting and often arranged very elaborate parties in the country at enormous expense, where everyone enjoyed themselves'.[43]

In fact, although the Nymphaeum takes up the ideal of the suburban Roman villa, it was not so much a house as a holiday pavilion in the country, set in the midst of nature, to be used for parties and short visits in the summer. But, like the Belvedere courtyard, it was also a building for shows: the streams that ran in front of it could be dammed with a dyke and the small valley opposite could be turned into a lake for representations of sea-fights. The shows and the surrounding countryside could be admired from the broad portico of the house, as if from an enclosed theatre. The façade, which was almost like a *scenae frons*, could in its turn form the background for a show viewed from the slope opposite. Memories of the Antique (e.g. baths, villas, even a few Byzantine features) were very much alive and vividly expressed. References to Bramante's style and preoccupations in Rome are apparent: in the articulation of the outside wall by as many as four archi-

118, 119

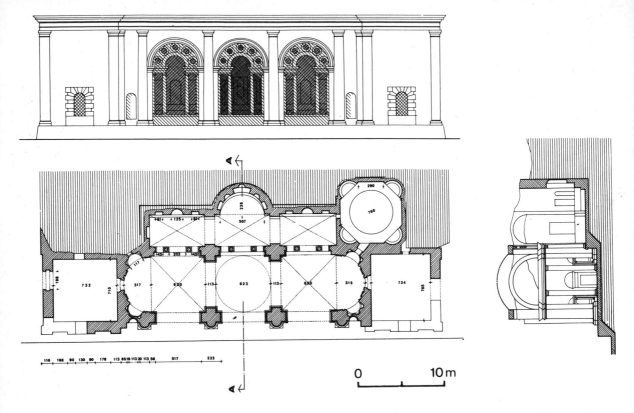

118 Genazzano, 'Nymphaeum': reconstructed elevation, plan, and section along A-A. Bramante here used attached half-columns, and the motif commonly known as a 'Palladian window', invented by him. Compare the use of oculi set in arches with S. Maria delle Grazie (Ill. 57).

tectural orders of different dimensions; in the interest in space in itself, partly built and partly hollowed out of the material; in the unorthodox way in which style and Classical grammar are handled. But here too a specifically 'illusionistic', theatrical character is given to the whole design; its free asymmetry in plan, suggested by Roman buildings, is unified, in typically Bramantesque fashion, by a dynamic emphasis on the central visual axis, set against the transverse axis, which is longer but less stressed. On the façade, the intention to create depth through perspective is shown particularly by the already Mannerist treatment of the 'Palladian window' motif. Three of these are placed between the back piers of the vaulted loggia, of which the front consists of a row of three arches framed by half-columns below an entablature, and they form a transparent screen between the loggia and the curve of the nymphaeum proper beyond it (a raised stage, perhaps for musicians or spectators). Their columns support arches pierced by oculi, a characteristic Bramante motif, which he had already used in Milan and, at about this time, was using in the choir of St Peter's. They stand on a high podium which greatly reduces their height, and although their cornice continues that of the adjacent pilaster, their complete entablature is deeper than that of the pilaster and extends below it. By this device, the Palladian motifs, which are anyway made up of elements smaller than those of the loggia, appear on a markedly 'distanced' plane behind it. And the whole visual schema – hemmed in as it is between solid blocks which flank it on either side – seems to separate into a succession of screen-like structures set in different planes in an illusory depth, terminating finally at the back wall, with its exedra and hollowed out niches. Once again the image is expressed in terms of painting, of *spettacolo*, given urgency,

119 Genazzano, 'Nymphaeum': detail of one of the Palladian windows

however, by visual hints that are full of meaning, rich in complex memories and influences and dynamic contrasts of style.

The Nymphaeum of Genazzano, Frommel suggests, marks the end of the transition from the late fifteenth-century suburban villa type, with a central loggia and projecting sides, like the villa of Innocent VIII (1484–87) and later the Farnesina (1505–09), to Raphael's more complex and articulated Villa Madama. And the Belvedere complex was the prototype of any number of plans for villas and open spaces, including urban spaces, in later centuries. So in the field of villas too Bramante led the way to a new kind of architecture, even providing models for it. Perhaps to a greater degree than any other man, he expressed the social context in which architecture was to develop from the Renaissance to the Baroque and right up to the eighteenth century.

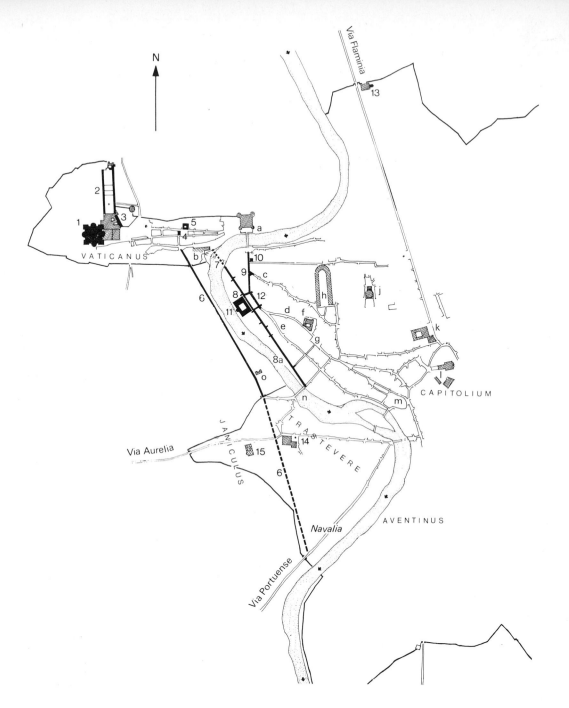

120 Rome: plan showing the works projected, and partly executed, by Julius II and Bramante (in black, 1–15) and other landmarks (*a-o*)

1 St Peter's, 2 Belvedere, 3 *logge* of S. Damaso, 4 House of Raphael, 5 palace of Cardinal Corneto, 6 Via della Lungara (the southern extension is conjectural), 7 Ponte Giulio or Ponte Trionfale (conjectural positions), 8 Via Giulia (8a: see Ill. 133), 9 Via dei Banchi Vecchi (del Banco di S. Spirito), 10 S. Celso, 11 Palazzo dei Tribunali, 12 piazza in front of the Old Apostolic Chancellery (Palazzo Sforza-Cesarini), 13 S. Maria del Popolo (choir), 14 fountain at S. Maria in Trastevere, 15 Tempietto of S. Pietro in Montorio

a Castel S. Angelo and bridge, *b* Hospital of S. Spirito, *c* Via dei Banchi Nuovi, *d* Via Peregrinorum, *e* Via Monserrato, *f* Cancelleria, *g* Campo de' Fiori, *h* Piazza Navona, *j* Pantheon, *k* Piazza Venezia, *l* Campidoglio, *m* Theatre of Marcellus, *n* Ponte Sisto, *o* Villa Farnesina

Chapter seven

Bramante's
image of the city

THE BELVEDERE, with its varying levels, its 'forum' courtyard, its staircases, its garden and its fountains, might be a whole district of a city (and in fact the inscription on the outer wall and a commemorative medal of Julius II called it '*via*'). Its seeming denial that the single building could be architecturally significant except as part of a total scheme, and the central role which it assigned to empty space as an element in its own right, give it an ideally 'urban' value, a value made even more emphatic by its great size. It was no coincidence that it was followed by a series of projects based on the idea of the *spettacolo*: not just large villas and gardens but, in the sixteenth century and the Baroque age, whole city districts. Bramante's interest in town planning, and in the building considered almost as the model for a possible urban space, characterizes nearly all of the works of his Roman period. It probably originated in Lombardy, perhaps under the influence of Leonardo, and was brought to fruition by commissions like the piazza at Vigevano and by Ludovico il Moro's proposals for rebuilding the area around S. Maria delle Grazie and opposite the Castello Sforzesco (in which Bramante may have been involved, as well as Leonardo).

Bramante's urban interests seem to have grown more intense in his later years, stimulated by the general enthusiasm under Julius II to reshape Rome completely and to revive the architectural splendours of Antiquity. Indeed, contemporary witnesses tell us that it was he who persuaded Julius that demolition and reconstruction were necessary; and that, far from being exploited, it was he who exploited Julius's 'imperial' ambition with daring and novel ideas (restrained only by Julius's proverbial meanness).

One of Bramante's contemporaries, Egidio da Viterbo, brings out his strong town-planning interest very clearly, in connection with St Peter's and the cutting of new streets. And Andrea Guarna, in an amusing play called *Simia,* written only two years after Bramante's death, represents him not only exercising persuasion on the Pope very cleverly by showing him his daring plans, but then, having died and arriving at Paradise, telling St Peter that he would enter heaven only on condition that he could rebuild it:

I want to get rid of this hard and difficult road that leads from earth to heaven: I shall build another, in a spiral, so wide that the souls of the old and the weak can ride up it on horseback. Then I think I shall demolish this paradise and make a new one that will provide more elegant and comfortable dwellings for the blessed. If you agree, I shall stay; otherwise I shall go straight to Pluto's house, where I shall have a better chance of carrying out my ideas . . . I shall make an entirely new hell and overturn the old one.[44]

This almost looks like an exaggeration of ideas which Bramante actually put into practice, particularly in the Belvedere: an easy ramp in the form of a spiral, negotiable on horseback, leading to the 'paradise' of the Pope, the earthly symbol of the celestial paradise (a possible interpretation of the plan of the Belvedere). (It may be significant, too, that in his *Momus* Alberti had shown Jove regretting that he had not asked the architects for a plan to rebuild the world.)

Bramante's concern for town planning during his Roman period emerges, as we shall see, in certain very bold ideas (never used, but probably by him) for the total replanning of St Peter's

5,
56

20

117

93,
152,

153 and of the Vatican buildings and even in the
141 project for the replanning of the Tempietto of S. Pietro in Montorio; it characterizes some very Bramantesque plans, which take up the theme of the open space; it appears in certain urban
131 schemes in Rome and possibly also at Civitavecchia. Even a work like the west wing of the
121 present courtyard of S. Damaso (under construction in 1508–09 and, according to Vasari, completed after 1514 by Raphael), was more an expressive urban feature than a functional building. It was to be the show façade of the 'imperial' Papal Palace, facing the Piazza S. Pietro, a character that comes out clearly in some of the early views, particularly those by Maerten van Heemskerck. It was probably the only part actually built by Bramante of what was, according to Vasari, 'a very grand scheme for restoring and improving the palace of the Pope' (perhaps the one documented in Uffizi
93 Arch. 287, already referred to).

Bramante's conception of a *courtyard,* an open space, as the model for a *piazza,* within a city, also appears in a few projects for buildings outside Rome, such as the remodelling of the court-
122 yard of the Rocca or fortress at Viterbo.[45] This was planned about 1506; in 1508 Bramante received payment from Enrico Bruno, Bishop of

Taranto, Pontifical Treasurer in charge of the work at St Peter's. It was still unfinished at Bramante's death and was completed in a modified form many years later by other architects. He had to work within an existing medieval building and to use part of its structure. He planned a rectangular space, with the entrance in one of the long sides, flanked on the short sides by symmetrical arcades and loggias of four bays, with an unusual, almost Mannerist, elevation. The transverse axis is thus closed by a 'solid', the middle pier (as at S. Maria della Pace), which prevents the eye from lingering: as in the Belvedere, the arcades on either side function simply as the wings of a stage-set and, again as in the Belvedere, direct attention along the longitudinal axis. This axis begins at the entrance and is marked at its half-way point by a fountain. It was planned to end at the far wall (part of the existing structure) in some feature that was never built, topped by a tower (which again was already there but would have been suitably remodelled). The arcaded 'wings' along the sides, the axial pointer with the fountain in the centre and the tower closing the visual axis, are all features which make this courtyard at Viterbo, even in its unfinished state, a precursor of Michelangelo's Piazza del Campidoglio. And,

121 Rome, Vatican: view of St Peter's and the
Vatican Palace by Maerten van Heemskerck,
c. 1550, showing the tall west range or *logge* of the
unfinished courtyard of S. Damaso. In the
foreground is the fountain attributed to Bramante
by Vasari (see p. 72 and Ill. 76). (Vienna,
Albertina)

122 Viterbo, Rocca: reconstruction of Bramante's
scheme for remodelling the courtyard. A entrance
from the city, B tower in the city wall, C portico of
Paul III, D portico of Julius II, E staircase

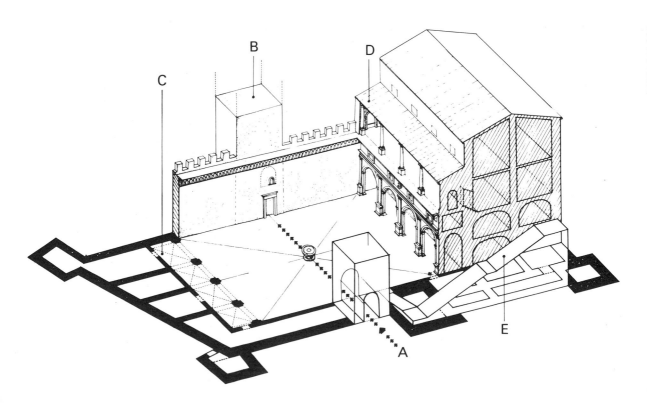

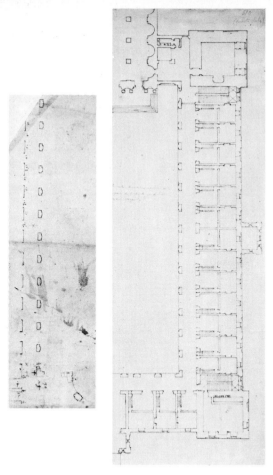

123 a, b Loreto, Palazzo Apostolico and piazza:
variant plans of the left and right sides, drawn
by Antonio da Sangallo the Younger (Florence,
Uffizi, Arch. 921v and 922). The church is at
the top. (a), probably closer to Bramante,
incorporates an exedra at the bottom; (b) shows a
modified design.

together with the stress on the organization of
space in itself as distinct from the structures
which define it, they prove its significance as a
town-planning concept.

The theme of the courtyard-piazza in a town
turns up again in 1507–10 in the plan for the
123, Palazzo Apostolico at Loreto. Here, too, Bra-
125 mante did no more than make plans and a
definitive model in wood (1510). Cristoforo
Romano directed the works from 1509 to 1513
and Andrea Sansovino carried on until 1517.
They altered Bramante's design considerably,
and further changes were made by Antonio da
Sangallo the Younger. The drawing in Uffizi
123b Arch. 922 is annotated in Sangallo's handwriting: 'S. Maria di Loreto in La Marcha, that
is, the palace facing the church, started by
Bramante, badly directed by Sansovino, needs

to be corrected.' The drawing would thus appear to represent Bramante's project overlaid
by the alterations of Sansovino and of Sangallo
himself. Kathleen Posner suggests that Sangallo's changes were so sweeping that the drawing in fact represents a complete restructuring
by him of Bramante's design;[46] and that something of Bramante's original design appears in
another drawing by Sangallo (Uffizi Arch. 123
921v), which shows a large but not very deep
exedra on the side opposite the church, framed
by two bays of the portico and flanked by
sturdy pilasters. According to this plausible
hypothesis, one is seeing here the return of
themes characteristic of Bramante, and probably inspired by imperial Roman buildings, especially the stadium or 'Hippodrome' on the
Palatine.

In any case when faced with the problem of
planning a building to complement the existing
church at Loreto, and one which was to have a
multiple use – to be at once sanctuary, fortress,
hospice and dwelling – Bramante (as in the
Belvedere) used a unified open space axially
planned, which would be simultaneously courtyard, piazza, and atrium to the church. From a 125
distance the complex of buildings on the hill,
with its towers, its walls, and the apses and
dome of the church, was meant to appear not
only as an outward and visible affirmation of
Julius II's imperial power (like the Vatican
buildings and St Peter's), but also, with a precise
biblical connotation, as an earthly image of
the heavenly Jerusalem rising on the sacred
hill. But to someone approaching the church
from the only point of entry, and above all
to someone looking out from the central
bay of the upper loggia of the exedra – namely
Julius II, like an emperor in ancient times
exhibited for the *adoratio* of his subjects –
the large open space must have appeared as an
Antique forum, a space in the 'city of the
ancients' marked out by two-storeyed colonnades and ending at the façade of the church.
(Bramante's unexecuted design for the façade 12
appears on a medal of Julius II dated 1509: it has
two towers, like St Peter's, and a large dome.) 14

Obviously the idea came from the layout of
ancient forums, in particular the Forum of
Caesar, with at the end the Temple of Venus
recorded by Vitruvius. Perhaps a deliberate
parallel was intended between Caesar and
Venus and Julius II and the Virgin of Loreto.
The Forum of Nerva, the Forum of Trajan, and
the Palatine Hippodrome are other possible
sources, especially for the apsidal ending of the
side facing the church. And there were also
spaces like the *quadriporticus* (noted in a draw-

124 Loreto, church: foundation medal illustrating Bramante's unexecuted design for the façade, 1509 (Rome, Vatican)

125 Loreto: air view of the Palazzo Apostolico and church

ing by Leonardo) in front of the church of S. Lorenzo in Milan, which also had a façade crowned by a cupola and flanked by two towers. Bramante never forgot this church. Like the lower courtyard of the Belvedere, the 'forum' of Loreto had the proportions of Vitruvius's 'Latin forum', roughly the 1:2 ratio laid down by Alberti. But, again as at the Belvedere, these historical precedents were less important than the idea of creating a rich and complex *spettacolo* in which architecture, town planning and 'stage-set' were fused in a single significant image. Indeed, it was a double *spettacolo*, one for someone approaching the church, another for someone leaving it, the curving wall of the entrance side reflecting the façade of the church, between the permanent 'wings' of the porticos. Bramante perhaps saw Loreto as a small-scale trial run for ideas that he was contemplating for the layout of the Piazza S. Pietro in conjunction with the new basilica.

Meanwhile, on 14 December 1508, Julius II laid the foundation stone of the coastal fortress of Civitavecchia.[47] Because of its proximity to Rome and even more because of the alum mines nearby at Tolfa (which provided Agostino Chigi, who leased them, with a substantial income), Civitavecchia was bound to be near the Pope's heart. Reviving the ideas of his predecessors Nicholas V and Sixtus IV, Julius made it the main pontifical naval base on the Tyrrhenian Sea and a useful commercial port. In view of the

24, 158 98

126– 131

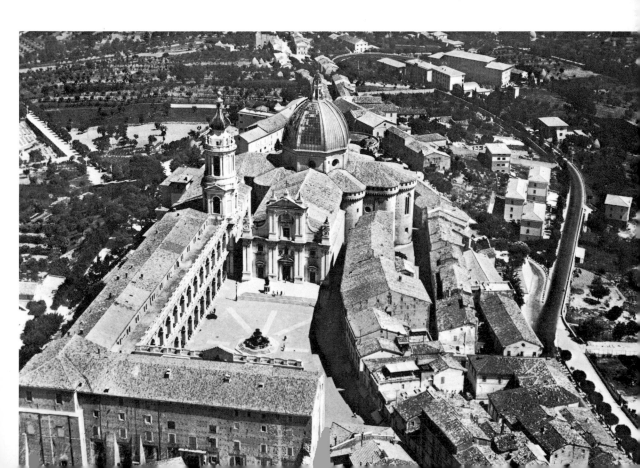

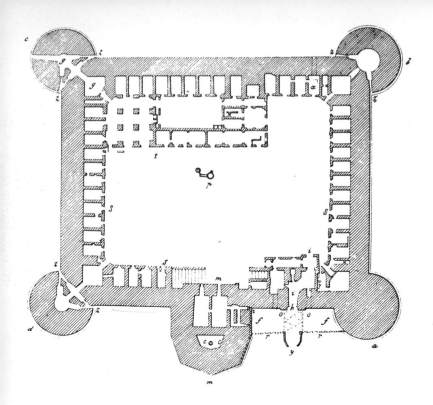

importance of this work, the Pope's architect – who, according to an eye-witness, Paride de Grassis, 'traced the lines of the building on the site' – could only have been Bramante, although he is not named in any written source. His presence as director of the harbour works at Civitavecchia is, however, documented in 1513: Giulio Massimi, we read, was to excavate the dock according to the 'judgment of brother Bramante'.

The courtyard of the fortress must have presented a perfect opportunity for the creation of an ideal urban piazza. The work was never completed, however, and was later altered, so that it is not a reliable guide to its designer's intentions; but it must have been meant to be a
126 large rectangular space with chamfered corners
98 (as in the statuary court in the Belvedere), with storehouses all around it. The latter had an
127 unusual elevation of two storeys and there were
128 four corner bastions, possibly planned to be
129 polygonal. The whole scene was dramatically dominated by a large tower in the middle of one of the long sides, forming a keep connected with spacious apartments for the commander. The validity of this design as an urban model is confirmed by the use of the rectangle with chamfered corners in later town planning (e.g. the Place Vendôme in Paris). The whole ensemble, which may look back to the Castello Sforzesco in Milan, takes up motifs used by Bramante

Civitavecchia, coastal fortress

126 Plan (from Guglielmotti). The front to the harbour is at the bottom

127 One of the chamfered corners in the courtyard

128 The fort from the harbour

129 Foundation medal, showing the fort overlooking the harbour

in the Rocca at Viterbo, at Loreto and in the Palazzo dei Tribunali (see below), and combines them into a theatrical arrangement of spaces and volumes. The military importance of the fortress (which was also remarkable for the originality of some of the techniques used) must have been partly subordinated to its role as a political symbol.   122, 123, 176

The design of the building, as it appears on the foundation medal, includes a number of architectural features which were not strictly necessary in a purely military building (some indeed were dysfunctional), but which would create an impressive image for anyone entering the harbour. However, the new fortress was probably not intended to be a *spettacolo* on its own, but part of a larger one. It is not improbable that Bramante, with the intention of restoring the ancient Centumcellae and producing an *exemplum* of a 'maritime city in the manner of the ancients', actually made a design (once again unrealized) for the rebuilding of the whole port, with its buildings and its equipment, and possibly of the whole town. His competence in harbour-works is shown by the fact that in June 1511 he was consulted about the building of the 'Julius Harbour' at Porto Recanati. Bramante's scheme for Civitavecchia may be reflected in some of Leonardo's sketches in the Codex Atlanticus, particularly in f. 271r, f. Leonardo went to Civitavecchia some time be-   129   130

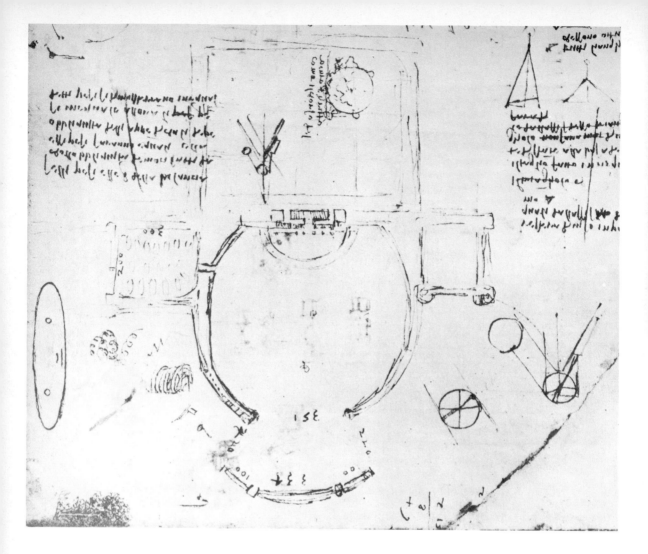

tween the end of 1513 and 1516 (perhaps, as Pedretti argues, at the beginning of 1514, when Bramante was still alive), probably to deal with technical problems connected with some part of the harbour, and he looked at the city's ancient buildings.[48] If our hypothesis is correct, then Bramante, with his knowledge of Antique medals, of ancient ruins, of the famous descriptions by Pliny the Younger and Rutilius Namatianus of the old Trajanic port, and possibly of drawings by Francesco di Giorgio (who also knew the ancient buildings of Civitavecchia), may well have imagined the port in the

131 form of an amphitheatre with symmetrical semi-circular quays, or moles, bordered with steps and ending in towers. In this marine amphitheatre, as in an ancient *naumachia*, shows could have been staged, such as the one organized in the harbour itself in 1509 in honour of Julius II.

According to Leonardo's sketch, a traveller entering the port from the open sea would see in the centre, projecting through the city wall, a large palace-like structure with a portico, and perhaps lateral towers and flights of steps behind, facing a gigantic waterside piazza or semi-circular quay, whose convex curve (as in other designs by Bramante) is contrasted with the concave curves of the projecting quays. Further back on each side, where these quays meet the city, stood two large fortified buildings, alike though not identical: on the right the 126 new coastal fortress, on the left the dock basin 129 (an idea of Bramante's for this area may have been developed by Antonio da Sangallo the Younger, in Uffizi Arch. 946). Both have a curtain wall, corner bastions and a tower-shaped keep on the side facing the harbour. At the back are the walls and buildings of the city, rebuilt on a chequerboard plan. The whole of Civita-

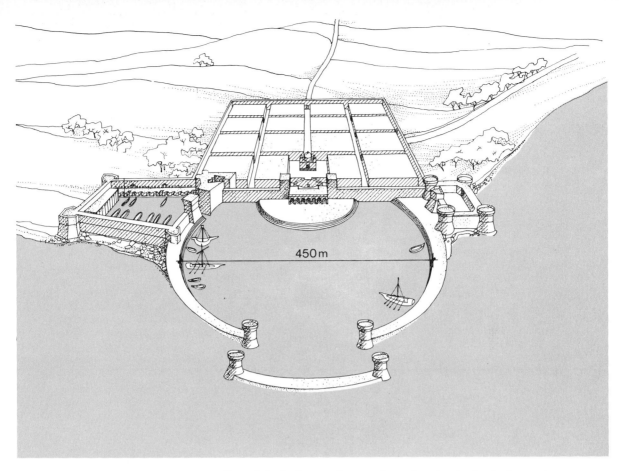

130, 131 Civitavecchia: projected remodelling of the harbour and town, shown in a sketch plan by Leonardo (Milan, Biblioteca Ambrosiana, Codex Atlanticus, f. 271r), and in a bird's eye view reconstruction. On the left is an enclosed, fortified dock, on the right the new fortress (Ills. 126–129). The road opposite the harbour mouth leads to Tolfa, site of important alum mines, that on the right to Rome.

vecchia must therefore have been considered neither as a functional military installation (as Antonio da Sangallo the Younger was to make it when he worked there after 1515), nor as an 'ideal' city, but as a grand *spettacolo* – about 500 m. wide and at least as deep, rich in political meanings but all with the same message. As in a single building, visual unity was to be guaranteed by the organic disposition of certain key accents, large structures acting as visual points of reference. These would enclose, pull together and articulate the scene in depth: a method of organizing space in an illusionistic and psychologically evocative way. The unity so achieved, of course, presupposed an ideally privileged viewpoint.

Imagine the scene as it would have been in real life, bursting with life, with the picturesque forms of the ships and their merchandise on the wharves; enlivened by people, and lit by

the sun (it faces south, as does the Belvedere, and as Bramante seems to have hoped St Peter's would), leading back into 'aerial perspective', surrounded by the sea and the sky: seen thus the space becomes definitely 'townscape' and 'landscape' in quality. But its essentially visual character still remains and it can be seen purely as a work of art. In that work, the essential multiplicity and endless flux of the real city is caught by Bramante in a fixed perspective image. It is the familiar humanist illusion of mind dominating the visible world.

But Bramante's interest in town planning had already found expression in Rome, after 1506–07, in actual large-scale works within the 120 medieval city, carried out between 1508 and 1512, which were necessary to Julius (who gave tax concessions on 20 December 1507 to those who proposed to build) as an *instrumentum regni*. He seems to have intended not so much to promulgate the imperial myth as, in a more realistically political way, to break up the medieval social fabric of the city (small areas controlled by particular baronial families) by breaking up the old network of buildings, and by establishing rapid communication between the various parts of the city and between them and the headquarters in the Vatican. He needed wide, straight streets – for keeping the coaches, processions, crowds of pilgrims, and troops moving; for striking promptly at disorders in the turbulent working-class districts around Campo de' Fiori and in the area of the future ghetto, in Trastevere and the port of Ripa; for ensuring that the Vatican could be safely provisioned from across the Tiber; and for aiding the influx of pilgrims to St Peter's. The works would also bring healthier conditions and all kinds of social benefits to the districts along the Tiber; and finally they would give the capital city of the 'empire' a new urban dimension and a new dignity.

Egidio da Viterbo called the Pope's plan 'Bramantis architecti clarissimi consilio'. Other sources confirm this. Although it was not a true plan for the whole city, it did constitute a realistic attempt to reorganize it in a way that reflected the political programme which Julius was trying to carry out. It operated equally against the interests of the old feudal families and against any plebeian revolution; but it was aligned with the rising capitalist power of an emergent middle class. Julius was not building an 'ideal city'; nor was he encouraging a large increase in population, as the *Addizione Erculea* of Ferrara had done in 1492. He was going back to the programmes of his predecessors Nicholas V and Sixtus IV, and emulating the achievements of Caesar and Augustus. Working rapidly and decisively upon the fabric of the old city, he was making it conform more closely to his own political dreams. The medieval city on the banks of the Tiber was left as it was; indeed, its medieval character was stressed; but it was enclosed by a ring of new roads consisting of two long, straight, parallel streets, on opposite sides of the river, Via Giulia and Via della Lungara, linked by the existing bridge of Sixtus IV and further up by a new bridge named after Julius, a rebuilding of the former Ponte Trionfale.

120, 133

The Via della Lungara was to lead directly to the Borgo Vaticano, and the Via Giulia would lead to it across the new Ponte Giulio: together they would deflect towards St Peter's the interest and traffic that had for centuries focused on the only approach to the Vatican, the bridge and fortress of S. Angelo. In addition, according to a rough sketch probably by Bramante (Uffizi Arch. 136v), the Via Giulia was apparently also to have been linked directly to the bridge and fortress of S. Angelo, and via them to the Borghi, by the Via dei Banchi or 'Canal di Ponte' (now Via del Banco di S. Spirito), which was an older street widened by Julius.[49] To the south this road would have led to a large piazza (about 55 by 110 m.) in front of the Palazzo dei Tribunali, which Bramante, as we shall see, began to build on the Via Giulia itself in 1508. The piazza, of which the Palazzo dei Tribunali would have formed part, was to contain several offices of the Papal Curia and all the city's law courts on one side and on the other the Apostolic Chancellery (the 'Old Chancellery', home of Galeazzo and later Sisto della Rovere, Julius's nephews, and now the Palazzo Sforza-Cesarini). It would thus have proved a major focus for the city's business and would probably have led to further embellishment by Julius II (*Restaurator urbis* like his uncle, Sixtus IV) and his family. It would also have been a crucial junction linking the new streets along the Tiber with the Via dei Banchi Vecchi and Via Monserrato (leading towards Monte Savello and the Theatre of Marcellus) and Via Peregrinorum (leading towards the Campo de' Fiori and the Campidoglio). Sixtus IV had already done something to both these routes.

176-180

Thus the directional accents of the city were linked in a unified system: the Vatican, seat of the highest political and religious authority; the Castel S. Angelo, Papal Treasury, prison and fortified place of refuge in case of danger (linked directly to the Vatican by the 'corridor' of the Borgo on which, according to Vasari, Antonio da Sangallo the Younger worked under Bramante); the district of the banks, of business and of the economic power of the great financiers connected with the pope, in the Via dei Banchi ('*forum nummulariorum*'); the new Papal Mint (at the intersection of the present Via del Banco di S. Spirito and Via dei Banchi Nuovi), founded by Julius II and later built by Antonio da Sangallo the Younger; the new piazza containing the Tribunali and the (old) Apostolic Chancellery; the Campo de' Fiori, the centre of the city's social life; and the Campidoglio – the old *caput mundi*, seat of the city's civil authority. This organic scheme for the whole area explains the new works – mentioned in documents but apparently of only marginal importance – undertaken in the Via delle Botteghe Oscure and the Via Rua (later Via Judeorum, in what was to become the ghetto): they were necessary in order to integrate the areas around the Campidoglio and the Theatre of Marcellus into the new riverside system.

Across the Tiber, the Via della Lungara (which was partly on the line of a Roman road) was not only to link the Borgo Vaticano with Trastevere but, as Andrea Fulvio described it in 1527, to go on northwards through the Porta S. Spirito to a point beyond Leo IV's walls of the Vatican, and southwards through the Porta Settimiana to beyond those of Trastevere. Cutting through the middle of Trastevere in a very long straight line, it was also to link the *platea Sancti Petri,* and therefore the Vatican Palace, directly with the *navalia sub Aventino,* the harbour of Ripa Grande, at the end of the Via Portuense, which was the landing-stage for sea-borne goods and supplies brought up the Tiber. (Julius had dredged the river to improve navigation, and built a road alongside to allow barges to unload; in 1508 he also built bridges across the Tiber's tributaries.) The connection of the Via della Lungara with the Via Portuense, and indirectly the Via Aurelia, also provided links with the ports of Fiumicino and Civitavecchia, giving the scheme an enormous importance both commercially (it was no coincidence that Agostino Chigi built his own house actually on the Via della Lungara) and militarily, and gave the whole plan a 'political' dimension.

A few decisive strokes restructured the city into an organic whole, uniting the old and the new in a practical way, breaking the tightly knit but disconnected medieval city and opening it up for further possible developments. But the complete plan was only partly carried out, and in the long run it came to nothing. It can however be seen as perhaps the most integrated effort to restructure the city prior to the plan of Sixtus V. We do not know how far it was influenced by the earlier ideas of Nicholas V and Sixtus IV, nor how much it owed to Julius himself and how much to Bramante. Probably the unifying concept of a 'riverside city' between the two poles of the Vatican and the Campidoglio, the new power and the old, was provided by Julius II (who also wished to recreate the Rome of Julius Caesar and Augustus), and the detailed planning was by Bramante.

33   It is not difficult to believe that the Via Giulia was in fact, as Vasari said, 'directed by Bramante' and that it was he within the context of the general programme who gave it a definite character, that of an *exemplum* of a city street (as the Via della Lungara was an *exemplum* of a suburban street). Like a banner standing out against the old fabric of the city – the beginning of an artificial, built landscape – it was for Bramante another piece of perspective scenery, a stage set. It was a permanent version of those civic decorations, somewhere between theatri-

cal scenery and street furnishings, which temporarily changed the face of the city when courtly or triumphal entries were held, and with which Bramante must certainly have been involved in Milan, as we have seen, and in Rome, too, probably during Julius II's pontificate and certainly at the coronation of Leo X. Something similar is also suggested by the stage sets that Serlio illustrates in his treatise, and by an engraving of a street scene attributed 132 to Bramante himself. But, as André Corboz has pointed out, 'the metaphor of the theatre in its turn becomes a metaphor for an order which is identified with an idea of society' and of the world; an order expressed through an 'ordering' of space in which, as at the Belvedere and at Civitavecchia, Bramante tries to catch and pin down time, movement, and flux, using this 'ordering' as an instrument of visual control over the city, yet allowing it its own individual elements, and thus the informal variety of life.

The unified structure of the city space is held firm by two fundamental elements: the layout which gives shape to the perspective simply as space, and the strategic positioning of complexes of buildings rising out of that space. These 120 complexes are conceived as stressed accents in the pattern or image as a whole, and as parts of it – interruptions, disjointings, perspectives, and at the same time as expressions and tangible symbols of the relationships of power. Thus, between the traditional poles of the Vatican and the Campidoglio, and as a kind of conceptual and topographical complement to the Castel S. Angelo, but in opposition to the Campo de' Fiori, to the Piazza Navona, and above all to the Campidoglio, the symbol of civic and baronial independence, Bramante set the Piazza dei Tribunali, the symbolic new centre of the imperial and pontifical state of Julius II, *liberator urbis et ampliator imperii.* The just State, as conceived by humanistic thought, was to be symbolized in the centre of the New Rome by the castellated image of the great Palace of Justice; the State 176 was just because it was 'rational' and therefore capable of ensuring the peace and concord of the *res publica,* which was an affirmation in the urban community of the same order which lay at the root of cosmic harmony. Julius might be hailed as 'Father of the Heavens and the Planets', in courtly style, but the *justitia cosmica* of Plato and the humanists was now the Pope's justice, serving an ambitious political plan.

All these considerations probably came into Julius's programme for the re-planning of the city. But the laying out of the Piazza dei Tribunali must have given Bramante scope for putting his own ideas into practice: two sym-

132 Engraving after Bramante of an imaginary Antique street, *c.* 1500 (London, British Museum)

bolically significant palaces facing each other and the corners, this time very definitely, left empty, as if broken through by the streets. But even before Julius's death, the programme's implementation had been interrupted. Possibly Bramante once more considered proposing to Julius's successor a new and even vaster transformation of Rome. Indeed it would seem, though this has never been proved, that he suggested to Leo X (possibly immediately after the flooding of the city in November 1513) that a large canal should be cut in the area east of Rome to take the overspill from the Tiber and thus prevent further floods. He knew something about hydraulic engineering and may have remembered Caesar's plan to divert the course of the Tiber: his idea was to take the excess water from the river upstream from the Porta del Popolo and then discharge it outside the city, beyond the Porta S. Giovanni and Porta Latina. The Tiber would have remained the city's commercial artery, but this new 'grand canal' (roughly parallel to the present Via del Corso) would have served as 'a pleasant route for boats for the convenience of the inhabitants at all times', as Bonini said when he described the plan in 1663.[50] As a useful waterway, subsidiary to the road network, it would have been a major enterprise (the cost estimate seems to have been 'a million in gold') of great urban significance.

Bramante's interest in town planning is of fundamental importance for the later development of Renaissance architecture, even though it was inevitably concentrated upon those aspects and spatial qualities of the city which could be used to express the Pope's political, social and economic ideas. It characterizes all his Roman works; and it grew out of his view of architecture as something primarily three-dimensional and concerned with space, and also, perhaps, out of a typical decision to push to the limits Renaissance methods of organizing and visually controlling architectural space (in this case urban space as well), and to test their presumed universality in as many specific situations as possible. This urban concern is therefore something which we shall keep finding (combined with other qualities) in the works of Bramante's full artistic maturity.

133 Rome, Via Giulia: view from the level of the Palazzo Falconieri (8a on the plan, Ill. 120)

Chapter eight

The Tempietto of S. Pietro in Montorio

OF BRAMANTE's project for an elaborate *memoria* marking the place of St Peter's crucifixion on the Janiculum, within the walls of the convent of S. Pietro in Montorio, only one part, the famous Tempietto, was actually built.[51] Even that was later altered in some details, especially the cupola. However, we have a woodcut in Serlio's treatise showing the plan of the whole project, some sixteenth-century representations, and the Tempietto itself as built, to give us a rough idea of what Bramante had in mind and show us fairly precisely what he was trying to do and what problems confronted him at this period of his 'mature' manner. It was a manner which was at once recognized as embodying the most profound and noble ideals of the High Renaissance. Serlio and Palladio ranked the Tempietto with the great buildings of ancient times, as an example of the 'good and beautiful architecture' which Bramante himself had first restored to the light of day.

The programme behind this work is highly significant in itself, for it showed the most superb effort yet made – except, perhaps, for Raphael's frescoes in the Stanza della Segnatura in the Vatican – at reconciling humanist and Christian ideals in a new, more complete synthesis, expressing their 'universal' values fully in a visual form. The Studiolo and the chapels at Urbino were earlier attempts.

The meaning of Bramante's idea, and the solution he proposed for it, can be understood only within the framework of this programme. It is in fact the concrete architectural manifestation in humanist, pagan and at the same time Christian terms, of an essentially religious and political theme. The Tempietto had no practical, physical, function: it was simply celebrative. When he was evolving its architectural layout and working out its component elements, Bram-

ante must have kept one single purpose uppermost in his mind: the exaltation of Peter as the *Roman* pontiff. For when Peter had set up his *cathedra* in Rome he had confirmed the city's 'universal' status, originally established by the emperor-priests of the ancient world.

In Bramante's project the Tempietto is a circular building standing in the centre of a small circular courtyard. From ancient times until the Middle Ages and on to Neoplatonic humanism, the circle had represented the world and divine perfection itself. In Renaissance thought a circular building was, as Palladio was to say of the Pantheon, 'an image of the world', a conceptual and visual expression of the numinous, suggesting the divine reality of the cosmos.

More specifically, the circular figure was suited to a temple dedicated to St Peter. Servius, a Classical commentator on the *Aeneid,* says that round temples were dedicated by the ancients to Diana (or the moon), and above all to Vesta and to Hercules (or Mercury). Palladio explained that the Temple of Vesta, the symbolic divinity of the Earth, was round because it was made 'to resemble the element earth, by which the human race is sustained' and from which it draws its food. St Peter, too, is the *earth,* the rock on which the Church is founded and from which it derives its origin and sustenance. And, as Vesta is the guardian of the great family of the State, so St Peter is the guardian of the Christian family, the Church. Moreover, the founder of the circular Temple of Vesta was Numa Pompilius, king and first high-priest of ancient Rome, buried, according to legend, on the same Mount Janiculum where Peter, first king and high-priest of the Christian world, was said to have been crucified. Thus in Peter the origins of the Church of Rome were symbolically linked with the origins of the ancient Roman religion.

134 Rome, Tempietto of S. Pietro in Montorio: view from the entrance to the courtyard, the farthest point from which the whole building can be seen (compare Ill. 142). (The dome and lantern in their present form date from the seventeenth century.)

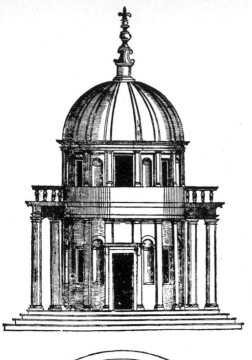

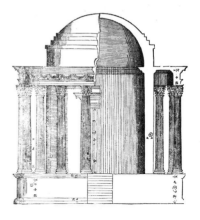

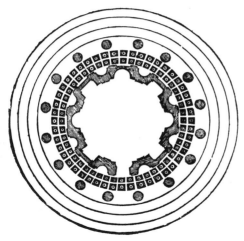

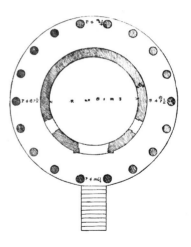

Numa Pompilius might be considered a pagan 'type' of St Peter. The origins of Rome and those of the Church were also connected through the location of the place were St Peter was crucified: 'in monte aureo sive janiculo, inter duas metas'; it was between the *meta* or Pyramid of Romulus (an ancient monument between the Castel S. Angelo and the Vatican hill) and the *meta* of Remus (identified with the Pyramid of Cestius). Peter, founder of the new city of God, was therefore placed between the twins who had founded the ancient city.

Palladio goes on to say, possibly paraphrasing Servius, that circular temples were dedicated to the moon and the sun. And Peter could also be compared to a heavenly body which governed the Church, and from which the light of faith shone down upon mankind. He was also a 'hero' of Christianity, a kind of Christian Hercules: just as round temples were suitable for the sun and for Hercules, so a round temple was suitable for him. Then again, the ancient god Portumnus, another form of Janus, to whom the Janiculum was dedicated, could be seen as another pagan 'type' of the Apostle. Portumnus was in fact the god of harbours and of gates (*porti* and *porte*), and was often represented with a key in his hand, just like St

132 133

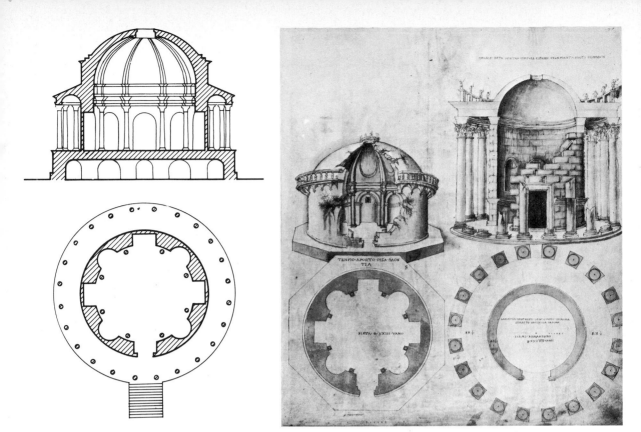

The Tempietto compared to Antique circular temples (see p. 142)

135 Rome, Tempietto of S. Pietro in Montorio: elevation and plan according to Serlio (Bk III, ff. 67v, 68)

136 Tivoli, Temple of the Sibyl or of Vesta: elevation, section and plan by Palladio

137 Porto, Temple of Portumnus: reconstructed section and plan (compare Ill. 138, left)

138 Porto, Temple of Portumnus (left), and Rome, 'Temple of Vesta': elevations and plans drawn by Giuliano da Sangallo. The Temple of Portumnus had lost its encircling colonnade: compare Ill. 137. (Rome, Vatican Library, Cod. Barb. Lat. 4424, f. 39)

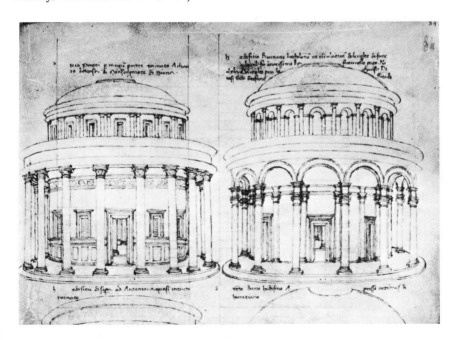

139 Rome, Antique circular temples, drawn by Francesco di Giorgio (Turin, Biblioteca Reale, Codex Saluzziano, f. 84)

Peter, the keeper of the gates of heaven. So
135 Bramante's Tempietto can be compared architecturally with the 'Temple of Vesta' type, as it
136 appears in Palladio's illustration of the so-called
Temple of the Sibyl at Tivoli, and with the
Temple of the Sun (formerly on the Quirinale)
and the Temple of Hercules the Victor (formerly
at the Velabro), all of which Bramante must certainly have known; and it has even more
obvious analogies with the circular temple
137 thought to be that of Portumnus at Porto.

In Bramante's time, it must have seemed to
the humanists that the circular form was most
suitable of all for St Peter's *martyrium*. There
was also a tradition, which may or may not have
been known to Bramante, that Constantine himself had erected a building commemorating St
Peter on the Janiculum in the form of a circular
shrine. For a building dedicated to a Christian
'hero', forceful, strong, 'Herculean' in fact, the
Doric order was the obvious logical choice.
These decisions, which determined the Tempietto's appearance, were not therefore motivated by merely aesthetic preferences, but
sprang from the programme.

There were certainly more considerations of
the same kind. Bramante had probably also
been given the theme of St Peter as founder of a
universal authority, both political and religious, set at the centre of the earth and spreading throughout the world. The dynamic centre
of the Church's action in space and time
originated at a precise moment, that of St Peter's
martyrdom, and in a physically definable place
– the spot on the *monte aureo* upon which his
cross was set up. At that moment and in that
place, which were to be celebrated in Bramante's
memoria, the Apostle, the Vicar of Christ, had
launched the Roman Church as an institution
both temporal and divine, and active in cosmic
history. From then onwards Rome, by virtue of
Peter and his Church, became the centre of the
world: the new Jerusalem, more splendid than
the ancient city because it was more universal,
a place where the values of the ancient pagan
world met in a synthesis with those of the
Judaeo-Christian world.

Bramante's plan quite deliberately developed
the idea of centrifugal expansion; from the
centre of the Tempietto, where St Peter's cross
had been set to the ground, this expansion
141, radiated out towards the circular horizon for-
142 med by the outer wall of the small colonnaded
courtyard. The Tempietto in the centre was the
symbol of Peter and of the Church of Rome, the
new Jerusalem whose action radiated out
towards the four points of the compass. It was
as if one of St Paul's ideas had been translated

into architecture: 'Christ is the head, and on him
the whole body [the Church, the Mystical
Body of Christ, represented by St Peter]
depends. Bonded and knit together by every
constituent joint, the whole frame grows
through the due activity of each part, and
builds itself up in love.' (Ephesians IV, 16).

In elevation the Tempietto consists of three
distinct parts one above the other, like the
Temple of Portumnus at Porto: a dark, underground crypt; a cylindrical body surrounded by
a Doric peristyle; and a hemispherical cupola
on a fenestrated drum. The crypt may be taken
to represent the lower regions, the Underworld,
the depths of the earth into which, with St
Peter's cross, the seed was planted in Rome.
That seed was the leaven of the earth mentioned
in the Gospel from which, through St Peter, the
new Moses, the water of life would pour out to
regenerate the world. Under another image it
can also represent the Roman Church of the cata-
combs, which only after a period of underground preparation could with Constantine
begin its ascent to the light and its expansion
through the world.

The main body of the Tempietto, with its
peristyle, may represent the 'tabernaculum
Dei inter homines', the Church Militant, dominating the terrestrial sphere in the world. The
cosmatesque floor of the Tempietto may be an 147
allusion in medieval terms to the 'labyrinth' of
human life. The main elevation with its columns 134
can stand for the order and authority of Peter
and his Church, based upon the theological
virtues (possibly symbolized by the three steps
at the bottom) and founded upon the doctrine
of the four Evangelists (whose images were
later placed in the four niches on the interior) 147
and of the four doctors of the Church, which
shines out from Rome to the ends of the earth.
The four corner chapels planned for the court- 141
yard may allude to the four quarters of the 142
earth. But if *in terris Petrus, in caelis Christus.*
The upper part of the Tempietto, with its cupola
on the high drum, obviously represents the
higher sphere, the Church Triumphant with
Christ at its head in celestial glory.

A number of details in Bramante's Tempietto
seem to confirm this interpretation. In particular, the forty-eight metopes of the Doric 1,
entablature of the peristyle (with that of the 140
Belvedere, one of the first examples of Doric 104
with triglyphs in the Renaissance) contain representations of twelve liturgical objects, which
are repeated four times. They refer in particular
to the dignity of the priesthood, with obvious
reference to the pope of Rome, and to the liturgical function of the Mass, in particular the Mass

of Maundy Thursday, in which the sacrifice of Calvary is re-enacted and through which Christ's working and presence in the Church is renewed. On the metope in line with the entrance door, on the one on the opposite side, and on the one on the side facing the church of S. Pietro in Montorio, the eucharistic image of the chalice and paten appears: this is the symbol of the bond between earth and heaven (seen also in Raphael's *Disputà* in the Stanza della Segnatura, and, for instance, in the marble frieze in the fifth-century church of S. Sabina). In line with the side door, facing the Vatican, is a representation of the *padiglione*, the basilical umbrella, symbolic of the pope's status as spiritual king or *basileus,* and thus perhaps alluding to the Basilica of St Peter. It is flanked by representations of the crossed keys and the incense 'boat', an allusion to the apostolic barque of the Church, the image of which also appears on the altar of the Tempietto. These would seem to be references to the seat of the Roman Church in a sort of 'hieroglyphic' language, which, as Vasari notes, would have appealed to Bramante's quixotic imagination and humanist background.

The idea of the decorated metopes can thus be attributed to Bramante. On the one hand it looks back to Antiquity – in particular to the representation of pagan liturgical objects in the entablature in the Temple of Vespasian. But on the other it represents, quite unambiguously, an essentially Christian religious and political programme. It celebrates St Peter as the *primus pontifex* of a Church that is not only a spiritual institution, but the guardian of the liturgy, able to transmit grace through the sacraments – the living fountain gushing from the symbolic rock – to strengthen the bond between God and man.

36– The round peripteral temple was an ancient
139 architectural 'type' whose significance was confirmed by the surviving examples and by Vitruvius. To the humanists it became in addition a concrete symbol of the philosophical idea of God and the perfect cosmos. Uniting the pagan *heroön* and the Christian *martyrium,* and placed in the centre of a circular courtyard, it conveyed a specific religious and political message.

Some Antique monuments, such as the Maritime Theatre in Hadrian's Villa, may have had some influence on the plan as a whole, but (as with the Tempietto itself) no one ancient building can be shown to have been the model for what seems to have been Bramante's own most 'Antique' work. The idea of a building in the centre of a circular or semicircular space had sometimes been suggested in the fifteenth century, but nothing like his project had yet

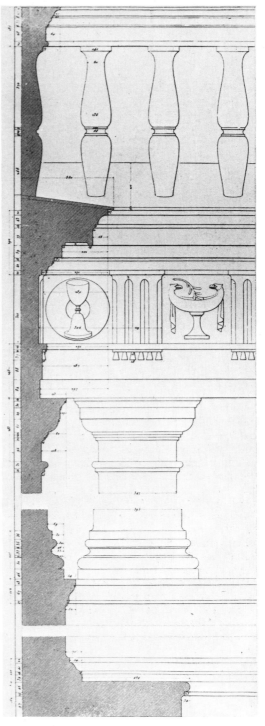

140 Rome, Tempietto of S. Pietro in Montorio: details of the Doric order and balustrade. The metopes shown are the chalice and paten and the incense 'boat': compare Ill. 1. (Letarouilly)

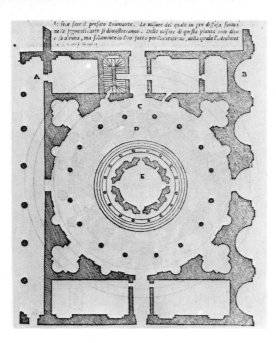

141 Rome, Tempietto of S. Pietro in Montorio: plan showing the Tempietto in a circular colonnaded courtyard, according to Serlio (Bk III, f. 67)

appeared. It is highly representative and charged with significance, the culmination of a process of cultural synthesis, a microcosm drawing sustenance from the ancient world but rooted in medieval Christianity, which at this precise moment came to maturity. Significantly, 142 the image of the circle inscribed in a square, which characterizes Bramante's plan, with the emphasis upon main cross axes and diagonals, also suggests the famous 'Vitruvian figure' of the *homo ad circulum* and *ad quadratum,* illustrated by Francesco di Giorgio, Leonardo, Cesariano and others, which Bramante must certainly have known: this too was full of hints of the medieval cosmos.

142 Bramante imagined an ensemble made up of three fundamental elements – the Tempietto, the open circular 'ambulatory' zone and the surrounding portico. It thus consists of a tight succession of four concentric zones, strictly proportioned to one another and varied in their design: the cylindrical *cella,* the peristyle, the open space, and the circular colonnade. Such a plan in concentric rings readily suggests the Platonic image of the ideal city as it was conceived by the politicians and architects of humanism. It was a small-scale 'built landscape', an urban plan in miniature, well suited to sym-

bolize the city made perfect and 'divine' through the action of the Church. Bramante's feeling for urban design can be seen in the highly geometrical nature of the planning by which the Tempietto and colonnaded courtyard are fused together: the four main cruciform axes, subdivided into two, give the eight main axes of the building, and then, subdivided again, the sixteen axes of the structure of the Tempietto and the circular colonnade. It is the system which Renaissance theorists believed that Vitruvius advocated for the organization of a city: starting from the four points of the compass and from the direction of the eight winds and successively dividing by two or three, as Cesariano, for instance, does, explaining that this method may be used for 'planning not only cities and towns but any other sort of building'.

But there is another point which needs to be noted. Throughout the building certain numbers, which clearly have symbolic meaning but which also affect the plan, seem to have a special significance and keep recurring, both through the repetition of certain architectural motifs and through the proportions of the building itself. *Sixteen* (the *teleion,* the perfect number according to Vitruvius, Bk III, chap. 1), the number of the columns of the Tempietto and of the circular colonnade, may be the key. This, as Vitruvius explains, can be divided into 10 + 6 (numbers which are also perfect, one according to the Pythagorian and Platonic tradition, and the other 'according to the mathematicians'), and so unite two systems of numeration, the decimal and the duodecimal; or else it can be divided into 8 + 8. So it 'contains' all the fundamental numbers: 2, 3, 4 and 5. In particular its half, *eight,* which is the number of the main axes of the plan, could be used – according to symbolism going back to the early days of Christianity – to illustrate the concept of salvation, regeneration and resurrection (Christ rose after eight days of the Passion; the earth was created on the eighth day). It could also stand for the regeneration of Rome through Peter and his successors and for the founding of the Church as a tangible institution after Peter's Passion. Finally, *three,* the divine number of the Trinity, and *four,* the cosmic number confirmed and sanctified by the cross of Christ, are contained in sixteen. Not surprisingly, therefore, there are *three* entrances to the Tempietto, *four* entrances to the courtyard, *eight* windows, *eight* niches, *forty-eight* metopes in the peristyle: three for each space between the columns (3 × 16 = 48) or, counting another way, twelve subjects repeated four times. The relationship between the diameter and height of the whole Tempietto is 3:4, 14

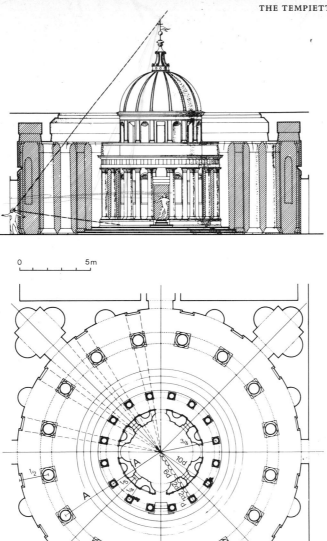

0   5m

142 Rome, Tempietto of S. Pietro in Montorio: conjectural reconstruction of the elevation and plan of Bramante's project for the Tempietto in a circular courtyard, based on Serlio's illustrations (Ills. 135, 141) and the existing building.

In plan, the 4 main axes are successively sub-divided into 8 and then the 'perfect' number 16 (the number of columns in both peristyles). The proportions of the whole reveal a module, A, sub-divided into various fractions. In the Tempietto itself, the two 'perfect' numbers 6 and 10 are used: the distance from the centre to the inside of the

cella wall is equal to 6 diameters of one column; from the centre to the inside of the columns is 10 diameters (the cella wall is 2 diameters thick, and so is the open space between wall and columns). The size of the two orders of columns is determined by lines radiating from the centre; but the pilasters' width is in fact governed by their respective columns, not by the tangential radii (see p. 136).

In the elevation, the sight-lines are indicated from the most distant point. The fact that the Tempietto could be seen only from close to determined its design (see Ills. 134, 148).

143 the relationship between the diameter of the peristyle and its height 3:5, and so on.

This language of numbers, through all kinds of interconnected references to the wisdom of the ancients and to Jewish and Christian symbolism, was surely another way of expressing the profound, universal meaning of the building, with a subtlety that was present from its very conception. The 'universal' message formulated in this programme was thus communicated to visitors in a variety of ways, corresponding to their varying levels of understanding. The same is true of all the 'universals' of Bramante's new architectural manner.

In the overall plan of the Tempietto we can see an image being given substance, an image that is simple but at the same time rich in meaning. Bramante is keeping faithfully to the humanist concept of the world as a harmonious microcosm, echoing with its *concordia discors* the harmony of the macrocosm. Bramante felt that he had so firm a grasp of the method, of the basic 'principles' which according to the theorists were fundamental to any 'modern' architecture which aimed at reviving that of the ancients, that it was unnecessary for him to follow any exact model or even Vitruvius's pedantic advice about the 'peripteral temple'. Although his building alluded to an Antique 'type', he wanted to challenge the ancients; to design a modern building which

135– would seem planned *in the manner* of the ancients
139 (partly following Alberti's theories on church building in *De re aedificatoria,* Bk VII, chap. IV, V, X and XI); a building that would have the prestige and authority of the ancient Roman monuments. He therefore confined his references to Antiquity to a few very specific motifs, which would be enough to arouse an emotive

1, response in the observer: the door, the shell
140, niches, above all the Vitruvian Doric order with
144 triglyphs. This order was in fact far removed from Vitruvius and from any ancient example, but it served as a statement of intent, a cultural manifesto: it was the symbol of a new, and to all appearances more exact, 'scientific' and 'archaeological' approach to Antiquity.

Once he had decided on the basic concept and had begun to work it out in practice, Bramante had to select the right architectural forms to express his purpose. Once again he turned to Antiquity. Renewed study of the Antique enabled him to clarify, to a greater degree than had ever been done before, the precise meaning of the Classical language of architecture. The column, understood as part of an organic system, that of the order, is no longer a simple 'ornament', as it had been for Alberti: it must

clearly return to its original function as a support in a post-and-lintel system, uncompromised by arches. In the same way, the 'wall-ness' of the inner wall is underlined by its continuity, 14 its articulation and its gentle curve. The pilaster, with its 'double nature' as a projection of the column on to the wall and at the same time as a rhythmic element in the wall itself, forms the natural link between the post-and-lintel system and the wall system. The problem of combining these two systems, which historically, structurally and conceptually are totally distinct, had already troubled Alberti, as Wittkower has shown: Bramante here solves it, in a deliberate, consistent way, without sacrificing either of the two and without involving any hybrid mixtures.

The unity of every aspect of the design – its style, its proportions, its perspective – is then ensured by building it round equidistant radial axes. Indeed, from the plan published by Serlio, 14 it appears that Bramante thought of deducing not only the *positions* of the single elements (columns, niches, etc.) from these radii, but also their *dimensions*. For instance, two lines drawn 14 from the centre and touching each side of a column of the Tempietto at a tangent would also, when extended, be tangential to the columns of the courtyard, which would therefore have to be correspondingly bigger. (The columns of the peristyle are re-used Roman columns, and their size would thus be a given factor.) This simple law, through which the structure and dimensions of the whole could be fixed, could, Bramante must have thought, tie the Tempietto closely to the circular colonnade. It could also show what the whole building meant, in both its plan and in its perspective arrangement, leading the eye straight from the large columns of the colonnade to the smaller ones of the Tempietto, pointing directly to the centre of all these axes, the place which was symbolically and actually the most important in the whole building. It could also suggest an illusionistic distancing of the Tempietto and an apparent enlargement of the space around it, rather like a *sotto in su* view, without any need for the bold, sophisticated perspective deceptions used in the Belvedere. The differences in size between the various bearing elements, determined by their tangential radii, would also be consistent with the law of statics which says that the larger the spaces, the larger the supports. Bramante and his contemporaries must then have found this plan 'perfect', the logical, consistent result of a rigorous method. And it was 'universal' because it was based on the theorists' ideal principles, the profound expression of a

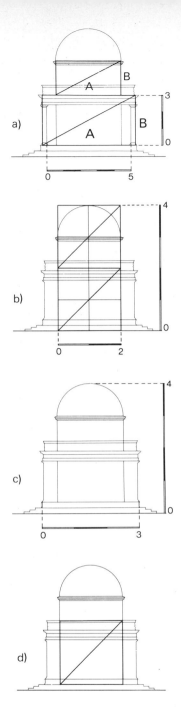

143 Rome, Tempietto of S. Pietro in Montorio: four analyses of the proportions of peristyle, drum and dome. *a* the ratio of the height of the peristyle to its inner diameter is 3 : 5, and the drum of the dome has the same proportions as the peristyle. *b* The ratio of the height of the cella and dome to their diameter is 2 : 4. *c* The ratio of the total diameter to the total height is 3 : 4. *d* shows an alternate reading of the cella as a square (compare *b*).

humanist view of the world that believed in the cosmic *coincidentia* of every aspect of reality.

Unfortunately the project for the Tempietto and the circular colonnade was never realized in its entirety. But such a rigorous system must have involved Bramante in a series of problems, and some signs of them are still visible in the Tempietto as it was actually built.

For instance, in Serlio's illustrations of the plans of the whole complex and of the Tempietto (which may both be based on a project by Bramante) the pilasters on the wall of the Tempietto and on the wall of the courtyard are shown respectively smaller and larger than the corresponding columns, proving that their dimensions were taken from the tangential radii. This is perfectly consistent with the general 'rule' of the plan and with Bramante's whole cast of mind, and would appear not to be an invention of Serlio's but a reflection of an early idea of Bramante's. But it also contradicts every example in the ancient world and every theoretical principle that says the pilaster (considered as the ideal projection of the column on the wall) should be the same width as the column. Indeed, perhaps in order to avoid problems, in their small round temples the ancients never put pilasters on the *cella* walls (in large buildings, such as the Theatre of Marcellus or the Colosseum, the great radius meant that the discrepancy was not noticeable).

Bramante felt that he had to put an order of pilasters on the surface of the *cella* wall, in order to show the overall geometric and perspective plan and to coordinate the parts strictly and completely.[52] Yet, contrary to what Serlio shows in his plan, he dared not follow the radiocentric idea so far as to use pilasters that were narrower than the corresponding columns: as their height was fixed, their proportions would then have been incorrect; and, although he made them shallow in order to minimize them as much as possible, he based their width on the diameter of the columns. But as a result the proportions of the section of wall between the pilasters seem distorted in comparison with those of the space between the columns. Once again, Bramante, working experimentally, had discovered a contradiction: he had shown that the rules were not universal.

Another fundamental principle of humanist architecture (expressed clearly for instance by Luca Pacioli, a friend of Leonardo and probably also of Bramante in Milan) maintained that the Classical rules, method and style were absolute, whatever the physical dimensions of particular cases. An architectural order might be only a few centimetres high or tens of metres high but

135,
141,
142

144

144 Rome, Tempietto of S. Pietro in Montorio: looking up in the colonnade. Note the compressed placing of window and niches.

it would still be an 'architectural order'. A whole building, in theory, and at least within certain limits and with certain modifications, could be doubled or trebled in size, while keeping its elements exactly the same. All architecture was a 'model', which had its own validity, quite apart from its physical dimensions. In Rome, Bramante seems to have sought to test the universal validity of this principle: in the Tempietto, for instance, he examined the limitations of the very small and, in St Peter's, the limitations of the immensely large. But the very small scale of the Tempietto produced problems which were difficult to solve.

The geometrical law which regulated his plan involved, as we have seen, the placing of sixteen pilasters on the inner wall, corresponding to the sixteen columns of the peristyle. Bramante placed them without hesitation. But when the voids (doors, windows, niches) had to be fitted into this tightly subdivided cylindrical wall, there were serious difficulties. Because of the limited space between the pilasters, all these 1, elements, however small, are so hemmed in 144 that they can only expand vertically, as if they were being squeezed by the pilasters. Against all the rules, the wall spaces between these elements and the pilasters are reduced to a 144 minimum. The window-frames, in fact, are not placed on the wall-surface at all; they are inserted ambiguously, and with unprecedented boldness, into the thickness of the wall, and when seen from a distance acquire a new value of their own in terms of the wall-articulation. Well aware of the visual problems of the whole, Bramante is working delicately in tiny thicknesses and minute sizes. The entire *cella* wall has a dynamic rhythm consisting of slight projections, deep and shadowy hollows: at once continuous and broken, constantly in tension. The result, springing from the very restraints imposed by a strictly logical general method, yet tackled entirely on the level of feeling, makes this outer wall of the *cella* one of the high points of Bramantesque poetry.

Difficulties always stimulated him to his greatest and most personal inventions. The 'relativity' of supposedly universal principles is illustrated again, very dramatically, in the 1 main door. For reasons that were partly symbolic – it was the entrance to the Church, the kingdom of the faithful under Peter, the only way to the gates of heaven – the main door to the Tempietto had to be stately and solemn. But the space between the pilasters is extremely small (about 77 cm.), scarcely sufficient for the side doors (66 cm.) and totally inadequate for a 'Doric' door worthy of its role and modelled on

Antique examples. Bramante accepts the contradiction; indeed, he flaunts it without inhibition. Perhaps recalling the main door in the façade of Alberti's S. Sebastiano at Mantua (which may however not be part of Alberti's original design) but pushing the solution to its very limits, he designed a door that was wider (about 97 cm.) than the space available. This meant cutting abruptly into the pilasters, ex- 1 tending the moulded door-frame far over their surface, and breaking the vertical continuity with a decisive cornice at the top; in other words, negating the original bearing function of the architectural order represented by the pilasters, a function which elsewhere he had been at pains to emphasize. Above all, this main door is 'out of scale' with the rest of the building and contradicts the 'structural' organization of the whole. And it occupies an ambiguous and discordant position in the perspective scheme which was supposed to unify all the elements of the *cella* wall. Starting from principles and rules, and from a rigorous logical method, Bramante once again arrived at a result that foreshadows the virtuoso artificiality of Mannerism; a sign of the inner contradictions in a system that was intended to be universal.

Even greater difficulties appeared when he had to arrange the interior of the Tempietto. Here, where the circle was even smaller, it was no longer possible to follow the plan consistently; that is, to place sixteen pilasters on sixteen radial axes to correspond with those on the outside. If proportions similar to those of the outside pilasters were kept, there would hardly be any space left on the walls for doors, windows and niches. Bramante must have understood the problem straight away and have decided at once to halve the number of pilasters in the interior, thus partly renouncing the idea of following his 'unifying' scheme to its logical conclusions. The first solution that occurred to 145 him must have been to place each internal pilaster at an equal distance between two external pilasters. This more 'academic' solution is the one which appears in Serlio's plan, which as we have seen may reflect an early project by Bramante. But even here the space is so small that it would still have been difficult to fit in the niches, doors and windows. Bramante was forced to give up altogether the idea of matching interior and exterior. The pilasters inside the Tempietto are placed on the walls according to a completely self-contained scheme. They are linked in pairs flanking the diagonal axes 148 and set very close together, squeezing in the tiny windows (about 45 cm. wide) between them; and they draw away from the main cross-

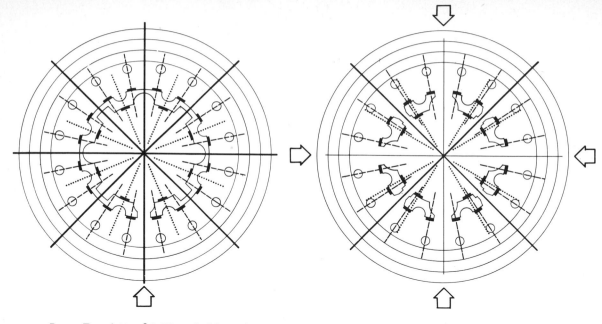

Rome, Tempietto of S. Pietro in Montorio

145 The position of the pilasters on the outer and inner walls, in Serlio's plan (left; and see Ill. 135) and in reality. In the actual building the pilasters are grouped in pairs on the diagonal axes, making the square-ended bays smaller, and allowing the apsidal niches on the main axes to expand.

146, 147 Looking up into the dome, and towards the altar. The large niches and flanking paired pilasters can be read as triumphal arches. Niches and windows (here shuttered) are compressed between the paired pilasters. Note the inlaid stone floor. (The dome is not original.)

148 Perspective section, drawn before the dome and lantern were altered. Note the *cella*'s height in proportion to its width (Ill. 143), and the placing of windows between pilasters or pilaster-strips on the diagonals (compare the exterior, Ills. 134, 135). (London, Sir John Soane's Museum, 'Coner Codex', f.31)

axes to allow the niches of the cella, three of which are pierced by doors, to expand.

146– A rhythmic movement, like a heartbeat, thus
148 animates the cylindrical interior. The rhythm of the coupled pilasters overcomes the limitations of the tiny scale. This more than anything else suggested the idea of a central space spreading outwards along the cross-axes and halted, almost compressed, by structures arranged transversally along the *diagonal* axes, which is the basis of the plan for St Peter's. It was the development – and a possible conclusion – of the same spatial impulse that first led to the visual reduction of the corners of the court-
90 yard of S. Maria della Pace and then to the idea of the octagon with unequal sides used in the
98, statuary court of the Belvedere, in St Peter's, in
158, S. Biagio, in S. Celso and possibly in the court-
180, yard of Civitavecchia. The basis of this idea was
166, the search for the greatest degree of three-
126 dimensional spatial centralization, the impulse to dispel once and for all the Quattrocento concept of a perspective space as merely what results from combining separate two-dimensional surfaces. The tiny interior of S. Pietro in Montorio is possibly the most successful development of this idea.

Here, as happened in another form and on another scale in St Peter's, there appears to be a distant, metaphorical reference in uniquely Bramantesque terms to the theme of the Roman
146– triumphal arch, transferred to the interior and
148 repeated four times; a reference that might be justified by the wish to celebrate St Peter's triumph. But the link between this theme and the circular space is ambiguous; the space is animated by the distribution of the light in an almost Late Antique way, emphasizing the unusual verticality and also the symbolism of the articulation. It is characterized by some extremely bold ideas that make the building seem complex and ambiguous, such as the four small windows below the small niches, which are squeezed in between the pilasters on the diagonal axes, thus piercing the 'solids', the walls, which, ideally, should have a bearing function.

The interior of the Tempietto is certainly one of Bramante's highest achievements. But considered as a part of the whole, it contradicts the pre-established rules of the plan; above all, it contradicts the Renaissance concept of the building as an organism – the Albertian assumption, reaffirmed several times by Bramante in his work, that a building is like a living body, an *animans* formed of strictly interrelated parts ruled by a single principle. This is the result of applying the method strictly. And if Bramante,

by trusting to his creative instinct, after all achieved a high spatial quality in this interior, he may well have felt that it was so much the worse for 'universal' principles.

When he began planning the whole project and tried to reconcile it with the small site available, Bramante must have seen the sort of problems that were going to arise in the definition of the exterior of the Tempietto, in that of the outer colonnade, and in their relation to each other. The colonnade was never built, and we can only guess at its treatment. But it was certainly the fact that the Tempietto would always be seen only from very close to, in a 134 restricted space and from below (as it still is), 142 that led Bramante to emphasize its height and raise the cupola well above the peristyle, quite 135 apart from its importance in the programme as a whole. This is the fundamental idea which characterizes the little building, decisively removes it from any model in the ancient world 136 and places it almost in the realm of fantasy. But 139 it also generated problems and led to results which acted against his intentions. The elementary geometrical solid (cylinder plus hemisphere), which is almost an incarnation of the Renaissance deal of the building as a pure three-dimensional object in space and an affirmation of 'harmonious' cosmic significance, visibly divides into two different parts. These two parts stand in sharp opposition to each other in various ways, for instance their degree of illumination. If this is a clear expression of the contrast between the 'earthly' and the 'heavenly' sphere, as the programme demanded, it can also be read in a way that is not simple and unequivocal but ambiguous and polyvalent, already approaching Mannerism.

The design set Bramante a number of problems: he had to decide on the height of the drum, how its surface should be treated, and how it should be linked visually with the Doric peristyle. The first two problems were closely connected. For a number of reasons he could not raise the drum high enough to allow it an order of columns like the one below, but neither could he leave the wall surface without pilasters, as well as niches and windows, to link it visually with the lower part of the building. He fixed the height by basing it simply on the overall proportions: Serlio's woodcut and other six- 13
teenth-century drawings suggest that he may at first have thought of introducing a 'dwarf order' of pilasters of the kind that sometimes appears in the attic storeys of Roman triumphal arches. But he must have felt that such a solution was in several ways unsatisfactory. Once again he had to rely on artifice and to trust his

own instincts in matters of expression: he reduced the upper entablature to a minimum, a simple strip with a small cornice above it; and in order to avoid losing height, he changed the pilasters into schematized projections, without capitals, surrounded by shallow moulding.

What we have here is the makings of a simplified style, not by any means close to Antiquity but with Classical elements 'synthesized' (Bonelli's word). It was to return in later works and to suggest new stylistic developments in Cinquecento architecture. But because of it the upper part of the Tempietto contrasts even more emphatically with the lower. Bramante had to find something that would be a visual link between them and would soften the division between their styles and scales. So he inserted a small, continuous balustrade, functionally quite useless but, with its light, openwork mass, exactly right as an imaginative transition from the entablature of the peristyle to the drum. It seems to give the drum a further perspective dimension, emphasizing its recession and its height, and it confers something of a 'heroic' dignity upon the tiny building as a whole.

There are further examples of Bramante's trust in his own artistic instincts and refusal to be bound by rules. Since the small lantern of the cupola (which also had no practical function) was visible only from very close to and in foreshortening from below, he raised it very high, to proclaim its pivotal importance in the entire plan as the vertical axis which, with obvious symbolic significance, flies like an arrow from the earth on which Peter's cross had stood towards the heavens in which he was glorified. Bramante designed not so much a traditional lantern as a spire, a kind of slender candelabrum holding aloft the light of Peter's power and supremacy above the city and above the world. It strikes an almost Gothic note of fantasy, in open contradiction to the Vitruvian rules and 'Classical' programme of the Tempietto.

The whole scheme, especially if we imagine it surrounded by the intended tall circular colonnade, resolves itself once more into a *spettacolo*, an illusionistic image. Serlio clearly saw the illusion (Bk III, ff. 67–68):

although [in the illustration] this temple appears too high, being twice as high as it is wide; nevertheless, in the building itself, by the window openings and the niches, which help to give an impression of width, this height does not offend; indeed, through the two cornices that go round it and steal much of its height from it, the temple appears much lower to the onlooker than it is in fact.

Like any other building, it is 'distorted' by the fact that it has to be looked at in foreshortening. When Alberti's 'musical' proportions are transferred from the flat two-dimensionality of the drawing-board to the solid three-dimensionality of Bramante's design, which is in addition curved, they lose their metaphysical values and become merely one of the means of determining an image, and this image, although in fact built, is nevertheless thought out in terms of pictorial perspective. The means used to achieve this effect are typically pictorial: the contrast or gradation of light and shade, the search for luminous and atmospheric effects attained through the chromatic, optical and tactile qualities of the various surfaces. A number of materials are used: travertine, granite, marble, plaster, stucco, but their tone is mostly light, and they combine to form a kind of monochrome; yet there is still some faint colour in them and their surfaces vary – porous, smooth, matt, shiny. It is as if a painter were trying to make his image look like a real object and to give actual vibrant life to his perspective composition by adding further effects of illusionistic space. In this realm of 'suspended disbelief', elements taken from Antiquity with archaeological care are displayed to make a building whose concept and meaning are in fact rooted in the early Cinquecento appear 'Antique'. These Classical elements are brought together and fused with others either invented by Bramante or freely reinterpreted by him to form a new synthesis; and the result is rich and at the same time daring, a sort of balancing act with forms of contrasting meanings and differing origins.

It is here in particular that the building's almost mysterious and miraculous vitality appears. It permits a number of critical interpretations; it is charged with intellectual ideas; it is programmatic; it is progressive. Yet in the end perhaps it has to be approached emotionally, and in the final analysis subjectively, simply in terms of the visual effect which it produces on the onlooker. 'Classicism', 'Mannerism', even 'Baroque', seem to co-exist in this strange work, which repels almost as much as it fascinates. That quality of 'novel invention' which (to use Vasari's words) both Bramante's 'judgment' and his 'gift for free inventions' produced out of 'artificial difficulties' must look for its counterpart not so much in the learning (*scienza*) of Brunelleschi and Alberti as in the gift (*grazia*) of the Neoplatonist Ficino: something which for contemporaries such as Pacioli had an almost theological connotation – a special favour and privilege reserved by heaven for the elect.

149 Rome, St Peter's: the foundation medal of 1506
by Caradosso, almost certainly showing the elevation
of Bramante's first project (see Ill. 154).
(London, British Museum)

Chapter nine

St Peter's and Bramante's late style

ALMOST ALL the buildings which would have constituted the most significant examples of Bramante's late style were tragically the victims of their own daringly ambitious scale. Their construction was interrupted first by the death of Julius II, and then by that of Bramante himself. Afterwards they were altered or in many cases demolished. Such was the fate, first and foremost, of St Peter's; then of the Palazzo dei Tribunali; of the church of S. Biagio; of S. Celso; of the church of Roccaverano; of Loreto; and of the House of Raphael. Even the Belvedere has been left like a dismembered corpse, a blurred shadow of itself. A better idea of the value of these works can be gained from the admittedly incomplete and contradictory evidence of drawings than from the few parts that do survive; and this means that it is often hard to make any profound examination or criticism of them as they actually stood. However, their historical importance is such that it is impossible to neglect the problems they raise and the possible solutions open to Bramante.

His work on St Peter's is the key to his whole final period in Rome. It led him to a rethinking of his whole aesthetic language that has few parallels in the history of art. And at least as far as the building of churches was concerned, it was the *summa,* the culmination, of his career; in a way, the 'unique' work which summed up his whole mature period in Rome. It occupied him off and on for about eight years, and all his previous experience was drawn upon in its preparation. Many of the buildings which occupied him from 1505 until his death can be considered broadly as 'trial runs' or tests, the development of ideas, hypotheses and problems born during his consideration of St Peter's. His ideas for St Peter's were always in flux. Some stages might at times seem to have reached a pro-

visional conclusion, but at any moment some unforeseen development might necessitate a change. And this process went on even after Bramante's death – at least as far as Michelangelo, Maderno and Bernini. Such constant reformulation of the project, combined with the scarcity and ambiguity of available information, makes any reconstruction of Bramante's work extremely difficult.

Bramante must have fired the Pope's enthusiasm for his Belvedere plan not later than the spring of 1505, and must have begun to work on the new Vatican basilica by the end of the winter of 1505 (in rivalry with Giuliano da Sangallo and Fra Giocondo).[53] An early project may possibly belong to the summer or at the latest to the autumn of 1505, when Julius II, who was anxious to find a worthy setting for his own tomb which he had commissioned from Michelangelo, must have decided to demolish the dangerously ruinous Constantinian basilica and rebuild it. This first project – possibly the result of 'an infinite number of drawings', as Vasari says, but probably not completely definite in all its parts – was probably the one of which the plan is shown in the so-called 'Parchment Plan' (Uffizi Arch. 1) and the general 154 elevation in Caradosso's famous medal, twelve 149 of which were placed with the foundation stone in the base of the first pier on 18 April 1506. But this design, as we are told by a note on the back of the drawing itself, 'was not carried out'. Indeed Egidio da Viterbo, an influential man at the court of Julius II, tells us that an early plan which Bramante presented to the Pope was not accepted by him. Bramante proposed to turn the building round by 90° and to place its entrance not at the east, on the old *platea Sancti Petri,* but at the south. This would have given pilgrims approaching St Peter's simultaneous

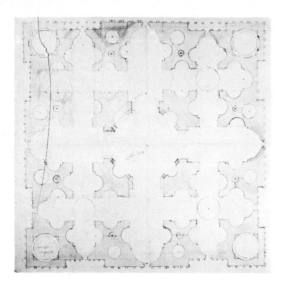

150 Rome, St Peter's: plan of Giuliano da Sangallo's third design (Florence, Uffizi, Arch. 8)

views of the façade of the new basilica and the ancient Vatican obelisk; the association of the obelisk, traditionally attributed to Julius Caesar, and the new church built by Pope Julius, would have reaffirmed to them, once again, the idea of Julius's *renovatio imperii*.

But Bramante's plan meant that the Apostle's tomb and the papal altar above it, if left *in situ,* would not be in the geometrical, ideal centre of the new church; nor could the whole consecrated site of the old basilica be included in the new one. Although, according to Egidio da Viterbo, Bramante declared himself ready to take responsibility for moving St Peter's tomb without touching it, Julius was adamant. Bramante had to make another project, the working out of which undoubtedly presented great difficulties because of the very strict limitations imposed: he had to keep the tomb of St Peter exactly in the centre, under the dome; he had to cover the whole area of the old basilica, fitting the new building into the fabric of the existing city around it; and he had provisionally at least to incorporate the choir which had been begun by Rossellino under Nicholas V and carried on by later popes. These limitations meant keeping the old symbolic orientation with the entrance at the east, and giving up the idea of a centralized plan in favour of a design which could eventually be extended by a nave and aisles in that direction.

In any case, serious disagreement and anxiety were aroused by the decision to demolish the age-old basilica of Constantine, with its vener-

ated monuments; although it was maintained that it was not a question of destroying but only of renewing (*instauratio*). One thing which must have stood in the way of a really careful consideration of the problems was Julius II's impatience to see quick, concrete results. Bramante probably also had to defend himself against the rivalry of Giuliano da Sangallo (architect to Julius since he had been a cardinal), who produced plans in competition with Bramante's and whose presence must have been both a stimulus to Bramante and a source of ideas. Actually on the back of a plan by Giuliano (Uffizi Arch. 8), a sketch in red crayon, probably by Bramante, hints at a new solution, with a longitudinal plan and three apses with ambulatories. The same solution, taking account of the exact position of the structure of the Constantinian basilica and Rossellino's choir, appears in another plan (Uffizi Arch. 20), which is also almost certainly by Bramante. However, we do not possess any definitive plan by him, and do not know whether, at the moment when the first stone was laid for the first pier of the crossing (later known as the Veronica Pier), he was working to a longitudinal plan, as Förster has suggested, or a centralized one, as the Parchment Plan almost certainly shows. Indeed, we do not even know whether there ever existed a real, complete plan by Bramante in which anything was more precisely set down than the position and the form of the piers destined to support the dome (the diameter of which was to be about 42·5 m., like the present dome), placed so that the papal altar would be exactly in the centre, underneath it.

Bramante's plan was probably not definite in every respect even when the other piers were started in 1507, or even later, when work went ahead with remarkable speed up to the death first of Julius and then of Bramante. By then, under Bramante's own direction, the four main piers had been built, together with the arches between them which would support the dome, and the adjacent structures had been begun.

In 1516, Guarna, in *Simia*, makes St Peter say: 'We still don't know where to put the doors of my church', and Demetrius, known as Simia, says: 'That's true. They say that when Bramante died he forbade any decision to be taken about the doors until he rose from the dead; in the meantime, he would be considering where to put them.' This probably also means that it had not yet been decided whether the church was to have a central or a longitudinal plan. To Julius and Bramante, the important thing must have been to get on with the building, following a plan in which, what-

150
158

157

154

157

157

151,
157

151 Rome, St Peter's: the church under construction, drawn by Maerten van Heemskerck before 1536. The design is basically that of Bramante's second project (Ill. 160). On the right is the choir of Nicholas V. Note the use of Doric pilasters on its exterior, and Corinthian pilasters inside the crossing (see p. 148). On the far left part of the nave of old St Peter's can be seen. (Berlin-Dahlem, Kupferstichkabinett der Staatlichen Museen)

ever else happened, there had to be a central nucleus with the dome, four chapels at the corners and cross-arms ending in ambulatories. It is likely that in 1506, and possibly during the next few years, Bramante concentrated on finalizing his designs for the various parts of the crossing and left the question of the plan open (just as the question whether Rossellino's old choir should be retained or demolished was probably undecided as well, although Bramante seems to have completed it both internally and externally). He was probably still arguing for a central plan, perhaps like the one shown in the sketchbook now in the Mellon Collection, dated between about 1513 and 1520–22, attributed to Menicantonio de' Chiarellis, who was Bramante's assistant on St Peter's. According to Serlio, the central plan was the one chosen by Peruzzi, while the longitudinal plan was taken up by Raphael in the time of Leo X (Bk III, f.65).

After the deaths of both Julius II and Bramante, when the work was going forward more slowly under Leo X and Clement VII, those parts which had probably been left vague by Bramante were given definite shape, but his general design was still followed. Because of the slow progress, and the interruption caused by the Sack of Rome in 1527, the intriguing views by Maerten van Heemskerck, who was in Rome from 1532 to 1535, show us the central nucleus of St Peter's in all but a few details, substantially as Bramante conceived it, and before the alterations by Antonio da Sangallo the Younger and especially Michelangelo and Maderno gave it its present appearance.

The symbolic programme for the rebuilding of St Peter's which was drawn up in the time of Nicholas V, expounded by Giannozzo Manetti and followed by Rossellino in his project, must have been partly in the minds of Julius II and

Bramante when they began to plan their new church. Rossellino's St Peter's, Manetti writes, was to be like the human body, a microcosm made in the image of the world and of God, glorified by the incarnation of Christ. At the same time it was to be like Noah's Ark, a symbol of the Church, a ship steered by a single pilot, the pope, outside which there was no salvation. Even elements retained from the Constantinian basilica, which was a cross between a basilica and a *martyrium,* were to have an obviously symbolic meaning in Nicholas V's St Peter's: the twelve columns placed in the transepts were to recall the Apostles; the *campanili* flanking the façade and the apse were to allude to the towers of the City of God. As Battisti has suggested, the whole ensemble was to express the theme of the Heavenly Jerusalem, symbol of the *Ecclesia triumphans,* built in Rome on the Vatican Hill.[54] These themes turn up again in Bramante's plans for St Peter's. But – as with other centrally planned churches before and after St Peter's – behind these particular ideas lay a more general purpose: the wish to express as fully and as completely as possible the new 'philosophical' religion of humanism. This was at the same time Neoplatonic and profoundly Christian: the church conceived as an organic, harmonious microcosm, made in the image of the Divine.[55] It should express the ideal form of the universe, schematized, according to a Classical tradition inherited by the Byzantines, as a cube (the earth), extended into four arms (the four quarters of the earth) and surmounted by a cupola (the sky).

In the fifteenth century this idea had found architectural expression at various levels of complexity, not only in the Neoplatonist circles of Florence, but in designs by Filarete and Leonardo. In some of these it had taken the form of a cross inscribed in a square, which, as we have seen, Bramante had proposed as early as 1481 in the *Ruined Temple* drawing engraved by Prevedari: this was used by his disciple Cesariano, who did not know any real Roman examples, in his edition of Vitruvius to illustrate a typical plan of a 'temple according to the ancients'. Although the cross inscribed in a square is one of the themes which appear most often in actual late fifteenth-century buildings in Lombardy, it must have appealed particularly to Bramante's taste and feeling for space. (Two plans for churches in the form of an inscribed cross, in the Biblioteca Ambrosiana, Milan, F. 251 inf. 55r and 145, may possibly also be by him or his circle.) In any case, such a plan must have seemed to him outstandingly suitable for the new St Peter's, which was to be not just a

church in a general sense (*tempio*) but also a *martyrium* (as Old St Peter's had been), the mausoleum or imperial tomb of the first pope and of his successors. In different architectural terms and on a gigantic scale, he had to express a symbolic programme which was to some extent like that of the Tempietto of S. Pietro in Montorio. Here too the pivot of the whole scheme had to be underground: the Apostle's tomb, the Petrine *rock*, the buried seed from which the Church sprang. Above that must be the sphere of the terrestrial world dominated by the Church Militant and Triumphant, spreading to the four corners of the earth; and at the top the celestial sphere, the region where Church and pope, Christ and the saints exist in glory, represented by the dome.

But St Peter's, far more than the Tempietto, was to be 'il tempio': the eternal church of a universal religion, not merely the *tempio* of the ancients and the Renaissance theorists, but also the final definitive reconstruction of the Temple of Solomon, the centre of the world, the place where 'God hath his dwelling among men'. The prophet Ezekiel and St John the Divine were certainly among the literary sources which influenced its planning. Both the temple described by Ezekiel and the Jerusalem described by St John in the Apocalypse were enormous buildings; and they were square in plan, and their height equal to the side of the square, so that they were cubic. A square wall surrounded the whole building. The interior was reached through twelve doors (as there were twelve tribes of Israel and twelve Apostles), three on each side of the square. All these features can be seen in Bramante's plan and also in some of Giuliano da Sangallo's plans made at the same time. The Doric order on the exterior (used by Bramante in Rossellino's choir) must allude, as it does in the Tempietto, to St Peter as hero, the Christian Hercules, but the large Corinthian order of the interior, with its 'olive leaf' capitals, may recall the Trees of Life which, according to St John, grew in the court of the Heavenly Jerusalem and bore fruit twelve times a year. (Twelve pilasters in each arm of the cross appear in both Bramante's first and second plans.) The new St Peter's was thus a compromise. In general its allusions to the grandeur of Antiquity were meant to express Julius's 'imperial' sovereignty. But at the same time Bramante had to work within the limitations imposed by a clearly defined and complex symbolic programme and by a series of liturgical and practical requirements. All this prevented his design from being (as it can easily seem) an abstract, ideal, 'theoretical' plan, unconcerned

159
161

43

25

154
150

15]

175

with a specific, concrete situation or with topography.

The symbolic programme, and in particular the idea of the Heavenly Jerusalem, square and enclosed by a wall, must also have suggested the plan which appears in a sketch (Uffizi Arch.104) which is in the style of Bramante and may very well be by him, and which must be more or less contemporary with the Parchment Plan. Like the Tempietto of S. Pietro in Montorio, but on a gigantic scale, the new St Peter's is here represented at the centre of an enormous square space, surrounded by colonnaded buildings which reflect the plan of the church by having exedrae in the centres of each side (possibly suggested by the Forum of Trajan) and tower-shaped blocks at the corners. This grand screen of palaces around the new church was probably intended to keep the consecrated area of the old basilica within the new complex and separated from the city. But to achieve it would have meant demolishing most of the Vatican Palace. A similar idea, worked out in more detail, appears in the Mellon sketchbook; in the centre is St Peter's, which is here shown according to Bramante's second project. It is even richer in references to Antiquity – especially to the plans of Roman baths – but is also rich in originality, and mindful of the demands of the symbolic programme. It gives the church an effective spatial context of its own, and at the same time sets it effectively within the fabric of the city.

But at the project stage and right from the very beginning Bramante's greatest problem must have been that of the enormous dimensions of the building he was designing. The inscribed cross plan, as it appears in the first Parchment Plan and in preliminary studies (e.g. Uffizi Arch.3), would have solved this problem better than any other. It was organic and at the same time allowed for great diversity of forms. The large square could be organized into a series of spaces arranged in a hierarchy of scale and culminating in the great central dome; and these spaces could be coordinated through the use of a number of similar systems, made up of architectural order-plus-arch, arranged three-dimensionally in space. But how was the spectator going to grasp the enormous size of the central space under the dome? Bramante's solution appears in the Parchment Plan and in subsequent plans (Uffizi Arch.8v and 20). It was to make the central space and each of the four corner 'chapels' similar in design and proportion, but to relate the two by a ratio of 1:2. Since the chapels are almost as big as a normal cathedral-size church (e.g. S. Maria

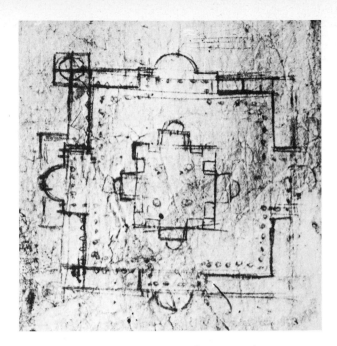

152, 153 Rome, St Peter's: projects for surrounding the church with vast colonnaded buildings. Above, a drawing possibly by Bramante based on his first project (Florence, Uffizi, Arch. 104). Below, a drawing based on the revised project (Ill. 159), attributed to Menicantonio de' Chiarellis (?) (Collection of Mr and Mrs Paul Mellon).

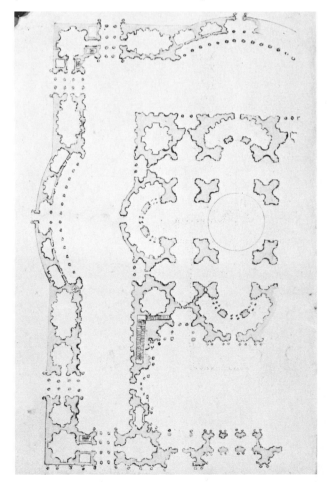

delle Grazie at Milan), the spectator at once appreciates the unprecedented immensity of the central space and of the whole building by a direct, visible and measurable comparison of scales. It is an emotive appeal to the eye through the juxtaposition of 'like' images.

From his memory and from his earlier experience as an architect – from Piero della Francesca's Brera Altarpiece, from S. Andrea at Mantua, the chapel of S. Satiro and S. Lorenzo in Milan, the cathedral of Pavia, S. Maria delle Grazie – Bramante forged a new image. The 'Byzantine' organization of space, which he had been advocating ever since the period of the Prevedari engraving, had now to be translated into more emphatically 'Roman' terms without losing its intensity of expression, and indeed gaining in richness and significance. Here, even more than in the Belvedere, Bramante needed his experience of Antiquity in order to speak 'the language of greatness'. The tradition that he wished to 'place the dome of the Pantheon on the vaults of the Temple of Peace' (as the Basilica of Maxentius was then called) may be expressing a concrete reality, though one which, as Murray suggests, again sprang from a symbolic idea:[56] the dome of the Pantheon, which since the early Middle Ages had been the church of S. Maria ad Martyres, could well represent heaven, or, equally, the Church Triumphant nourished by the blood of the martyrs and rising from a structure alluding to the *Pax Romana,* which Julius, like the Roman emperors, intended to establish in Rome and in the world. The arrangement of the arms of the cross – perhaps, as Metternich suggested, roofed with large groin vaults like the Roman baths with the sides opening into barrel vaults – recalls that of the Basilica of Maxentius. The dome, contradicting the Quattrocento tradition, goes straight back to the type used in the Pantheon. The circle of columns around the drum is a translation into three-dimensional, load-bearing terms of the order of small pilasters which runs round the upper part of the Pantheon drum on the inside. Bramante had done the same thing, though in a less 'mature' way, at Milan, in the interior of the dome of S. Maria delle Grazie.

But if this was all there was in the first plan for St Peter's, we should have to say that it was certainly very ambitious and full of meaning, rich in invention and skilfully worked out – perhaps, had it been built, Bramante's greatest work to date – but not yet more than a design of exceptional range. What makes it different *in kind* from anything that had gone before is above all two specific elements: his solution of the problem of the piers bearing the dome and, even

more, a totally new way of conceiving the relationship between spaces (voids) and walls (solids).

By placing the piers which carry the arches below the dome *diagonally,* Bramante not only solved the tremendous problem of statics in a masterly way. He also managed, by an extreme readiness to experiment, to produce in the completest possible way that image of the *square with chamfered corners,* that *suppression of the corner* which was for him a means of accentuating the centrally planned, three-dimensional quality of the building. It was something he had already tried to do to some extent in Lombardy and in the cloister of S. Maria della Pace in Rome. The diagonal pier of St Peter's (which he repeated in the corner chapels and was later to use again in other churches) is therefore highly revealing about Bramante's way of manipulating space; and it is also one of his most extraordinary spatio-structural *invenzioni*. It not only denied the corner its traditional function as a spatial caesura, but fundamentally upset the whole, rather mechanical, scheme of the inscribed cross; it conditioned the entire spatial arrangement of the building; it became the generating element of the whole image; it reverberated in every part of it; and its presence produced a totally new play of solid and void.

It was a remarkable step forward to the 'Baroque' vision, if one can call it that. The central space defined by four diagonal piers was to be an accepted solution for all such buildings until the eighteenth century and beyond. The geometrical Renaissance plan, the embodiment of abstract, 'perfect' proportion, was challenged from within, in a way that was particularly decisive and explicit. The diagonal pier introduced an element of subjectivity, of 'judgment', into the predetermined proportional scheme of Renaissance tradition. According to the architect's judgment, the corner could be more or less chamfered, making the central space more octagonal or more square, not by obeying certain geometrical rules, but by pursuing aims which involved expressive form as well as sound structure, and which had very little to do with the search for abstract, absolute proportions.

The stressing of the diagonal axes, of which the piers of the crossing are an example, was only one of the ways in which this entirely novel conception of space was made manifest. By means of a large number of visual devices, the old Quattrocento regularity of proportion and perspective was broken and replaced by a new urgency. The Parchment Plan at once shows that for the first time since the Romans, and far

14, 28, 24, 46, 55

166, 180

156

155

40

154

15

more richly, Bramante was concentrating his interest on the 'void', on 'space in itself', much more than on the walls which enclosed it. It is not the plan of a building determined by its walls and piers, those separate planar and linear elements which would automatically produce spaces and delimit voids: it is a building conceived primarily as a series of voids. They are the architecturally 'positive' entities. It is the solids, the walls and piers, which are now seen as 'negative', assuming the forms they do only in response to the requirements of the voids. The spaces appear to be the result of *hollowing out* a homogeneous material that is moulded by their dynamic expansion. The various components which make up this space are richly articulated. Built up and linked together in a hierarchy established by the overall plan, they seem to come alive individually. They are the product of a dialectic between empty space – functioning like an expanding fluid – and the material bonds which constrict it. Only the void is *form*; no longer, in Ackerman's words, 'a mere absence of mass', but 'a dynamic force that pushes against the solids from all directions, squeezing them into forms never dreamed of by geometricians'; consuming them, to the furthest limit of physical possibility, in an irresistible movement of expansion.[57] For the first time since the Romans, architecture becomes the *direct, tangible presentation* of space itself, displayed for its own sake as 'pure' space. Here is a direct challenge to the traditional view that the function of structure and enclosing surfaces is to articulate lines of force. Bramante had not forgotten Gothic, and in the Prevedari engraving and at Pavia he had clearly shown his understanding of that tradition. But at St Peter's the function is transferred from structure to space, which acquires a subjective, emotive, yet completely controlled expressive power.

26
49

Bramante must have learned a good deal of this through his study, and his new understanding, of Roman baths. Ancient buildings must also have suggested to him that walls could be treated like scenery in a theatre, that enormous weight and thickness could be suggested where in fact the material used was often fined down to the point of being a mere membrane. This way of seeing a building as an image, a *spettacolo* of spaces formed by the opposition of apparently 'boundless' enclosing walls, is not only consistent with Bramante's whole aesthetic vision but was also to some extent forced upon him by the task in hand. He had to evoke the 'imperial magnificence' of the ancient world in enormous structures to be built in the shortest possible time (as Thoenes has pointed out[58]), and using a

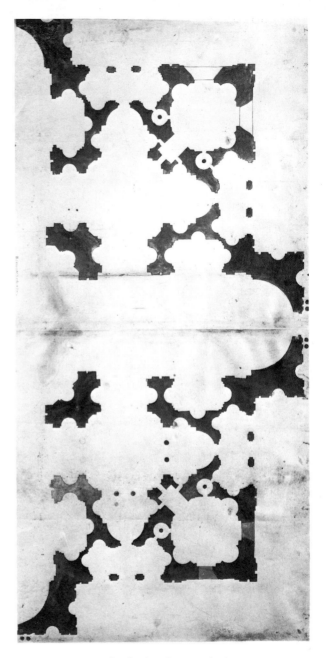

154 Rome, St Peter's: the 'Parchment Plan', illustrating Bramante's first project (Florence, Uffizi, Arch. 1)

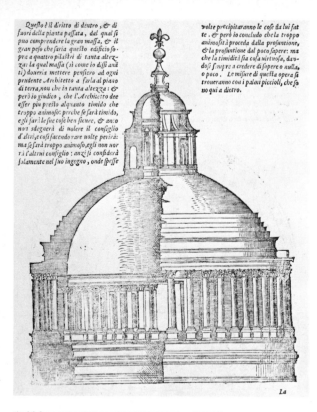

Questo è il diritto di dentro, & di fuori della pianta passata, dal qual si può comprendere la gran massa, & il gran peso che saria questo edificio sopra a quattro pilastri di tanta altezza: la qual massa (sì come io dissi anti) doueria mettere pensiero ad ogni prudente Architetto a farla al piano di terra, non in tanta altezza: & però io giudico, che l'Architetto dee esser più presto alquanto timido che troppo animoso: perche se farà timido, egli farà le sue cose ben sicure, & anco non sdegnerà di uolere il consiglio d'altri, & così facendo rare uolte perirà: ma se farà troppo animoso, egli non uorrà l'altrui consiglio: anzi si confiderà solamente nel suo ingegno, onde spesse

volte precipitaranno le cose da lui fatte. & però io concludo che la troppo animosità proceda dalla profuntione, & la profuntione dal poco sapere: ma che la timidità sia cosa uirtuosa, dandosi sempre a credere di sapere o nulla, o poco. Le misure di questa opera si troueranno con i palmi piccioli, che sono qui a dietro.

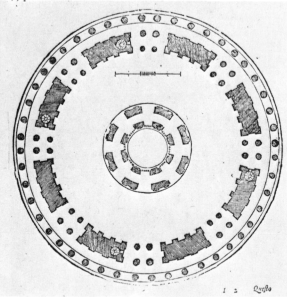

155 Rome, St Peter's: section, elevation and plan of the dome as designed by Bramante, from Serlio (Bk III, ff. 66v, 66)

relatively modest work force, certainly much smaller than had been available to the Romans. The Roman system of building with concrete cast on the site was the technical method Bramante intended to use, to ensure the maximum speed. But it was also the method which suggested and permitted the new relationship between spaces and their structural 'envelopes' which he was introducing. By reviving the constructional use of concrete to express his new ideas, Bramante was inaugurating a new era in architectural theory and practice.

Almost our only source for the exterior appearance of Bramante's first design for St Peter's is Julius II's foundation medal. However sketchy this picture may be, it tells us that if the interior was essentially a *spettacolo* of three-dimensional, fluid and hierarchically organized *spaces,* of varying size, expanding outwards from the void beneath the dome, the exterior, in its turn, was to be essentially a *spettacolo* of three-dimensional *volumes,* of varying forms and dimensions, also hierarchically arranged around the large central dome. As foreshadowed at Pavia, at S. Maria delle Grazie, and in Leonardo's sketches, the three-dimensional unity of the building, the complete correspondence between interior and exterior, the whole and its parts, means that the idea of an architectural organism as an *animans,* a living, human organism, which had been Alberti's unrealized ideal, is successfully given form. The Quattrocento tradition of plane surface and line is replaced by a conception of the interior as *space* and the exterior as *volume.* That is, the building is completely expressed in primary three-dimensional architectural terms.

One consequence of this is that many of the traditional problems simply disappear. Designing a façade, for instance, had meant for Alberti visualizing a flat elevation which would somehow convey by the articulation of its surface the interior spaces behind it. But with Bramante's centralized cross-in-square plan, the volumes of the building themselves form their own composition. The key elements here are the domes of varying size. Beside the large central dome the visitor would see also the smaller domes of the corner chapels. But a 'façade' was probably demanded by the commission, and Bramante took advantage of this to provide greater enrichment. On the medal the semi-domes of the apses are shown as domes themselves, illusionistically represented as being placed on drums and crowned with lanterns. In reality they are only the large apses in which the arms of the cross end; but Bramante wanted the new St Peter's to seem to have the

149

48, 59, 41, 43

149

156 Rome, St Peter's: conjectural elevation and section based on the Parchment Plan, Ill. 154 (by F. Graf Wolff Metternich)

largest possible number of domes, of all sizes, building up as a pyramid around the large dome. For this reason the half-cylinders of the large apses are not carried down to the ground (as they are in Leonardo's sketches and in S. Maria delle Grazie). Their lower part is concealed behind a substantial wall, leaving only the upper part visible; and this upper part, compartmented by pilasters, pierced by windows and topped by a semi-dome and a small lantern, looks to the viewer no longer like an apse but like a complete dome-on-drum rising above a cubic block, the front of which functions as a façade. Once again, an illusionistic expedient had been called in to solve the problem of creating a façade without giving up the idea of expressing the whole through its volumes.

The exterior, therefore, becomes once more a composition conceived in terms of volumes but drawing upon illusionistic perspective; a build-ing that rises gradually until it culminates in one dominating feature, which (as Metternich observed) is not so much the dome itself as the enormous colonnaded drum. Dome and drum together are a sort of temple in the sky, a ceremonial canopy raised over the Apostle's tomb and weighted by the heavy lantern at the top. The minor domes (four intermediate in size, which as we have seen are not real domes, and four more real ones which are smaller) seem like reflections of the central dome and – as in the interior – act as comparisons by which to measure its immensity. The *campanili* at the side (possibly to be built only on the main front) frame the architectural picture; at the same time they form part of it by helping to indicate the depth of space behind them.

Four small domes; four feigned domes; four projections at the corners of the building. In all, *twelve* elements rising around the great central

155,
156

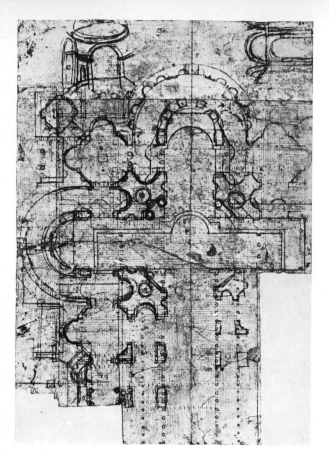

157, 158 Rome, St Peter's: drawings, possibly by Bramante, showing a revised plan (similar to Ill. 159) combined with a longitudinal nave. The drawing above (Florence, Uffizi, Arch. 20) shows the outline of old St Peter's in relation to the new nave and crossing and the outline of Nicholas V's polygonal choir (Ill. 151), and includes sketches of the crossing in elevation. In the drawing below (Arch. 8v), parts of two other plans are visible—those of S. Lorenzo (top: compare Ill. 24) and the cathedral (bottom) in Milan.

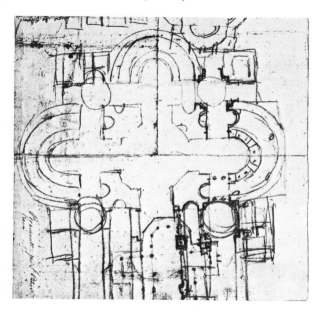

dome. Perhaps they symbolize the twelve Apostles on whom the Church was founded (and possibly the two *campanili* on the façade stand for Peter and Paul), surrounding Christ.

But, as we have noted, the Pope rejected this first project, and although Bramante remained substantially faithful to the plan and to his initial idea, he was forced to start thinking afresh. He seems to have considered two alternative solutions, one with a centralized plan and another with a longitudinal plan, although the nucleus with the dome and the corner chapels was retained in both. The Pope's demands obliged him to look at the plan again and gave him a chance to consider it critically; first of all in the matter of statics (which in the Parchment Plan might have created problems), and secondly with a view to achieving greater spatial compactness. The new plan took up the scheme of the Parchment Plan but with some essential innovations. The length of each arm of the cross remains the same as in the earlier plan (the same as the length of Rossellino's choir and the nave of the Constantinian basilica), but the dome is significantly larger, and its centre now coincides exactly with the tomb of St Peter. The crossing piers are more massive; and corresponding to their thickness Bramante has provided an ambulatory round the end of each arm, separated from the main space by colonnades. The curve of the apse thus becomes a transparent screen offering the eye no finite boundary. This looks back explicitly to Bramante's buildings in Lombardy and it is not by chance that the plans of S. Lorenzo and Milan Cathedral are jotted down in the margin of Uffizi drawing Arch.8v, which seems to be a preliminary study for this second plan in his own hand.

Using the methods of ancient Roman architecture, Bramante wanted to translate certain spatial values characteristic of the Late Antique into contemporary terms. The tendency is to centralize space more and more around the greatly enlarged dome; to synthesize the whole building into a stronger image, more strictly organized and more emotively effective than that of the Parchment Plan; a space dynamically transfigured by light, but more compact and unified, emphasized by the unusually vertical proportions of the arms of the cross (twice as high as they are wide), and by the sheer power of the huge structures, a power emphasized by dramatic jumps in scale; yet still quickened by the tense, unresolved struggle between material and space. Space is still the active element: it pushes into and models the concrete masses, it expands from the centre, spreading out in all directions like an advancing fluid whose irresis-

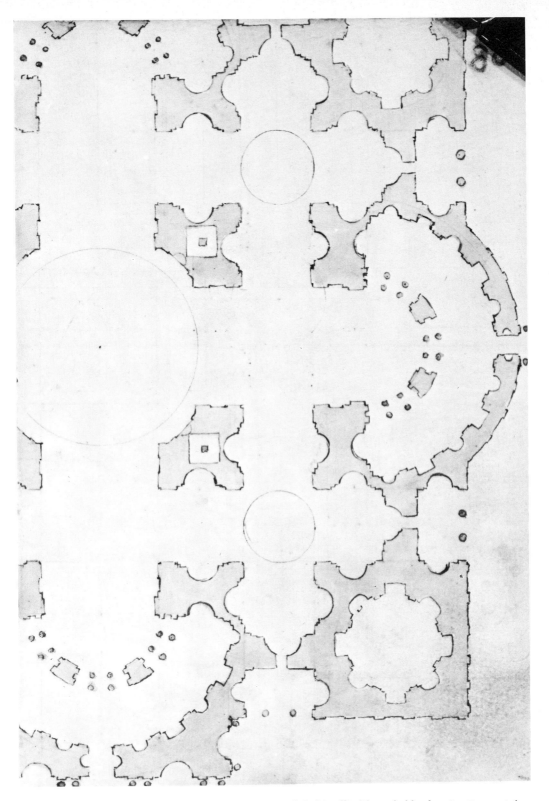

159 Rome, St Peter's: plan attributed to Menicantonio de' Chiarellis (?), probably showing Bramante's second, revised scheme. Compare the Parchment Plan, Ill. 154. (Collection of Mr and Mrs Paul Mellon)

160 Rome, St Peter's: conjectural axonometric reconstruction of Bramante's second project. Compare contemporary views, Ills. 151, 175. (Question-marks indicate areas of uncertainty.)

tible movement breaks through its containing limits, pierces the apses, and flows beyond them as far as the eye can see. The apses at the 159 ends of the arms no longer close the interior 154 space as they had done even in the Parchment Plan. Rather they act as temporary halts, curbing the expansion of space and defining the main internal spaces of the arms of the cross, but not the space of the church as a whole. This feature looks back to the Late Antique, and to some extent forward to Palladio's Redentore. At several different levels – optical, pictorial, atmospheric, chromatic – it was a way of combining Bramante's two basic ideas: space conceived as an immense *spettacolo* and volume conceived as a perspective composition, evoking, as on a stage, the great imperial wall masses of the ancient Roman baths.

This second plan, which was the one Bramante 159 began to build and which, in spite of later 160 modifications, determined the main nucleus of 175 the building as it stands today, is a clearer and simpler idea than the Parchment Plan, fascinating though that is. It is perhaps less personal, less suggestive, some would say less 'artistic'; yet more mature, more unified and 'universal'. Through his almost incredibly rich historical knowledge and through the experiments in planning which spanned his whole life, Bramante had attained complete mastery of his forms of expression, though he had not reached the point of defining every detail. It was a mastery which seemed elementary and simple in its complexity, but which was in reality a concentration and summary of a whole range of Renaissance thinking on the subject of the 'temple'. This second plan, had it been worked out and realized in all its parts, would have constituted an almost symbolic conclusion to humanist Quattrocento architecture, and at the same time the beginning of a new era in which the pupils and followers of Bramante would of necessity have been the leaders.

With his characteristic impatience and mercurial temperament, however, and with his restless urge to experiment and to put everything to the test, Bramante may not have been entirely satisfied. The uncertainty of the programme made it hard for him to work, and he dissipated his ideas inconclusively. And although the building of the nucleus of the church went ahead fast, Bramante, as Serlio says (Bk III, f.64v), 'interrupted by death, not only left the building imperfect, but the model also remained imperfect in some of its parts'. The parts which were not carried out under Bramante's direction were no doubt those furthest from the crossing: in particular, probably, the ambulatories, the *campanili*, the corner sacristies or

chapels, and the façade. The choice between the centralized plan and the longitudinal plan must have been left undecided as well.

The problem of the façade must have been particularly important in this decision. The Pope, whatever happened, wanted it to be on the main front of the building. The 'illusionistic' solution shown on the medal must have been 149 considered insufficiently grandiose, and perhaps also functionally inadequate (for instance, no benediction loggia is indicated). An idea of Bramante's for a façade may appear in a drawing 161 in the notebook in the Mellon Collection already mentioned, which seems to refer to a project with a central plan and which also shows part of the section of the building in which the sacristies at the back are surmounted by a kind of round temple similar to S. Pietro in Montorio. In this drawing, which marks the beginning of a whole series of designs which were to lead, via Antonio da Sangallo the Younger and Peruzzi, to Maderno's final solution, the large Corinthian order of the nave interior is carried over

161 Rome, St Peter's: elevation showing façade (left) and partial section, possibly related to Bramante's second project, from the sketchbook attributed to Menicantonio de' Chiarellis (?). Compare the plan of the second project (Ill. 159) and Metternich's reconstruction of the first project (Ill. 156). (Collection of Mr and Mrs Paul Mellon)

on to the façade. Two pairs of gigantic pilasters, corresponding to the coupled piers of the crossing, frame the centrepiece at the sides and support a large triangular pediment, evoking the idea of the Classical temple, but with a hint of the Pantheon and perhaps even of S. Andrea at Mantua. Two minor orders of superimposed columns, perspectively 'recessed' behind the giant order, are fitted into it and extend beyond the centrepiece on either side, forming colonnades and galleries which link up with the Doric order surrounding the whole complex.

As far as we know, the other parts of the building shown in the Mellon drawing (particularly the dome with its lantern, the other lateral porticos, and the small domes of the corner chapels) correspond to Bramante's second plan. The date of the drawing is not later than 1520–22 and it may represent a project conceived in the last years of his life, or at least derived from one of his ideas. In any case it is a remarkable idea, completely unprecedented and mature; it conforms to his plan so faithfully and at the same time so freely that, unless definitive proof appears, it is hard to attribute it, as has been done, to one of his successors – Raphael, Peruzzi or Antonio da Sangallo the Younger.

The idea of a giant order combined with a smaller one as part of a façade design reappears in the church of Roccaverano, almost certainly planned by Bramante before 1509, though partly altered during construction. It had been commissioned by Enrico Bruni, Bishop of Taranto, Superintendent of Works at St Peter's. Here Bramante again used the inscribed cross plan of St Peter's, though reducing and simplifying it in a way not unlike that which he was using at the same time for the (now destroyed) church of SS. Celso e Giuliano in Via dei Banchi in Rome.

As Wittkower has pointed out,[59] a first step towards an organic solution of the Renaissance problem of the façade (which Alberti had many times tackled, without coming to any convincing conclusion) is embodied in a drawing in the Louvre in Paris which perhaps reflects an idea of Bramante's. This drawing was at one time thought to be a design for the façade of S. Maria presso S. Satiro, but one cannot be sure: it may possibly be an exercise of Bramante's inspired by Vitruvius's description of the basilica of Fano (one of Vitruvius's own works) and incorporating ideas from Alberti's façade of S. Maria Novella and project for S. Andrea at Mantua. In it, a large Corinthian order is the main element of the façade and supports a large arch at the centre flanked by small pilaster-strips and surmounted by a triangular gable (corresponding to the nave), while the sides finish in two half-pediments (corresponding to the aisles). Two small superimposed orders fit into the height of the main order, possibly to express on the façade the interior form of the basilica described by Vitruvius. But the problem of integrating façade and interior into a single organism and giving what might be called a faithful perspective representation of this organism on a flat surface is not entirely solved. The large central arch is placed above the order like something extra, and it is not very clear whether the small pilaster-strips without capitals which support the pediment are meant to be read as 'order' or as 'wall'.

In the façade of Roccaverano, on the other hand, a giant order set on a pedestal marks the central part of the façade and directly supports a triangular gable that looks almost like the front of a large temple in antis projecting from centre of the building. Within this, and slightly recessed, is a large arch which is to be understood as the projection upon the façade of the internal barrel vault of the nave. This large central arch is supported by a minor order which is continued at the sides, forming the wings of the façade; these are surmounted by two half-pediments, and in their turn enclose smaller arches which correspond to the aisles behind. Two similar systems, differing in size but both based on the order-plus-arch, are thus logically correlated, and are used to translate without incongruity the spatial variations of the three-dimensional interior into terms of a two-dimensional elevation. At the same time, the façade can be read as a perspective composition, like a bas-relief, involving two Classical temple fronts which appear to be superimposed in receding space. Thus, by completely integrating the internal space and the external volume of the church of Roccaverano into one single organic work of architecture, the problem of making the façade into a two-dimensional perspective representation of that internal space is immediately solved. Or rather, Bramante simply denies that it exists at all as a separate problem, i.e. a problem of two-dimensional composition (disegno) divorced from that of the three-dimensional, spatial and volumetric organization of the whole building.

Some years later, this idea of Bramante's was taken up by Baldassare Peruzzi for the façade of the Sagra at Carpi (1514–15), and later still Antonio da Sangallo the Younger used it in some projects that were never built. It was fully developed only by Palladio, whose Venetian church façades, particularly that of the Redentore (1576), are versions of it as sophisticated

162 Roccaverano, parish church: reconstruction of the façade elevation. As in the Louvre drawing (Ill. 163), a central pediment is flanked by two half-pediments. (Drawn by E. Checchi)

163, 164 Design for a church façade, formerly thought to be for S. Maria presso S. Satiro (Paris, Louvre). The schematic analysis shows that it can be read as a central square (A) reflecting the width of the nave, flanked by two half-squares (*a*) reflecting the aisles, or as a composition of three squares equal in size to A.

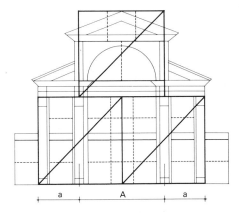

159

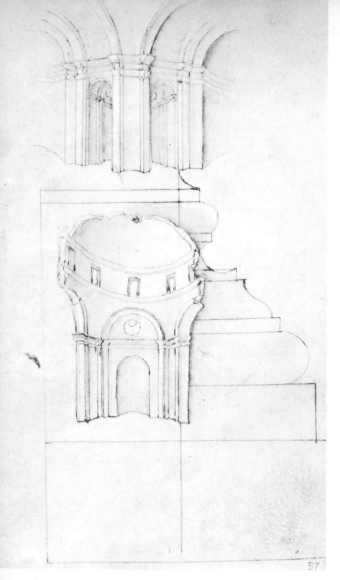

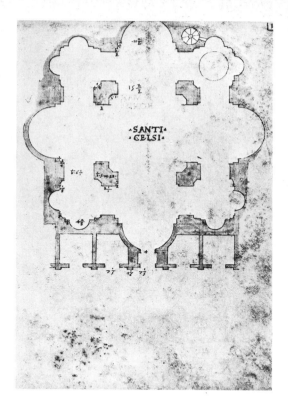

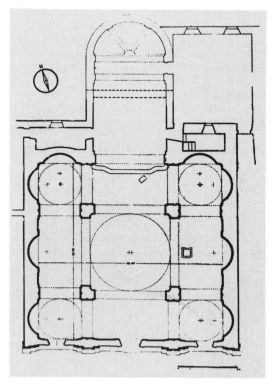

165, 166 Rome, S. Celso: views of the interior, from the sketchbook attributed to Menicantonio de' Chiarellis (Collection of Mr and Mrs Paul Mellon), and plan, from the 'Coner Codex' (London, Sir John Soane's Museum). The diagonal view, above, shows one of the piers set at an angle and the niches behind it (compare St Peter's, Ills. 154 and 159); in the axial view, below, we are looking towards the apse.

167 (right) Roccaverano, parish church: plan (drawn by E. Checchi)

and intellectualized as they are lucid and original. Once again Bramante's ideas are seen to be the foundation of later developments in sixteenth-century architecture.

A number of churches exist which have
167 centralized cruciform plans: Roccaverano and
166 SS. Celso e Giuliano in Banchi in Rome (begun *c.* 1509, left unfinished and later demolished), and two buildings which may not be connected with Bramante, S. Eligio degli Orefici in Rome (begun 1509–10 or 1514?, continued by Raphael and later by Peruzzi, but now much altered) and S. Maria delle Fortezze at Viterbo (begun 1514?). The usual assumption that they are preliminary studies for St Peter's is probably wrong: rather, they are experiments on a small scale with problems raised by the vast building. Bramante meant his greatest church to be the compendium, the living synthesis of the new architecture. But after the plan of the whole had been established, and even after the crossing had been built, there were still a great many decisions to be made. Until each part was actually finished, Bramante could keep his options open and room for experiment remained. He was not concerned to give every detail the stamp of his own personality: he did not hesitate, for example, to have the capitals of the large Corinthian order in the nave copied directly from those of the Pantheon.

168, 169 Rome, Vatican: *The School of Athens,* fresco by Raphael in the Stanza della Segnatura. In the background is a cruciform building whose four arms, covered by coffered vaults, converge on a dome with roundels in the pendentives, as in Bramante's St Peter's (Ill. 175). Below, a reconstruction of half the design, showing one of the arms, with niches between paired pilasters below coffered vaulting, leading to the central space.

170 Todi, S. Maria della Consolazione

But what did concern him was the organization of spaces and volumes, and he seemed to seize the chance of taking on almost any other work in order to experiment with the problems and themes he was encountering at St Peter's.

Furthermore, St Peter's was so large that work on it would have to go on after his death, as Bramante, being already old, must have realized; and with characteristic impatience he may have wished to see, and to be able to show the Pope, at least some image that would give an idea of what the final great St Peter's would be like. He wanted to leave works actually built as partial models which after his death would serve as a guide to his successors on the basilica.

Certainly the years around 1509 seem to have been a time when he was particularly pre-occupied in this way. At the end of 1509 or the beginning of 1510 comes the temple painted in the background of Raphael's *School of Athens* 16 (the design of which Vasari attributes to 16 Bramante), which, at least in its central space and great coffered vault, has some connection with the idea for the new basilica. And the 17 church of S. Maria della Consolazione at Todi 17 (begun in 1508–09) has elements which correspond to some in St Peter's. It develops a theme which also interested Leonardo and which is 41 found in Milan in the Bramantesque Cappella della Pozzobonella; but if the design of the Todi church did originate with him, it was certainly altered by the numerous architects who worked on it during its long period of building.

Neither of these works can definitely be attributed to Bramante, but they must spring from his circle. Other works certainly by him from these years involve themes comparable to those of St Peter's. The church of S. Biagio della 17 Pagnotta in the Palazzo dei Tribunali, begun in 18 1508 (see below, p. 169), took up the theme of the dome on diagonal arches and piers dominating a short nave. The idea of the *campanili* flanking a façade and framing a dome behind them appears on a medal of 1509 showing a project of Bramante's for the front of the church at Loreto. 12 The piazza-courtyard of Loreto, which would probably also have had a curved ending, exem- 12 plifies an idea which might have been used for the setting of St Peter's (as it is expressed, for instance, in the Mellon sketchbook). 15

If, as we have noted, the setting of the new church is echoed on a minute scale in the plan for the Tempietto of S. Pietro in Montorio, the 14 theme of a three-dimensional colonnaded building based on radial axes which Bramante had used in the Tempietto returns on a gigantic scale in his ideas for the dome of St Peter's. And 15

161

145

moreover, as we have also seen, buildings rather similar to the Tempietto surmount the sacristies in the drawing in the Mellon sketchbook. Problems similar to those which faced Bramante when he was deciding how to group the pilasters inside the Tempietto must have arisen, too, in the placing of the coupled pilasters on the lantern of the dome of St Peter's, which contradicts that of the columns of the drum.

71–
174

Similarly, the choir of S. Maria del Popolo (finished in 1509), and, to some extent, the small chapel in the papal villa of La Magliana,[60] probably by Bramante (1508–10), may be regarded almost as small-scale fragments of St Peter's. Certain themes directly or indirectly connected with the basilica appear in these works in several versions and on a number of scales. It was as if Bramante, especially between 1507 and 1510, was obsessed by the rhythms and complexities of St Peter's and its gigantic problems.

But a more general problem, which we have noted in dealing with the Tempietto, seems also to have preoccupied him in these years in Rome: that of architectural expression in relation to the physical size of the building. The problem may have originated from having to plan both very small buildings, like the Tempietto, and enormous ones, like the Belvedere and St Peter's. In buildings involving similar concepts but of different physical dimensions he could find out how valid the Classical rules really were. He seems to have perceived that outside the 'normal', medium range, size was extremely relevant. For instance, not only does the scheme of St Peter's have to be simplified in order to meet the more elementary requirements of S. Celso, but the actual architectural style is modified in accordance with the difference in scale.

165

In this group of fairly small buildings which take up themes from St Peter's, forms are summarized and simplified in a mature and very personal way that does not minimize – indeed, by careful use of lighting actually emphasizes – the spatial organization. Each building, though it was always an *exemplum* of universal values, has its own individual character and, far from being an abstract and purely theoretical model, acquires vitality through its response to a particular architectural scheme and a particular position within a town. S. Celso, for instance, being hemmed in by other buildings on every side, had to be lit entirely from above, and the careful filtering of the light from the central space to the corner chapels contributes very markedly to the way its spaces are experienced; it is a synthesis of the inscribed cross plan,

165,
166

organized as a series of linked parts, similar in shape but differing in size, opening out one into the other.

Since, as we have seen, nearly all these buildings remained unfinished and were later altered or destroyed, it is only the choir of S. Maria del Popolo, probably planned between 1505 and 1507, finished in 1509 and preserved substantially in its original form, that gives a valid idea of Bramante's manner in this period.[60a] Here the old choir of the church from the time of Sixtus IV (square, covered with a cross vault which Bramante was to transform into a domical vault, and preceded by a barrel vault) had to be restored and enlarged in order to include a mausoleum for the famous cardinals Ascanio Sforza and Basso della Rovere. It was a programme in many ways similar to that of the church of S. Maria delle Grazie in Milan, and, as he did there, Bramante unhesitatingly transformed the fifteenth-century church, producing a square space covered with a domical vault, preceded and followed by a barrel vault. It was the scheme of Brunelleschi's Pazzi Chapel; and perhaps Bramante was trying to revive and up-date a famous Quattrocento prototype. There, however, the barrel vaults had flanked the square bay; here they are placed on the longitudinal axis, increasing the feeling of recession into depth at this end of the church. (Luca Fancelli had done the same thing in the Cappella dell' Incoronata in Mantua Cathedral, perhaps following an idea of Alberti's.)

171–
174

171,
172

Today, the effect Bramante sought is largely destroyed by the clumsy Baroque altar which makes it impossible to see the choir from the nave: previously, the altar was smaller and did not significantly block the view. And while the central square of the choir, covered by its domical vault and strongly lit by large 'Palladian' windows (a new invention of Bramante's, seen in arcade form at Genazzano) had to appear as a proper funerary chapel containing the two cardinals' monuments, the new addition as a whole constituted a remarkable expansion in depth of the space of the old church, beyond the fifteenth-century crossing. Ideally, therefore, the church becomes a centrally planned building that has been drawn out at the far end – as at S. Maria delle Grazie – by an all-powerful dynamic force running through it. Bramante wished to convey the greatest possible impression of recession into depth of the apse with its shell semi-dome, and at the same time to emphasize the square bay in the middle. His choice of the exact form and size of the details needed to achieve these visual effects shows extreme subtlety and maturity of thought. He

171,
174
118

55

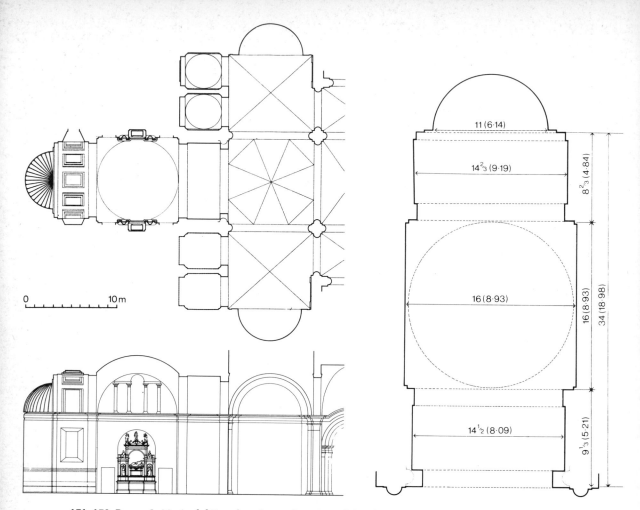

171–173 Rome, S. Maria del Popolo: plan and section of the choir and transepts (showing symmetrical chapels opening off the transepts: the fifteenth-century church is thought to have had only two semicircular chapels flanking the choir); measured plan of the choir, and view towards the apse. In the measured plan, dimensions are given in Roman *braccia*, followed by metres.

172 enlarged the central bay (16 Roman *braccia*) in relation to the width of the two barrel-vaulted spaces which precede and follow it (14½ and 14⅔ *braccia*), and slightly reduced the depth of the most distant one (from 9⅓ to 8⅔ *braccia*) to make the apse appear farther away. The effect was further enhanced by the careful handling of the wall surfaces and by the remarkable narrowing of the apse (11 *braccia*) in comparison with the width of the wall-space in which it is set.

173 The effective way in which this space is characterized is the result of a remarkable simplification of Bramante's stylistic language. The orthodox architectural orders, which he had used ever since Urbino and his early days in Lombardy, are eliminated. Simple pilaster strips now mark the junction between different spaces. Instead of capitals a pared-down form

of entablature indicates where the pilasters end without interrupting their solemn but dynamic thrust, which continues into the arches of the vault. The enclosing walls are articulated according to their specific spatio-structural functions, but their slight projections do not compromise the monolithic unity of the material, which is conceived as being hollowed out and modelled by the action of the interior space. A single colour – warm white on the walls, white slightly veined with brown on the structural members – emphasizes this unity. In this setting, the monumental coffered vault at the end was not merely a deliberate reference to Roman stylistic methods and a powerful way of suggesting the heroic: it was also a tangible demonstration of the new relationship between the spaces and the walls enclosing them. Per-

fect continuity is achieved between walls and vault: a continuity of forms cut into a single material, and also logically individualized, bound together and arranged in sequence. The profiles of these forms seem to take on a clear-cut, almost metallic quality: they seem to be absolute, outside time, charged with meanings that go beyond merely cultural values, images of extraordinary intensity.

Within the limits imposed by the architecture, sculpture and painting were also introduced to define more clearly the quality of the space, and to underline its method and its meaning. Bramante himself must have directed the work of Sansovino, sculptor of the two cardinals' tombs, of Pinturicchio, who decor-

174 ated the large central vault, and of Guglielmo di Marcillat (brought to Rome by Bramante, according to Vasari), who made the glass for the Palladian windows. Inlaid choir stalls and perhaps a Cosmatesque floor, like the one in the Tempietto, were probably meant to complete

172, the work. Sansovino's two monuments, their
173 complex architectural frames projecting symmetrically from shallow niches in the walls, inevitably set up a lateral movement in this bay in opposition to the prevailing longitudinal movement, so that the space as a whole takes on a rhythm of expansion and compression, either real or illusionistic, in its progress from one end of the composition to the other.

The white marble of the monuments, set against the warm white of the walls, introduces a vibrant variation of tone in the continuous monochrome of the surfaces, bringing them alive without depriving them of their homogeneous quality – indeed enhancing it by the contrast. The two monuments serve to link the walls with the columned Palladian windows of the lunettes and with the divisions painted on the vault. At the same time, the crowding together into a tiny space of small architectural elements and less than life-size statues only enhances the building's monumental scale.

It is quite possible that Bramante himself designed the architecture of the tombs in collaboration with Sansovino. He probably also

174 suggested the pattern of the vault decoration to Pinturicchio, taking as his model the stucco decoration of a room in Hadrian's Villa. (Bramante must have supervised the decoration of the Vatican Stanze and perhaps, before Raphael's arrival, may have suggested the scheme for the decoration of the vault of the Stanza della Segnatura, which has similarities with that of S. Maria del Popolo.) The painting of this vault was not intended merely to attract the onlooker's attention with its dazzlingly bright colours in

an otherwise monochrome building: it was a means of emphasizing even further the three-dimensional central area, of bringing in new illusionistic spatial ideas. The curved surface of the vault is divided geometrically by having a square with chamfered corners set into it diagonally; in the corners, resting on *trompe l'oeil* pendentives, are four Classical aedicules containing figures of saints. These figures carry on the small scale of Sansovino's monuments, and they emphasize powerfully the diagonal axes of the central space. What Bramante was trying to do in this novel treatment of space is to stress the ideal centrality of his new choir by making its small vault echo the larger octagonal vault at the crossing of the old fifteenth-century church.

Between the bright colours of the vault and the light monochrome of the walls and monuments below it, Bramante placed the windows, with their glass by Marcillat. Architecturally they echo the two tombs, while the glass, vivid in colour, carries the polychromy of the vault downwards and softens the division between vault and wall. As in a Gothic church, light filters through the stained glass, projecting shifting splashes of colour on the walls and floors; it colours the atmosphere, subdues the whiteness of the architecture, blending the different parts together, as if a painter had covered them with a veil of coloured shadows.

A new, revolutionary relationship is thus established between architecture and the figurative arts. As previously in Milan, light becomes the protagonist, accompanying, emphasizing and controlling the flow of space. The middle bay is alive with colour and sculpture and is lit by two large windows, but in spite of this, and contrary to all abstract logic, it is not the place of maximum luminosity, because of the stained glass. Bramante had not forgotten his original idea, that of an articulated space that had in some extraordinary way been hollowed out, not built. The old church was to seem as if it had been inflated by the bursting energy of the void within it. So the most vivid light was to be directed upon the most distant part, the part which had felt the effect of this expanding force the most – the shell of the apse and the great coffered 173 vault above it. At this point, on the right of the onlooker, he set a large window into the wall between the two pilaster-strips. But its light was reduced by the thickness of the window embrasure, by the projection of the pilaster-strip in front of it, and by the fact that there was originally a portico on this side of the church, so that only a faint gleam penetrated into the interior.

The main body of light comes from above, and only from one side, like a searchlight pointing downwards at an angle into the apse. Let into the lowest of the coffers of the vault is a deeply splayed window opening which catches the greatest possible amount of light from the sky and focuses the rays of the midday sun into the interior. The effect is very much that of a painted architectural background, as in the Brera Altarpiece or the Prevedari engraving. The slanting light from one side only picks out the sculptural qualities of the building, emphasizing the almost metallic precision and pure geometry of its forms with sharp highlights, *sfumato, chiaroscuro* and areas of dazzling brilliance. Architecturally, as we have seen, the choir is organic, regular and symmetrical. The emphasis of the lighting not only differs from the emphasis of the plan (the large central bay is not the most brightly lit): it throws the whole symmetrical scheme off balance. It is, however, wholly consistent with the dynamic drive towards the apse which was Bramante's overriding idea. Indeed, it brings that idea down from the realm of abstract theory to the actual world of experience.

The image thus becomes imbued with a wealth of meanings. It not only expresses a heroic, Antique dignity in keeping with Julius II's 'imperial' programme, but suggests whole layers of historical ideas with a fervour in which intellect, emotion and scientific curiosity are combined, and which gives an unprecedented unity of expression surpassing any prototype of the ancient world. It evokes some underground Roman chamber, a place hollowed out of the earth, its forms cast in solid concrete rather than built up out of separate elements, the light entering in painful stabs. Yet all its cultural references – from ancient Rome to Quattrocento Italy – are miraculously concentrated in a single image. They are subconscious allusions, suggestions, pointers which enrich it not only in visual terms but in meaning and significance. It is light, above all, which keeps all these conflicting aims in a precarious balance. In Bonelli's opinion, S. Maria del Popolo is 'perhaps Bramante's finest achievement as an artist', a work in which, through his newly forged, personal idiom, the image becomes 'the unequivocal embodiment of a creative moment'.[61]

Once he had established a new approach to the relationship between space and the enclosing walls, especially in St Peter's, Bramante was led to a reappraisal of the significance of the wall and ceiling, in both their internal and external functions. According to Vasari,

174 Rome, S. Maria del Popolo: domical vault over the central bay of the choir, painted by Pinturicchio, probably following a scheme by Bramante

Bramante 'discovered' at St Peter's 'the method of casting vaults in wooden moulds, in such a manner that patterns of friezes and foliage, like carvings, come out in the plaster'. The invention of 'plaster vaults after the manner of the ancients' is also attributed by Vasari to Giuliano da Sangallo, and the method had in any case been described by Alberti in *De re aedificatoria*. Nevertheless it was Bramante alone who deduced from this technical system a new treatment of the elements that enclosed space: he no longer saw them as 'built' structures, or even, as Alberti had, as proportioned walls and superimposed 'ornaments', but as architecture modelled out of homogeneous material. Indeed, Vasari goes on to say that he not only made moulded vaults, but 'directed the building, in the Borgo, of the palace which afterwards belonged to Raffaello of Urbino, executed with bricks and mould-castings [cast concrete], the columns and bosses being of the Doric Order and of rustic work – a very beautiful work – with a new invention in the making of these castings'. This technique changed the specific meaning of the elements used in building. Bramante may have thought that there was no longer any point in making Alberti's rationalistic distinction between the 'wall' and the superimposed 'ornament' forming an architectural

175 Rome, St Peter's: view of the building under construction, looking towards the apse, showing the *tegurio* protecting the papal altar in the centre of the crossing. This sketch after Heemskerck, of *c.*1534, also shows the vast crossing piers and coffered arches. (Berlin-Dahlem, Kupferstichkabinett der Staatlichen Museens)

order, which he had previously used in a strict and precise way. With the use of mould-made structures the only reality was the physical, or at least conceptual, homogeneity of the whole building. There was no longer any point in translating the order on a wall into strictly mural terms by representing it exclusively in

the form of a *pilaster*. Now half-columns too could be used to express the continuity, cohesion and central unity of the whole building, including its 'ornaments'.

Half-columns appear on the façade of the House of Raphael (*c.* 1510 or later: see below, p. 173); in the courtyard of the Palazzo dei Tribunali (*c.* 1508); on the façade of the Nymphaeum of Genazzano (*c.* 1508–11); in the refacing of the Holy House of Loreto (1509–10); and in the *tegurio* or shelter (1513) which was put up to protect the papal altar during the building of St Peter's. All these belong to Bramante's late period. 181, 182, 178, 118, 175

Starting from the idea of an architecture that is *moulded* (just as sculpture is moulded in plaster or bronze, after being modelled in clay or wax) and no longer *built,* Bramante sees wall and order, structure and decoration, of whatever material, as a single composite entity, homogeneous in concept but articulated on its surface by means of visually differentiated textures. To the 'pure' enclosed space of the interiors, which is tangible and hollowed out of the material, now corresponds a 'pure' enclosing medium, freely modelled and articulated, and expressed in painterly and sculptural terms. This gave the architect a freedom he had never enjoyed before. He could 'depict' his building by any means he chose – by optical devices, colour, sculpture or light – either using real architectural features and real materials (brick, travertine, marble, tufa) or representing them illusionistically in moulded concrete, unhampered by the physical limitations which they would have imposed. Such buildings could be made to embody all the emotive values of the ancient world whose forms they seemed to reproduce so exactly. In fact, the more they seemed to contemporaries to be 'copies' or reincarnations of Roman models, the further they actually were from them, both structurally and in their deeper meaning. In the same way, Julius II's *renovatio imperii* was a sort of illusionistic image for something that was in fact part of a political, social and economic reality very far from that of the Romans. But architecture, all architecture, was becoming 'false', a *spettacolo* of itself, produced by architectural means; no more than a branch of 'art', to be interpreted first and foremost in visual terms, like a painting or a piece of sculpture.

Two further projects must be examined as significant examples of Bramante's attitude at this time, especially in relation to the problem of the façade as part of urban design – the enormous Palazzo dei Tribunali and the House of Raphael. 176–182

Julius II's programme was to concentrate all power, including civil power, in the hands of the Church, and so the Palazzo dei Tribunali was to have contained all the ecclesiastical and civil courts of Rome, as well as the judges' apartments.⁶² The building was begun in 1508, stopped after about three years of intense activity, never completed and later almost entirely destroyed. Bramante's plan is preserved in the Uffizi (Arch. 136), though we know from another Uffizi drawing by Peruzzi (Arch. 109) that some details of it were altered during the execution. A square courtyard with sides about 35 m. long is surrounded by a large rectangular block, about 76 by 96 m., with towers at the corners. The entrance on Via Giulia is marked by a large tower rising above the rest of the building and terminating in an octagonal top which would serve as a *campanile*. On the opposite side of the courtyard is the church of S. Biagio della Pagnotta, which juts out towards the Tiber but is an integral part of the palace. The cruciform plan of the church, with a cupola and projecting apse flanked by two sacristies possibly heightened by *campanili*, would have formed an impressive formal composition set against the palace wall on the river side, possibly resembling the grouping shown on the foundation medal of St Peter's. From the annotations on Uffizi Arch. 136, which shows only the building's first floor, one can deduce that there were three storeys: a ground floor with shops (like the ancient Roman law courts, the basilicas) on the Via Giulia, audience chambers, and staircases, and two upper floors containing the apartments and offices of the judges of the four main courts, and the apartments of their families and servants. The top rooms of the corner towers may perhaps have been intended for use as prisons. Great care is shown in the arrangement and in the proportions of the various rooms in relation to their widely differing functions.

The plan and some elements of the building are partly influenced, as Frommel noted, by the medieval *palazzo comunale* (such as Michelozzo's at Montepulciano). Other features recall Roman cardinals' palaces such as the Palazzo Venezia or, in particular, the Palazzo della Cancelleria, which may have suggested the idea of the church and of the projecting corner pavilions. The handling of the volumes recalls the ideas of Filarete and the Castello Sforzesco in Milan, while the way in which the church is made to jut out beyond the line of the palace reminds one of Roman baths, such as those of Caracalla, Diocletian and Constantine. It is a type of plan which in various guises keeps recurring in Bramante's work during these years, for instance in the fortress of Civitavecchia and at Loreto. At the same time, the spatial organization of the whole – with a centrally-planned nucleus, the square courtyard, whose main movement leads forward but which is checked and halted at numerous points by spaces or features of various kinds along the longitudinal axis – shows (as Frommel points out) the characteristic duality between centralized planning and axial perspective which appears several times in Bramante's mature work and which we have seen expressed so clearly in the choir of S. Maria del Popolo.

Everything suggests that this project for the Tribunali, for which a model was made, was, along with St Peter and the Belvedere, one of Bramante's most important works for Julius II. Apart from what has already been said, very little is known about its elevation. But parts of it still standing and the meagre documentation available show that it must have been of very great interest. The foundation medal shows the façade on Via Giulia. There are two corner towers and a higher central tower, all with battlemented tops, battered bases and almost no openings; and between the towers there are curtain walls with arcades. But many details do not correspond to those in Uffizi Arch. 136 or to the building as executed. Possibly the medal shows an early idea which was later changed. What is certain is that the ground storey of the building (of which remains are still visible in Via Giulia) was rusticated, made of large, roughly-cut stone blocks of varying size interrupted by cavernous shops with arched openings, and string-courses with big moulded keystones. The source for this (as for the Porta Julia of the Belvedere and possibly for the Nymphaeum at Genazzano, being built at the same time) was ancient Roman architecture: the wall of the Forum of Augustus, the door of the Templum Sacrae Urbis in the Forum, etc. But what was entirely Bramante's innovation was to repeat the Roman motif of a rusticated arch and combine it with a wall to form the structurally articulated base of a palace. This invention was to be fundamental for the development of Mannerism in the sixteenth century (Giulio Romano, Peruzzi, Serlio, Vignola, etc.): as Argan observed about Serlio, it was the sign of a 'tendency to extend the concept of space beyond its identification with the concept of plastic form. Rustication itself, if defined naturalistically, cannot be part of a geometrical definition of space.'⁶³ It is another way of denying the abstract geometry, and with it the absolute rules of proportion, of the

Rome, Palazzo dei Tribunali

176 The foundation medal of 1508, showing the façade on Via Giulia (Rome, Vatican)

177 Surviving rusticated base-course in Via Giulia

178 Plan of the first floor. At the top, the church of S. Biagio projects towards the river (see Ills. 179, 180); at the bottom is Via Giulia ('Via Nuova'). (Florence, Uffizi, Arch. 136)

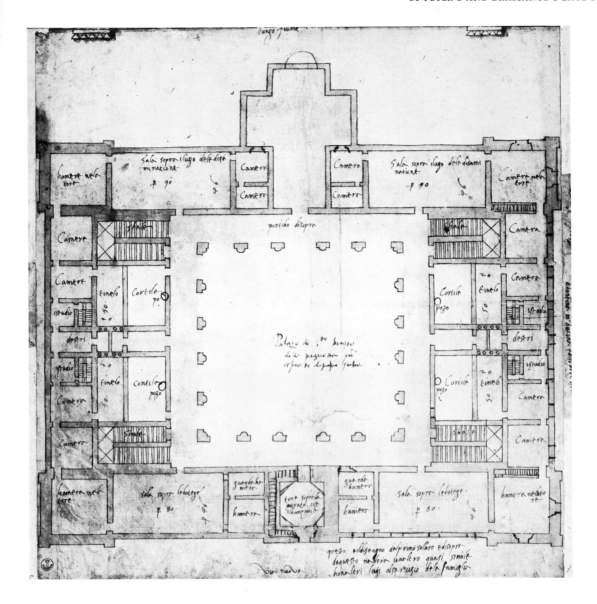

fifteenth-century tradition: a way similar to that shown in St Peter's, for instance, although expressed in another form; a way of reaching and touching the observer visually and emotionally rather than intellectually.

But there seem to have been other innovations in the Palazzo dei Tribunali. In Uffizi Arch. 136, the corners of the side towers are shown on the plan as having projections of such a size (almost twice that of the halfcolumns in the courtyard) that they suggest a giant order of pilasters, extending to the upper floors of the building, and possibly standing on pedestals, above the rusticated bases of the

178

corner towers. According to this drawing, there were no such projections on the central tower or on the curtain walls with the windowopenings. They seem to mark only the four corners of the building, the key visual points of reference for the *spettacolo* of the façade. It is not known exactly how the details were treated, whether there were smaller superimposed orders with arches or, as seems more likely, only windows and string-courses, rather as at Sangallo's Palazzo Farnese. The corner projections might also mean that the rustication of the ground floor was carried up as quoins on the upper part of the side towers.

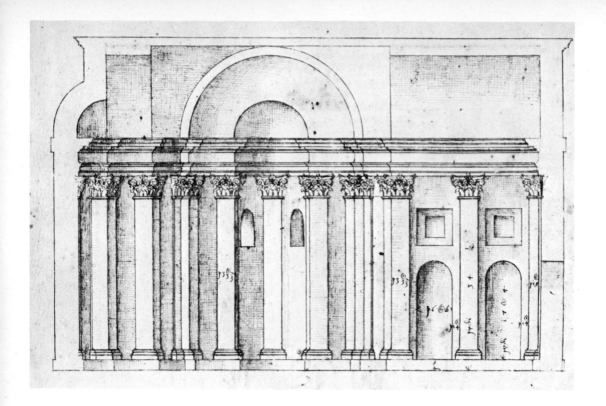

179, 180 Rome, S. Biagio della Pagnotta in the Palazzo dei Tribunali: longitudinal section, drawn by Palladio (Vicenza, Museo Civico), and plan from the 'Coner Codex' (London, Sir John Soane's Museum). The plan is reproduced on its side, to match the section; for its position in the palace, see Ill. 178, top. The theme of diagonally-placed crossing piers combined with a longitudinal nave is associated with Bramante's designs for St Peter's (Ills. 157, 158).

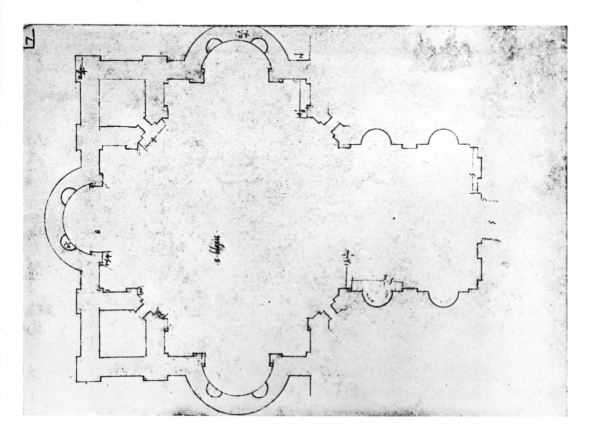

Perhaps, indeed, it may have covered the entire surface of the central tower. But whether rusticated quoins were used, or, as is perhaps more probable, giant pilasters, we are confronted with a remarkable enrichment of the traditional language of the Renaissance, which foreshadows later developments. If it was pilasters that Bramante used, developing the Brunelleschian idea of the Palazzo di Parte Guelfa in Florence and interpreting it in a three-dimensional way, then his design could be linked with Michelangelo's work in the Palazzo Senatorio on the Campidoglio (which uses several elements from the Palazzo dei Tribunali). If he used rusticated quoins, then it could be linked with buildings of the Sangallo type, such as the Palazzo Farnese. Another highly significant link with the Palazzo Farnese is the courtyard, although the two buildings differed completely in their treatments of wall and space. The courtyard of the Palazzo dei Tribunali must have had three storeys with five arches on each side, framed, at least on the first floor, by half-columns.

In the case of the Palazzo dei Tribunali we know the plan, but have only a rough idea of the exterior. The opposite is true of the House of Raphael, originally the Palazzo Caprini and later included in the Palazzo dei Covertendi. Although a date of 1501–02 is sometimes suggested, I consider it to be a late work of Bramante's, designed about 1510 or later. It was acquired by Raphael in 1517. The building stood on the corner of Via Alessandrina and the piazza later called Scossacavalli. Its plan is known only from the drawings of Ottaviano Mascherino, made c. 1591–1600, which already show it in altered form. Its street front, on the other hand, is recorded in a number of sixteenth-century views, of which the most detailed and reliable are a drawing attributed to Palladio (RIBA, London) and an engraving of 1549 by Antoine Lafréry. This façade is Bramante's most important work in Rome in the field of palace architecture.

Its basic arrangement is one that goes back to the Roman house and continued into the Middle Ages, with shops on the ground floor and dwellings above. Bramante makes a clear distinction between the two functions: the public or commercial function, and the private or dwelling function. The front consists essentially of only two elements, the lower rusticated part and the upper storeys (main and service floors) articulated by a single giant order. There are virtually no precedents either among fifteenth-century palaces or among ancient Roman buildings. It is unlike both the traditional Florentine palace (such as the Palazzo Medici) and those with superimposed orders (such as Alberti's Palazzo Rucellai and the Cancelleria) – though, in the treatment of the ground floor and upper orders, the closest precedents for the House of Raphael are the Cancelleria, some of Filarete's ideas, and possibly the palace of Cardinal Corneto. In the Tribunali the great stone blocks of the ground floor had conveyed a powerful impression of 'Roman' strength. The ground floor of the House of Raphael makes the same effect even more forcefully, although the material here is cast concrete, not stone. The unbroken solidity of this storey contrasts sharply with the openness of the order-plus-entablature above, here expressed in its most 'Greek' form, the Doric with triglyphs. The 'Greekness' of this order comes through in significant details, taken from Vitruvius, such as the corner triglyph and the removal of the metopes at regular intervals to make windows in the service floor. These two distinct, contrasting systems are unified (in concept rather than in appearance) by their common fabric – the traditional Roman brick and cast concrete. This finally explodes Alberti's theory that the orders must be seen as just an aspect of the wall, a theory to which Bramante, through his exclusive use of pilasters, had until now been faithful.

Each element is clearly defined and proclaims its precise static function – or rather *seems* to, because of course the whole front is an artificial composition. The only element which makes no attempt to seem anything but what it really is is the material. This Bramante conceived as homogeneous, something from which all the various parts are obviously seen to be made, like modelled and painted sculpture. The treatment of the corner is particularly striking. Renaissance architects had constantly striven to achieve this unity of effect while allowing each part its due weight as three-dimensional structure, but never before with such success. The great rough-hewn blocks *alla rustica* of the 'Roman' wall make it seem like a work of nature, cyclopean, primordial, timeless. But the 'Greek' order on top of it, like the colonnade of a temple on its high podium, speaks (with learned reference to Vitruvius) of civilization, of polish, of human hands moving with precision, refinement and reason. The 'natural' and the 'man-made' are thus shown as the two 'universal' alternatives of architecture. Although in opposition, neither permanently dominates the other. The lighter, finer, less solid but more 'noble' structure rests upon a foundation that is stronger but coarser, illustrating the natural

181, 182 Rome, House of Raphael (Palazzo Caprini), in Via Alessandrina: façade seen in an engraving by Lafréry (1549), and corner, in a drawing formerly attributed to Palladio. In the latter, note the corner triglyphs and the windows for the service floor inserted in the metopes above the main floor windows. The palace formed part of the 'Spina' of the Borgo, destroyed after 1936 to make the Via della Conciliazione. (London, Royal Institute of British Architects, British Architectural Library)

law of gravity and the social law of the time, according to which the intellectual and political activity of those who lived on the *piano nobile* rested upon the labours of the shopkeepers and artisans on the ground floor.

181, 182   So the building consists, as Serlio says of later works like it (Bk IV, f. 33), of a 'balance' or 'blend' of diverse parts, 'representing partly a work of nature and partly a work of artifice'. This 'invention', based on the opposition, in idea as well as in appearance, between two different parts of the same building, neither of which dominates the other, was one which the Mannerists of the sixteenth century were to find very stimulating. A taste that could already be called 'Mannerist' appears clearly in the *expressionistic* emphasis placed upon the structural meaning of the elements. On the ground floor, in particular, some odd details seem to point forward to the idiosyncratic 'licences' of Mannerism: these are the paired keystones above the shops; the 'illogical' emphasis upon structural strength in relation to the spaces for the tiny open windows inside the arches; the

ambiguous arrangement of the openings on the ground floor, which vary in contradiction to the uniform rhythm of the coupled columns above; and so on.

This, then, is a new kind of architecture, presenting a 'picture' of itself by means of illusionistic and perspective devices, in a material that is moulded, its forms, as it were, impressed upon it. Here fact and fiction converge, mingle and lose their distinction. In spite of appearances, no simple, single interpretation of a building will suffice any longer. We have entered the realm of the imagination. Now the architect is free to express his personality through any novelty, any innovation that he chooses. That innovation goes beyond the old *scientia* founded upon *Natura* and *Ratio,* and illuminated by *Historia.* It is a message which may proclaim itself to be universal, a thesis which may seem a paradigm of rationality. But it is more. For now both architect and observer are being invited to make their own interpretations of a work of architecture, emotionally and subjectively. The way to Mannerism lies open.

183 Bramante, sketched by Raphael for the fresco of the *Disputà* in the Stanza della Segnatura in the Vatican, c. 1508 (Paris, Louvre)

Chapter ten

Bramante's personality and influence

THE YEARS between 1505 and 1510 were Bramante's most productive period in Rome. He not only received a large number of commissions but worked intensively upon their execution. After 1510–11 the commissions begin to dwindle and the rhythm of his activity to slow down. Hardly any of the works put in hand by Julius II were completed when the Pope died. His Treasury had been drained by the expenses of war, and he had other things to worry about besides architecture. After having promoted the League of Cambrai against Venice in 1508, he re-established relations with the Venetian Republic early in 1510 and obtained from it freedom of navigation and trading in the Adriatic (which was why, in June 1511, he decided to build the port of Recanati near Loreto, on which Bramante was consulted). In October 1511, having allied himself with Venice and Spain, he moved against France. France, with the support of the Empire, retaliated by calling a General Council against Julius. It was convened at Pisa, but almost immediately moved to Milan, then to Lyons, provoking a schism. On 11 April 1512, the Pope was defeated by a French army under Gaston de Foix at Ravenna, but in May the Pope's own Lateran Council, at which papal supremacy was vigorously reaffirmed, opened in Rome.

Bramante's fame was now immense, and he was a close friend of the Pope. On 10 July 1510, Cardinal Soderini consulted him about his palace on Via Alessandrina in the Borgo, but, possibly because Bramante was too busy, he seems not to have become involved with it. At the end of 1510 he was with the Pope at Bologna: a letter of 13 December from there says that Julius, who had been ill, was 'now better and wanted to become learned in Dante,

so every evening he had Dante read and explained to him by Bramante, his learned architect'. According to Vasari, at this time Bramante 'occupied himself, during the whole war against Mirandola [a fortress which fell on 20 January 1511], on many ingenious things of the greatest importance'. 'He was rightly held worthy by the . . . Pope,' writes Vasari, 'who loved him dearly for his great gifts, to be appointed to the Office of the Piombo, for which he made a machine for printing Bulls, with a very beautiful screw.' This was the time at which Bramante's prestige was at its highest. The office of the Piombo, which carried the title Frate but could be conferred only upon a man who knew no Latin, brought very handsome rewards: indeed Saba da Castiglione (1549) relates that 'when Bramante was asked how his affairs were going, he said: "Excellently, for my ignorance pays my expenses."' According to Cesariano (1521), Julius 'made him rich and gave him gifts and offices which produced more money than he needed for a decent life and clothes for himself and his servants'. Vasari says 'he always lived in the greatest splendour, doing honour to himself; and in the rank to which his merits had raised him, what he possessed was nothing to what he would have been able to spend'. And in *Simia* Guarna makes him say: 'I cared not what I spent on good living . . .'.

But work now grew scarce, and the political and financial crisis forced him to concentrate his efforts almost entirely on St Peter's. Other building works slowed down or were abandoned altogether. However, from January to September 1513 some minor work on the villa of La Magliana (a project of Giuliano de Sangallo's) was undertaken 'by commission of Maestro Frate Bramante the architect', and also in 1513

149–161

126–
131 work was going ahead on the port of Civitavecchia, which proceeded 'on the advice of Frate
Bramante'.

On 21 February 1513 Julius II died. After a
brief interregnum during which work on the
sea-fort of Civitavecchia continued, the Florentine Giovanni de' Medici was elected pope on
11 March 1513 and took the name of Leo X. At
the beginning of his pontificate, after Whitsun
1513, as Shearman has established, work on
175 Bramante's *tegurio* was begun.[64] This was to be
a temporary protection for the papal altar while
the new basilica was being built. 'He preserved
only the altar of S. Pietro, and the old tribune',
Vasari writes, 'round which he made a most
beautiful ornament of the Doric Order, all of
peperino-stone, to the end that when the Pope
came to S. Pietro to say Mass, he might be able
to stand within it with all his Court and with
the Ambassadors of the Christian Princes.'
Vasari goes on to say that the work, interrupted
after Easter 1514, was completed by Peruzzi.
The *tegurio* was demolished in 1592.

But now Giuliano da Sangallo, a Florentine
and the Medici's chief architect, suddenly
came back to Rome from Florence. He had been
Bramante's most formidable rival and was to
some extent the leader of the 'Florentine party'
at the court of Julius II, a group which included men as remarkable as Andrea Sansovino and, most prominent of all, Michelangelo.
When the Medici fled from Florence in 1494,
Giuliano da Sangallo worked for the next two
years for Julius, while he was still a cardinal;
and then, between 1505 and 1507, he worked
for him again in Rome. But Bramante, whose
talents were more than merely professional, had
surpassed him, and had managed to win the
favour of the Pope and of influential people at
the Vatican court. In order to consolidate his
position, Bramante had helped older non-
Florentine artists with whom he was friendly –
174 such as Pinturicchio, Luca Signorelli and Perugino – and had brought to Rome artists like
Guglielmo di Marcillat and pupils of his own
from Lombardy, such as Bramantino. He had
also formed diplomatic friendships with pro-
mising young artists, even Florentines such as
Antonio da Sangallo the Younger and Jacopo
Sansovino, and the Sienese Baldassare Peruzzi
(a pupil of Francesco di Giorgio and the protégé
of the Sienese Agostino Chigi, the Pope's banker). And at the end of 1508 or the beginning of
1509, he had been instrumental in bringing
168, Raphael to Rome, as a counterpoise to Michel-
183 angelo.

Under Julius II Roman art and architecture at
all levels was dominated by artists and work-
men faithful to Bramante. In 1507 Giuliano da
Sangallo was forced to leave the papal court and
Bramante took over his works, such as the
villa of La Magliana. It was a serious defeat for
the 'Florentine party'. But with the election of
Leo X, and Bramante now old and infirm, the
situation rapidly changed. Already in July
1513, Giuliano da Sangallo, back in Rome, was
planning a large palace for the Medici family in
Piazza Navona; in September he was involved
in work connected with the Borgia Tower in
the Belvedere and on 1 January 1514 he was
associated with the direction of St Peter's
(until 1 July 1515).

Bramante and Raphael still enjoyed high
prestige, but the Florentines were recovering
their position everywhere. For instance, the
temporary wooden theatre put up in the Piazza
del Campidoglio in September 1513 for the celebrations conferring Roman citizenship upon
Giuliano and Lorenzo de' Medici was built by
the Florentine Pietro Rosselli, a friend of
Michelangelo's, and possibly designed by
Giuliano da Sangallo himself. Florentine work-
men returned to the villa of La Magliana; and on
22 June 1513 Andrea Sansovino was appointed
head of Bramante's workshop at Loreto.

From the day of his coronation Leo X had
stressed his intention to follow the wars of
Julius II with a new golden age of peace and
justice, in which the arts could flourish and
useful progress could be made in city and state.
Bramante was employed on the decoration of
the city to celebrate the coronation. But the
Pope's shrinking financial resources, his down-
to-earth politics, his nepotism, which limited
his horizons to the private sector, and his re-
nunciation of universal political claims ruled
out any large-scale architectural work. Bramante, as we have seen, may not have let slip
the opportunity to assert his position by presenting the Pope with a new scheme for the re-
planning of Rome. Its point of departure was the
need to find a remedy for the flooding of the
Tiber, and was perhaps connected with the idea
of redeveloping the area of the Piazza Navona
and the Palazzo Medici. Something like it was
actually carried out later in Leo's pontificate, in
1518, with the regularizing of the Piazza del
Popolo and the opening up of Via Ripetta.

But Bramante was now weary and ill. In his
last years Vasari says 'he could not work as he
had done before, being old and suffering from a
paralytic condition of the hands', and Antonio
da Sangallo the Younger was called in (along
with Peruzzi and others), Vasari continues, 'to
help him in the designs which he made . . . Bramante giving the order that he wanted, and

providing all the ideas and details necessary for each work'. Finally, at the end of 1513, when he was consulted about work on the cathedral at Foligno (where Cola da Caprarola, who had also been active in the Consolazione at Todi, was working), Bramante was in such a poor state of health that he declined the work. He grew worse and died in Rome on Tuesday, 11 April 1514, and was buried in St Peter's, 'borne to his tomb', according to Vasari, 'with most honourable obsequies, by the Court of the Pope and by all the sculptors, architects and painters'.

Although there is relatively little documentation about Bramante's personality, we can gain some insight into it, and thereby into his architecture, from scattered remarks by contemporaries such as Cesariano, Egidio da Viterbo, Guarna, Michelangelo, etc., from accounts by historians like Vasari, who probably drew upon first-hand sources, and from an examination of his other works, for instance his paintings and above all his sonnets. According to Vasari, 'Bramante was a very merry and pleasant person, ever delighting to help his neighbour. He was very much the friend of men of ability, and favoured them in whatever way he could.'

Andrea Guarna, who must have known him well, shows him in a very lively way in his *Simia* (1516). Bramante appears as an attractive, humorous talker but with a streak of cruel banter ('he told stories about everyone marvellously'). And a subtle mockery may be detected in the Classical-sounding sonorously obsequious way in which he addressed important people ('To the high shepherd of Christ's flock, Bramante, prone and reverent, sends greetings'). Yet with these same important people he could be disdainful, resolute and aggressive; a master of sophistry, he was quite capable of using them for his own ambitious projects and also for less noble purposes: indeed, he confesses to having 'lightened the Pope's purse a good deal'. Highly ambitious, arrogant, boastful, witty, quick and cutting in his speech, cynical, 'turning as fast as a potter's wheel', irascible and eccentric, a suspected homosexual, he was a man, according to Guarna, who recognized no moral restrictions: an uninhibited follower of Epicurus. 'Avoiding melancholy and boredom as far as possible', he confesses, 'I have always nourished my soul on happiness and pleasure.' Indeed, he goes on, 'Is not a free man, endowed with a free will, bound to live a free life? . . . What I am permitted to do, I think I also have the right to do': liberty to the point of licence, 'in the cause of his own genius'.

Guarna was no doubt caricaturing Bramante to some extent in this portrait. Nevertheless, wit, irony, a taste for clever and bantering raillery, are qualities which come through very clearly in some of his sonnets and even in some of his paintings; and certain aspects of his character revealed by Guarna are confirmed by the evidence of contemporaries such as Egidio da Viterbo and by hints from Vasari. Vasari emphasizes Bramante's desire to display his 'mastery over difficulties' and calls him an 'inventive genius', quoting some examples of his architectural ideas in support, as well as, for instance, his odd proposal to place an inscription in the Belvedere 'after the manner of ancient hieroglyphics . . . in order to show his ingenuity' (see above, p. 108).

Sixteenth-century witnesses show Bramante as a man interested in every kind of experience. Cesariano and other contemporaries refer to him as 'unlettered', but in the Renaissance this merely meant that he was lacking in knowledge of Latin and the classics. He was 'fluent in the rhymed verse of the vernacular poets', so he must have had some culture, however incomplete. He had a remarkable capacity for assimilation and, as Cesariano says, a 'great memory and power of expression'; this he must have developed through his contacts with the many humanists at the courts he frequented. For instance, Chastel notes that he seems to have known the ideas of Ficino, illustrated in the fresco in the Casa Panigarola where *Heraclitus* 37 *and Democritus* – tears and laughter – stand on either side of the terrestrial globe (similar to that which decorated the Platonic Academy). The Milanese poet Gaspare Visconti, a friend of Bramante's, celebrated him as a poet (and in poetry as a 'devoted admirer of Dante', which he certainly was) and as a man of many 'insights'. Saba da Castiglione recalled him as a 'cosmographer' and 'poet in the vernacular' and Vasari writes that he 'delighted in poetry and loved to improvise upon the lyre, or to hear others doing this: and he composed some sonnets'. In fact he left over twenty sonnets which are unpolished but full of life; some are humorous, others deal with love and religion, and they reveal some of the hidden sides of his personality.

In the field of artistic activity, too, his lively curiosity about everything made him, as Vasari says, a man who experimented in many arts. In fact, the very first documents about him call him *painter, engineer,* and *perspectivist,* as well as architect. Works of sculpture (such as those in the sacristy of S. Satiro) were also attributed to him and, as we have seen, he was certainly a theatrical designer, a town planner, and an expert in fortifications, machines, and hydraulic problems. Sixteenth-century writers, such as Doni and Lomazzo,[65] also attribute to him theoretical writings (now lost) on perspective, on illusionism, on fortifications, on the 'German style', i.e. Gothic, and on the architectural orders, subjects which reflect the range of his interests.

Echoes of his ideas can perhaps be traced in his contemporaries, including Pacioli, Cesariano, and Leonardo himself; and the famous letter to Leo X, though it may have been written by Baldassare Castiglione from notes by Raphael, contains observations which might well go back to Bramante (for example, the very shrewd remarks on the 'German style' and on Late Roman architecture). Nevertheless, as Argan has rightly emphasized, his interest seems always to have been directed towards concrete applications, towards that *Practica* which (according to Doni) seems to have been the characteristic title of one of his own writings. And as an architect, although he was always intensely concerned with visual effects, he must have had remarkable technical knowledge. Often he showed himself to be an extremely daring builder; indeed, as the contemporaries who condemned his 'foolhardiness' noted, he was quite frequently an imprudent, dangerous experimenter. Whether he was studying Late Antique and Gothic architecture in Lombardy, or Classical architecture in Rome, he was concerned not only with stylistic solutions, but also, deeply, with constructional methods. In Milan he invented 'a method of making drawbridges' which interested Leonardo; in Rome 'a method of making arches with suspended scaffolding' and similarly (according to Vasari) a suspended cradle for Michelangelo to use when painting the ceiling of the Sistine Chapel.

In general, Vasari notes, he combined knowledge and very good draughtsmanship with 'zeal, study and resolution' and with 'very good judgment'. His capacity for patient research, for analytical probing into technique and style – linked, however, with a remarkable gift for grasping the essentials – united with 'capricious genius' to produce that 'novelty' ('*invenzion nuova*') which Serlio, Vasari and Palladio all stress when discussing Bramante's works. There is a particular side to his character, however, which Vasari emphasizes a number of times: his impatience, the 'extraordinary speed', indeed the fury, with which he produced his architecture. Above all he was 'resolute, prompt and most fertile in invention', and, especially in Rome, rapidity of conception was matched by

speed and impatience of execution. He was always ready to start again from the beginning – as in St Peter's; he was adaptable and resilient in the face of difficulties. All this shows another side of his personality, a side that enabled him to face his financial difficulties and his not always easy relationships with clients and colleagues with a disillusioned irony that is revealed in some of his sonnets; this in a world where he was always basically an outsider, an alien. In the difficult, insincere world of courts he had to learn to move easily: apparently without descending to the base arts of the courtier he managed to maintain his own dignity while at the same time manipulating powerful men to achieve his aims. He was capable of deep religious feeling (as one of his sonnets makes clear) and in Rome was a lay brother, 'monachus conversus monasterii Fossenove', yet (as we can tell from another sonnet) he was critical of priests, and sometimes to get important commissions he must have stretched his moral principles. In the case of St Peter's, for instance, although admittedly his ideas were clearly better than those of his rivals, he did not act over-scrupulously: according to Vasari, he 'threw everything into confusion' in order to persuade the Pope to accept his proposal for the total rebuilding of the church.

He was ready to collaborate with colleagues and helpers so long as they accepted his authority and his role as coordinator. In Rome, perhaps for the first time in the history of architecture, he ran a professional studio – what Giovannoni calls 'Bramante & Co.' – which was capable not only of dealing with the very many jobs given him by the Pope and private clients but also of standing up effectively to competition from other artists, especially the 'Florentine party'. It would appear that his relations with Michelangelo were particularly tense and, according to the latter and his biographers (Vasari and Condivi), motivated by envy and ill-will. Condivi (1553) makes insinuations about Bramante's behaviour, not only in his relations with Michelangelo but also with regard to his honesty in matters of work. However, a copy of Condivi's work, with notes written in the margin by a contemporary, has recently been discovered.[66] They seem to be the first-person comments of Michelangelo himself, confirming or contradicting what his biographer says about Bramante. And Michelangelo, who, as late as 1542, was writing: 'All the discord which arose between Pope Julius and me was through the envy of Bramante and Raphael of Urbino', about 1546–47 admitted honestly: 'It cannot be denied that Bramante was as worthy in architecture as any other man from the ancients until today. He laid the first stone of St Peter's, not full of confusion but clear and uncluttered and luminous, and free-standing . . . and it was held to be a beautiful thing, as is still obvious: in such a way that anyone who departed from the design which Bramante had laid down, as Sangallo did [Antonio the Younger], departed from the truth.'

The conflict between the two men must have been largely a conflict of personalities. Apart from rivalry in prestige and economic competition, the dichotomy between Bramante and Florentines like Giuliano da Sangallo and Michelangelo was one which involved two different ways of conceiving architecture. Bramante's was the way of the 'painterly' and 'perspective' architect, founded by Brunelleschi, followed to some extent by Francesco di Giorgio and Leonardo and reaffirmed by Bramante, a way which aimed at the three-dimensional representation of complex spatio-structural organisms. The Florentine way was that of the 'sculptural' architect: this began with Ghiberti – in this Brunelleschi's opposite – and even Alberti in part, and continued with Giuliano da Sangallo and his brother Antonio the Elder, Andrea and then Jacopo Sansovino, and finally Michelangelo himself. Architecture, to them, was given its character through the decorative and sculptural qualities of its two-dimensional surfaces ('ornaments'); to Bramante it meant the invention of spaces and organisms whose voids had an active quality and forced the walls into three-dimensional forms more complex than those which could be derived from elementary geometry. The Florentine view of architecture could be called the marble one; Bramante's could be called the brick and concrete one – materials which were exploited both for their tectonic qualities and for their capacity to mould pictorial space. In their attitude to the Antique, the Florentines were more interested in triumphal arches, in the individual parts of buildings and in decoration than in the great spatial complexes like the baths that fascinated Bramante, or in the character of the Roman wall itself, so powerful that it needed no extra ornament. Bramante used the architectural order above all as a means of definition and spatial parameter, to measure and generate spaces and volumes that were syntactically coordinated; the 'sculptural' architects, on the other hand, used the architectural order above all as ornament, as a plastic element that was significant in itself, an autonomous sculptural form arousing an aesthetic emotion, like a statue. The orders, indeed, assumed very different characters in the hands of different architects. With Antonio da Sangallo the Elder they are expressive; with Jacopo Sansovino refined and exquisite; with Michelangelo they take on something of his own tormented personality.

In spite of this basic conflict, Michelangelo in his old age paradoxically confessed to Vasari that in completing St Peter's he was merely 'the executor of the design and arrangements of Bramante'. And in other works too, especially after 1546, Michelangelo, who came to approach the problems of architecture more and more thoughtfully, accepted the ideas and axioms of Bramante. (The same is true of the two greatest architects in the second half of the sixteenth century, Palladio and Vignola.) Once his memory of the conflicts of Julius II's time had mellowed, Michelangelo's 'terribilità', to use Vasari's term, must have responded to the *terribilità* of the aged Bramante. And the *terribilità* of Bramante's imagination, as Vasari pointed out, can be seen not only in the vast conception of St Peter's but in its details. For all his *terribilità*, however, and for all his vast ambition to do things on a grand scale, Bramante showed an inner balance, a lucidity and clarity of thought and purpose which seldom seemed to waver. His openness to the most varied influences meant that he was continually renewing himself and surpassing previous efforts; and his ability to change his approach so readily and so often (as is evident from his buildings), to remain almost always miraculously anti-conventional, can be disconcerting to those who would like to make him the father of so many academic conventions. Yet for all his anxiety to explore different possibilities, in all the forty years of his professional life he remained essentially faithful to his own vision.

Self-reliant, proud and active, Bramante seems to have had a fundamentally extrovert temperament. But this may have been only the outer shell. A defensive mask which, as Förster has observed, appears in some of his sonnets, seems to cover a profound melancholy and a consuming desire for love, born, perhaps, from his own restless loneliness. He had broken his ties with his own family and seems never to have married or had children. Behind his extrovert manner, uncertainty and profound uneasiness must have been hiding; seeking 'universal' certainties, he was dissatisfied with everything he achieved, and was forced into a spiral of ever-new experimentation. Hence his apparently inexplicable *voltes-face*. Bramante's personality seems to show in particular a sense of *time*, an awareness of the mutability of the world and of man within time, not in a cyclical rhythm, not

even in a sequence pre-ordained by provi-
dence, but in an ever-shifting struggle between
human freedom, 'Fortune' and 'Nature'. The
concept of a human, existential, time corrodes
from within both desire for and faith in the
absolute. And although Bramante put forward
models and methods intended to be universal,
independent of every temporal contingency,
he himself was in a continual state of flux. In
one of his sonnets he wrote: 'As time changes
in a moment, So my thought that follows it
changes too.' Nothing could be a surer indica-
tion of his personality.

Bramante's complex personality, and his
changeable, contradictory psychology, taken in
conjunction with his career as an artist and the
way in which his experiences changed him and
his ideas developed, is the key not merely to an
understanding of his work but to a realization
of its historical significance in the development
of sixteenth-century architecture.

Outwardly extrovert and open to any experience, cultural or otherwise, ready to listen
to every voice that spoke of 'possibilities' or
alternatives, both on the artistic and the personal level, he was, deep down, a man on his own; a
detached observer, endlessly and restlessly
curious, but not tied to any particular tradition
or conditioned by one. He refused to commit
himself to the circle of Urbino or to his own
family, he refused to stay faithful to his early
training: as soon as he could do so, he moved on
somewhere else, to another world. In Milan,
and later in Rome, he was in spite of his success
basically rootless and stateless, an exile, a
stranger, a man in a permanently precarious
psychological condition. Self-taught, his education was necessarily unsystematic, casual and
fragmentary, even if critically selective. This
detachment, this inner psychological isolation,
was at once his strength and his weakness. It
allowed him to strike out on new paths, un-
trammelled by convention and prejudice, but
it also produced in him a psychological instability and a duality, a contradiction between
outward attitudes and inner reality. This is no
doubt what led to that fundamental ambiguity
in his work which we have noticed. Looked at
in one way, it is clearly a search for certainty;
looked at in another, it seems to be questioning
that certainty, or at best to be treating it as
merely provisional, a hypothesis in perpetual
need of reaffirmation and proof, and perhaps
also, at times, a limitation on his freedom.

On the one hand, a reflective, critical,
'scientific' and rationalist attitude led him, from
his very earliest works, to search for principles

and methods which could claim to have the
force of axioms, universal and communicable
truths independent of time and change. On the
other, with extraordinary 'impatience' he wanted to 'change', to 'follow his own genius' and
his 'capricious' instinct for complete freedom,
a freedom which he coveted as a man rather
more than as an artist. This conflict of attitudes –
something which is very modern and already at
least proto-Mannerist – only rarely attained a
calm balance. More often if produced what
Vasari calls 'artificial difficulties', or occasionally 'impatience' towards the work itself, so
that plans and projects would be left unfinished,
or even abandoned half-built. Hence the ambiguity which seems inseparable from any assess-
ment of his historical significance.

Psychological isolation and critical detachment allowed Bramante from the very beginning
to select and evaluate the most important contributions of the Quattrocento 'modern tradition':
those of Brunelleschi, Alberti, Piero della Francesca, of the Urbino circle, of Mantegna,
Francesco di Giorgio, Leonardo, and Giuliano da
Sangallo. Within this 'modern' tradition, as we
have seen, he went beyond points of style and
ways of expression to 'universal' principles and
methods which govern the design process
according to a logically linked series of decisions.
To him at this period of his career, as to the
Quattrocento theorists, architecture was a
'science': its results could be verified, and they
occupied a place *in primo gradu certitudinis*.
Natura, the manifestation and image of the
divinity, and *Historia,* the human and intellectual experience of the ancients, examined by
human *Ratio* – all were consistent with one
another, manifestations of the 'harmonic' and
rational nature of reality. They were the founda-
tions of human, as well as artistic, action. In
architecture their effects are seen mainly in the
following ways: in the perspective planning of
space; in 'musical' proportions; in the concept
of a building as an organism (like a living human
body, in which each part forms an indissoluble
unity with the others and with the whole); in
the use of 'logical' architectural elements,
derived from Antiquity; and in the way in
which a building is conceived as having a symbolic meaning as well as a practical function
(this applied especially if it was a church – a
'tempio' – since that was understood as a
'harmonic', proportionate microcosm, just as
man and the world were). In the light of these
principles, the interpretation of a building programme produced in the architect's work an
'idea', an 'invenzione', imposing specific terms
of reference which closely defined the choices

open to him and enabled every part to be integrated into the overall plan. From this point onwards, it was possible to deduce successive decisions by an analytical process that separated out and isolated all problems, finally solving them and reassembling the parts into an organic whole. So logic and poetry coincide (as most Renaissance philosophers, particularly Aristotelians, had maintained). And it was from just this logical, analytical and 'problem-solving' method that the new *invenzione* arose. By means of this method, which was 'universal' because 'logical', and which could be communicated as an abstract theory without involving any subjective, arbitrary 'choices', Bramante hoped to discover a consistent architectural calculus, which could be used in every conceivable situation. Such a method, which was at the same time a research programme leading to the acquisition of knowledge and an ideal to be pursued, had led Bramante as early as the Prevedari engraving to the organization of a fully three-dimensional architectural space, even though that was only an interior represented in perspective. And before 1487 or 1488, possibly influenced by Leonardo's way of thinking, he was expounding with clarity the idea of the building as an organic 'macchina', a machine or mechanism, like the 'machine' of the universe, and above all, following Leonardo, the anatomical 'machine' of the human body: a 'macchina di tutto lo edificio', as the author of the *Letter to Leo X* put it, which knits together space and its enclosing walls, interior and exterior, in an integrated, indivisible whole. As with Leonardo, the logical, analytical phase was to be followed by an expressive synthesizing phase in which the vital unity of the architectural *invenzione* would virtually resolve itself into painting – structure as *spettacolo*. But meanwhile, concentrating all his interest on the 'machine' of architecture, Bramante expressed its total *three-dimensional* quality as it had never been expressed before and reduced it to its essential terms, *external volume* and, above all, *interior space*, displaying them as the fundamental elements of visible expression.

The psychological reason for this search for 'universal', rational, communicable methods and principles was Bramante's craving for stability, his need to base himself on absolute certainties. The particular forms which it took – the three-dimensionality of his work, the resolution of architecture into space and volume – were the result of his actual working methods, of his instinct to try out alternatives, to experiment, to examine everything critically, and above all of his own formation as a perspective painter used to expressing spaces visually. The origins of all this must surely be sought in his background, in his early activity in the complex intellectual atmosphere of Urbino about which we know so little. One other characteristic, even more fundamental than the search for universality, which runs like a *leitmotif* in varying forms and degrees through all his work in Milan and Rome, can also surely be traced back to Urbino, though it was nourished and strengthened by his experiences in Northern Italy: perspective illusionism, the representation of space virtually as if it were scenery on a stage.

With Bramante, as we have seen, the reality of architecture becomes its 'representation'; physical, concrete space becomes 'artificial' space, to be looked at rather than lived in; spatial reality as a whole resolves itself into the 'fiction' of a stage spectacle. This was for Bramante not so much an occasional expedient as a basic instinct, a way of thinking rather than a way of practising architecture. In the event, it turned out to be linked very ambiguously to the idea of universality. One can see them either as complete opposites or as two sides of the same coin. This illusionism may, as we know, be a flight 'away from experience and true logic'. Perspective, which had once been a scientific instrument used to achieve order, measurement and the humanistic mastery of space, became, in the words of the *Letter to Leo X*, the art of exploring 'distances that seem to be and are not'; or, as Castiglione put it in *The Courtier*, the art of 'making seem . . . that which is not': a means of persuading and suggesting, rather like a figure of speech in rhetoric, degenerating into a mere cultural exercise, a precious, courtly, intellectual game.

Although based on scientific procedures, therefore, perspective was in itself, at the deepest level, something which tended to undermine the formulation of humanist architectural theory in terms of pure concepts. It could make concrete the full potentiality of what the architect could imagine, while at the same time demonstrating the relative and essentially conventional nature of the theoretical premises by which space was conceived, and casting doubt on its pretended scientific 'universality'. In perspective representation understood in this way, the absolute idea, the 'universal', 'objectively valid' principles and methods of architecture shrink from the realm of *noumena* to that of *phenomena*: they become subject to the contingencies of human vision and the personal 'will' of the architect who decides in advance what will be seen. The 'universal' results re-

26

183

main valid in their *appearance,* but from only a single point in space; in order to keep their appearance of universality, they have to be 'distorted': they lose their metaphysical absoluteness, and in order to persuade the observer more effectively, they 'deceive' him.

On the one hand, then, architecture is a *science* because it is based on 'universal' principles and methods: as Alberti remarks, painters' perspective is something quite separate from it. But on the other, painters' perspective makes it into art, by making everything figurative. The *Letter to Leo X* says significantly that perspective is 'still useful to the architect . . . because with it he can better imagine the whole building'. Bramante felt that he could not do without it: it was a tool which stimulated his imagination to produce the *invenzione*; it was an outstandingly efficient instrument for defining space; it was able to extend the real into the illusory as a moving 'artistic' creation. The power to conceive architecture visually, and in particular the technique of painters' perspective, including illusionistic perspective, gave Bramante the sense of dominating space quite freely, unfettered by any physical limitations, of being able fully to realize his own creative potential by ranging beyond the world of reality. If principles and methods are the certainties of *science,* the security of a stable order, painters' perspective gave Bramante the 'freedom' of *art;* it was the means by which he could 'follow his own genius'. Perhaps it was even a means of psychological compensation, a way of relieving the tension and constraint implied in the idea of 'order', and channelling his subjective longings for freedom and the irrational into artistic expression ('It's all false' is thus a kind of game).

Bramante's dual personality – the *mask* that of an extrovert, a man of the world, a confident, arrogant and conceited character; the *face* that of a lonely, insecure, melancholy and unstable man – was perhaps reflected on the one hand in his search for 'scientific' and 'universal' certainties, and on the other in his introverted tendency as a 'free' artist to treat architecture as a *spettacolo.* Both mask and face are equally integral parts of Bramante's personality, and neither can be called any more 'true' than the other. In the same way his search for universal certainties and his need for artistic freedom are complementary poles, both true and both necessary, present at one and the same time, and mutually conditioning each other. Freedom on its own brings suffering and insecurity. The free imagination requires a structure to control it and to channel it into a creativity that is complete and can be communicated. And rational order and thought, without some 'wild freedom' flowing through it, is merely a dead, restrictive set of rules, unable to bear creative fruit. But the contradiction implied in the humanist assumption that architecture is both a universal science and an individual subjective art crops up all the time, producing the instability and changeableness that characterizes Bramante's personality and his whole life. By continuous switches of *persona* he sought to strike the mean between two opposite poles, to reduce freedom to order (and vice versa), science to art (and vice versa), the universal to the particular (and vice versa), in a difficult creative synthesis which could only rarely be achieved. In more general terms, he sought to reduce the forces of becoming, of motion, of the temporal world of flux, phenomena and experience, to the Absolute, to universal 'perfect' order outside time. Thus, for instance, as his ideas developed, the painter's technique of illusionism opened up new areas where they could be applied. The means used to attain his ends became subtler, more delicate, harder to detect, more apparently natural; increasingly 'universal', although remaining fundamental to his method of organizing architecture visually. In S. Maria presso S. Satiro the deception was obvious; the Casa Panigarola frescoes were pure illusionism; but in the Belvedere or S. Maria del Popolo, for instance, the same approach produces a display of 'universal' spatial values, a *spettacolo,* that is the more convincing because the machinery, so to speak, is now concealed. Each new work can be seen as a fresh opportunity to solve this immense problem of synthesizing opposites, to reach a point of balance that was highly controlled but never secure. It was a task which Bramante approached from many different directions. He had an extraordinary ability to expose the full significance of every discovery by pushing its implications to the limit.

In his early work Bramante was exploring two apparently irreconcilable opposites simultaneously. The first is blatant illusionism (seen in the frescoes on the Palazzo del Podestà at Bergamo, S. Maria presso S. Satiro, the Casa Panigarola frescoes, probably up to and including the *Argus* in the Castello Sforzesco). The second is an organic, three-dimensional architecture which he tried to achieve by generalizing the 'scientific' method that he inherited primarily from Brunelleschi, and up-dating its stylistic vocabulary (seen in the Prevedari engraving and Pavia Cathedral). S. Maria delle Grazie represents his first attempt at a synthesis. But immediately afterwards, around 1492,

17
37–
39
106
173

22
23
17
37–
39
54

26
50
57

while the Italian political situation was darkening, he showed signs of restlessness and impatience, possibly of a crisis. In the last decade of the century he vanished from Milan several times and may have gone to Florence and Rome. Perhaps he was seeking, in the two main sources of the architecture of humanism – Brunelleschi and the Antique – for a renewed security based on scientific, rational, universal principles and methods. In the works that followed, his means of expression became more strictly architectural; the concept of architecture as a perspective picture diminishes almost to the point of disappearing. His last works in Lombardy, the Canonica and cloisters of S. Ambrogio, show not only a more emphatic and definite preoccupation with space in itself, both architectural and urban, but a renewed rigour in theory and method, all of which connects them closely with his first work in Rome, the cloister of S. Maria della Pace.

61–
64,
72

80–
91

The style here has become restrained and purified, the method settled and exact. As soon as Bramante reached Rome he seems to have felt the need for an extensive and profound re-examination of his own attitude to the Antique and what he wanted from it. The result, as it appears for instance in the cloister of S. Maria della Pace, was not so much a spatial *invenzione* designed with a view to 'artistic' effect as the product of rigorous reasoning, almost the demonstration of a theorem. While the situation deteriorated, politically and in other ways, and the future grew dark, while faith in principles was wavering and Bramante's own fate seemed more and more uncertain, he sought for a new security, and in these works affirmed his belief that architecture could be constructed 'rationally'.

80–
91

With the accession of Julius II to the papacy Bramante's affirmation of 'universal' principles received an unexpected boost. His programme of an ordered, strictly scientific architecture corresponding to the divinely ordered harmony of the world, which had been the basis of architectural theory from Alberti to Leonardo, now coincided with the 'universal' political and cultural programme of the new Pope-Emperor. A re-examination of architecture on these lines had begun in Milan in the final years of the century, and had been carried on with renewed energy under Alexander VI. The pursuit of 'universality' was fundamental to Bramante, and it entailed his placing supreme importance on those aspects of architecture which could be held to embody absolute values, 'eternally' valid. The essential reality of architecture (in the philosophical, Platonic sense) resided in its ability to structure space and volume into an organism. It was this which constituted the three-dimensional 'machine of the whole building'. This led, in turn, to the formulation of *types*, and the suppression of the contingent, individual element. The multiplicity of separate projects tended to be replaced by a few ideal schemes calculated in relation to certain typical functions of human life. Buildings should exist not for specific times or places, but as absolutes, almost outside history altogether: the church, the palace, the villa, confined and open space, etc. The identity of *usefulness, structure* and *form* is affirmed in the way the parts are organized as visual equivalents of the 'fundamental laws' of the cosmic order. The idea of a *type* was extended even to the morphology of the elements of architecture, the so-called 'ornaments'. As the *Letter to Leo X* says, these consist of and are 'all derived from the five orders which the ancients used'. Features which can in some way be equated with each other and reduced to a single *type* (e.g. a straight architrave and the curved archivolt of an arch, or a door and a window) can be given the same form, made up from a limited number of *typical* mouldings.

In any case, the components of the building – the 'ornaments' – are merely parts, 'cogs', of the articulated machine which, with its volumes and spaces, constitutes the architect's essential contribution and alone shows his creativity. They cannot in themselves constitute architecture. Alberti's view, widespread in the late fifteenth century, was challenged by Brunelleschi's practice of 'standardizing' parts so that they become neutral or anonymous. If the overall design did not require any unusual features, the detailing might even be left to the builders. Bramante could, however, when occasion demanded, design mouldings, capitals and columns of an intensely expressive quality and with a definite character of their own.

Yet just as a mechanic can choose from a catalogue the screw or wheel that he needs for a particular purpose, so the architect can choose what he wants from the ideal catalogue of history. We know from the documents, for instance, that the columns of Bramante's Canonica of S. Ambrogio in Milan were copied from those in the church of S. Maria Greca and the capitals of St Peter's were copied from those of the Pantheon. In Rome he often actually reused the shafts of Antique columns. The case is not unlike that of a modern architect who utilizes components made available by industry. In *Vers une architecture*, Le Corbusier, urging architects to look at works of engineering, especially ships and aeroplanes, writes:

62–
64

'Les ingénieurs d'aujourd'hui se trouvent être en accord avec les principes que Bramante et Raphaël avaient appliqués il y a longtemps déjà', and he compares the *logge* of S. Damaso, stylistically one of the most impersonal of Bramante's works, with the products of modern engineering. If all architectural values are reduced to the absolute *idea* or universal concept (to use Platonic or Albertian terminology), the actual quality of execution becomes of very minor importance. It is notorious that nearly all Bramante's works, especially those in Rome, are very badly built.

Bramante's idea – or at least one of the aspects of his work which struck his contemporaries most forcibly – seems, then, to have been to formulate *exempla* of universal value. They originated in particular occasions but, as far as possible, acquired significance for values which were independent of time, and for an authority equal to, or greater than, that of ancient buildings. Seen in this way, all Bramante's works in Rome make up a sort of treatise or manual of exemplary models worthy to be placed beside the work of the Romans, as indeed they were in later architectural treatises. An essential part of his programme in Rome, and one which closely paralleled that of Julius II, was to make a scientific study of the Romans' stylistic language and to investigate the possibility of its revival, since he believed that they had used a 'universal' language which was in a sense objective and universally important.

Indeed, from the very beginning, the experience of history, of the *whole* of history, was fundamental to Bramante's work. But the relationship between his work and history was not constant and unchanging. In Lombardy, he had acquired a composite, conventional idea of Classical Antiquity through Alberti, Piero della Francesca, Mantegna and the culture of Urbino and Padua in general, sometimes coloured by literary influence. It gave him a stylistic tool for expressing the organization of space and the rules that govern it. But his understanding of Classical Antiquity was indirect, via the interpretation of others. Some of the 'ancient' buildings which we know interested him in Milan, such as S. Lorenzo or S. Satiro, were actually Early Christian or even medieval, though what preoccupied him here was not so much the details as the overall organic integration of space and structure. In any case his interest in the Classical style (of which he could have seen real examples in Verona, Brescia, Milan and, at least from 1492 onwards, in Rome) was not yet of a systematic and scientific kind, but wholly pragmatic and practical. The orders provided

him with a language, including a few regional or dialect usages, in which clear architectural statements could be made. What could be composed in that language was a tremendous, eloquent drama expressing all the meaning and value which he saw in 'santa antichità'.

Just because Bramante's notion of Classical Antiquity was so ideal and conventionalized, his approach to ancient architecture at this period was fairly free from problems. The style of Rome could comfortably accommodate features from the Middle Ages. His view of what was historically relevant was growing broader. Medieval tradition, both Romanesque and Gothic, could suggest particular ways of doing things, individual formal elements, methods and means of interpreting the arrangement of space, translating it into physical terms and treating it expressively. But it was not open to Bramante, as it was to some of his contemporaries, to work within a still-living local tradition. For him, as for Brunelleschi and Alberti, the continuity with medieval tradition had been broken. His relationship with the past, whatever it might have been, was not instinctive and 'natural'; it was intellectual, conscious and cultural. Every occasion when an aspect of ancient history was turned to account constituted a separate reference, suggesting a solution that could be directly translated into Renaissance terms. Such a use of the past was bound to lead to eclecticism. Far from limiting or conditioning the imagination, it only animated it and helped to bring it into focus. Even Vitruvius's rules and descriptions were read not as academic decrees but as stimuli towards the reconstruction of a world that Bramante idolized but scarcely understood.

This attitude to the past remains substantially the same in Bramante's work until at least his early years in Rome. His references to Antiquity in the ground floor of the cloister of S. Maria della Pace are still generic, ideal, second-hand, although a more specific attempt to assimilate the style of the ancients can be seen to some extent in his later works in Lombardy (in the upper storey of the cloister of S. Ambrogio and the façade of Abbiategrasso), and also in the Roman Palazzo della Cancelleria, if that can be connected with him. But after 1492 Antiquity played a more profound role in his work. It made him re-examine the whole question of how to set about designing buildings, in an attempt to get rid of every regional idiosyncrasy. His stylistic ideal, as it appears in the cloister of S. Maria della Pace, in the courtyard of the palace of Cardinal Corneto and in some of the works that followed, seems to have been a sort of pure, stripped-down, absolute essence of 'Antiquity', purged of any specific historical associations.

Soon, however, his references to ancient Roman architecture become a good deal more definite and precise, especially in those works datable to the time of Julius II. Vasari's mention of the fact that during his early days in Rome he studied ancient monuments (which 'he measured . . . and made great use of') is very important. It must have been an extremely profound study, first-hand, methodical, searching, and more penetrating than any before. Faced with real Roman buildings, Bramante saw how academic, how *literary,* the knowledge was that he had acquired from the architecture of humanism. Like the humanist philologists, from Lorenzo Valla to Politian, he seems to have felt the need to revive the original language of the ancients and to submit himself to it with patience, devotion and humility, in order to recover its meaning, the original thought uncorrupted by later interpretations or incrustations.

To revive the 'universal' language of the ancients was more than just a part of Julius's purpose in his *instauratio imperii.* To Bramante, it was above all a way of giving a visible, convincing form to an architecture which he wished to see accepted as a model, expressed in a vocabulary which was no longer that of a particular region or convention, but, like Julius's papal monarchy, truly 'national' and 'universal'. For him (as for the literary scholars in their own sphere) there was only one way of demythologizing Antiquity, of transforming it from a lost dream world or an ideal of abstract perfection into an instrument that could be mastered and used. And that was to study it, to know it thoroughly and to experiment with it.

There is a paradox here, though it is only an apparent one. The archaeological study of ancient monuments by Bramante and sixteenth-century architects and theorists had the effect of distancing the monuments and diminishing their power as authorities. Before they could recreate the past, designers had to see it with detachment. And Bramante had no feeling of inferiority towards the ancients. Pedantic Vitruvian rules could be refuted simply by pointing to his own works – to the precision of the circular colonnade round the Tempietto; to the drum of the Tempietto; to certain parts of St Peter's, the Belvedere, or the Palazzo dei Tribunali. He could evolve solutions which were totally new. From the many examples of Roman architecture he could choose those he found most germane to his purpose, using them merely as starting-points for the creation of 'modern' spaces. No building or stylistic feature from his Roman period, even those which seem closest to Antiquity, can in fact be equated with any specific ancient monument. Besides, as long as Antiquity and its 'rules' were still awaiting codification, there was the joy of research and discovery, of advancing in an exciting new world, rich in every kind of expression, a world far more vital and moving in its physical reality than in the exalted imagination of literary enthusiasts. It was not a fetter, not a convention, not an authoritative precept, but a stimulus to the imagination. As Vasari rightly puts it: 'the Greeks were the inventors of architecture, and the Romans their imitators', but Bramante imitated them 'with new invention'.

Bramante's programme involved testing Renaissance theories by putting them into practice. 'Universality' was a hypothesis to be proved by experiment. As Chastel says of St Peter's, it was a matter of 'solving a problem, not of applying a formula'. And logical necessity often turned out to be the mother of artistic invention. Specific architectural problems could point to completely untried solutions, on a stylistic as well as a structural level. But, as we have seen, the same rigorous logic might also reveal the fact that a problem was really insoluble because two 'universal' principles clashed and cancelled each other out. When that happened, resort had to be made to *artifice,* or the project would simply have to be abandoned. In such a case intuition and personal sensibility were still indispensable, though to use them meant giving up the logical method and contradicting the whole idea of 'universal' principles.

Still, to say it once again, this process is by no means foreign to the other side of Bramante's character, the secret, uncontrollable urge to variety, complexity, singularity, 'difference' – anti-order, anti-Classicism, anti-balance. The 'Dionysiac' was at war with the 'Apollonian' in his soul, fighting against his own instincts and his own tastes. It is the kind of conflict which was to characterize Mannerism, although here it was apparently devoid of drama and of compromise.

The results as they stand are thus a vindication of 'universal' principles and of a stylistic language 'like' the Antique. But at the same time they are a clear demonstration that such rules cannot be consistently applied everywhere. Sooner or later artifice has to enter in, and the language ceases to be Classical. Exactly when that point comes will vary in each case. Quite often the final building is the product of successive minor modifications, shifts of intention. One can see it as a sort of dialectic between theory and practice, premise and conclusion, or perhaps as the interaction of four distinct forces – logical method, alert critical sense, sensibility and creative 'frenzy'. Hence the feeling of uncertainty and ambiguity that is never far from Bramante. Can we penetrate deeper? Should we not see it as an expression of the ambivalence, the inevitable ambiguity of the human condition itself, a confession of the impossibility of achieving and holding on to anything certain and unequivocal? Surely it was the longing for certainty, for universal values, which generated in him, from one work to the next, such a continuous 'mental transformation', which drove him on with such urgency ('prestezza'), which aroused in him such a frenzy ('furia') to plan and to execute, to catch, and not to lose, the absolute, definitive form.

The underlying contradictions between theory and practice came to a head with the accession of Julius II, just when Bramante's reputation was reaching its peak. His hopes of 'certainty' were higher than at any time during the previous decade. His ambitions ran parallel with the Pope's, and his recent experience of the Antique was opening up an extraordinary range of new possibilities. Greater psychological security, perhaps still alternating with bouts of depression, allowed him to express his instinctive ideas more freely. He could test principles and methods in all kinds of remarkable projects, and at the same time put the stamp of his own artistic imagination more profoundly upon his work.

That imagination was above all that of a painter-architect, a perspectivist able to construct emotionally moving displays of space. And it is through this fact that Bramante can claim to be both the heir of the Brunelleschian tradition, whose values he was at pains to confirm, and the man who started it upon a new path. For by his expressive and theatrical manipulation of space – 'space in itself' – he was really suggesting that the metaphysical assumptions of the Quattrocento should be replaced by others that were primarily visual and psychological. He was not denying, indeed he seems anxious to reaffirm, the fundamental basis for a metaphysic of architecture: he was merely making the point that in *practice* architecture could not embody absolute values, for it was tied to physical man and a visual world. Metaphysical, 'musical' proportions, the organization of a building as a symbol of universal harmony, Antiquity as an ideal, timeless model – all these remained, but only as hypotheses to be tested, as remote goals.

Instead of presenting these ideas in absolute terms, therefore, he conveys them visually and psychologically. Musical proportions are made relative to the spectator, 'distorted' in order to seem more true. Indeed, absolute proportion can only work in two dimensions, and to a Quattrocento artist space was simply that which is contained by flat planes; this Bramante challenged in the name of recession into depth (three-dimensionality). In a similar way, *ideal* Antiquity becomes *real* Antiquity, rich in values which depend on its being *per*ceived rather than *con*ceived, bodied forth in actual monuments, emotive through the particular light that plays upon them, through the materials of which they are made, through their very condition as ruins, shorn of 'ornament', hollowed out, buried in the earth, but still alive through a thousand qualities of shape and colour. And the organization of a building as a harmonious microcosm of the divine macrocosm comes to stand not for a metaphysical 'reality' which is purely abstract, but for some earthly and historical order (e.g. the *imperium* of Julius, or the Catholic Church, or the life of the ruling class in town or country) and its power of persuasion resides in the way it *looks* to the spectator.

In thus bringing the absolute down 'from heaven to earth', Bramante could certainly be accused of denying it the sort of objective reality that the humanists claimed for it. Was not the whole thing no longer a geometrical theorem but a sort of scene-painting, a visual fiction? But the whole point resided in this feeling of conviction aroused in the spectator. The verisimilitude of his later buildings was that of a perspective painting. Their fidelity lay beyond physical reality, in the world of representation. It was this element which removed them from a particular historical context and gave them their quality of timelessness. Nor did they necessarily have to be *equivalent* to those of the ancient world. The important thing was that, even if they were very different, they should *appear* equivalent; that visually and psychologically they should persuade the spectator that they embodied universal principles and that the architecture of the ancients – the 'true, beautiful and good' architecture which 'until this time had been buried' – had at last been reborn. Even today, Bramante is sometimes mistaken for a Classicist.

Up to the time when he came to Rome, Bramante had worked within the mainstream of Italian architectural development, at least since the rise of humanism, and had taken its principles as far as they would go. In his Roman period he revealed the limitations and contradictions of those principles and of the method which sustained them. And his achievement – that ambiguous, illusory balance between order and freedom – opened the door to the crisis of Mannerism. The balance he arrived at turned out to be visually convincing but in reality precarious; the synthesis he put forward was authoritative, yet at its deepest level artificial and equivocal. His attempt to freeze the rebellious forces of movement – of *becoming* – in the absolute stillness of perspective representation, stopping time, focusing the whole space of a building into a single point of vantage from which man could indulge in the humanist illusion of being at the centre of the universe – all this makes Bramante, as Pevsner has pointed out, a precursor of the Baroque.[67]

But it was an illusion which could not last for ever. The whole of Baroque in the end seemed nothing but a stage-set, its persuasive power increasingly harnessed to some political or religious ideology. It took the Enlightenment and the Industrial Revolution, the inescapable reality of the new, giant, anonymous cities and factories, the 'anti-architecture' of the engineers, to finish with illusion once and for all. The miserable but undeniably 'true' reality of hovels and slums and ghettoes and working-class towns, plus the active entry into history of new, broader social classes, brought architecture back to *real* life; anti-artistic, perhaps, but truthful and serviceable to real men in a real world.

Bramante's work is an essential part of this process, a stage through which history had to pass before it could move forward. It was he who, after Brunelleschi, set Renaissance architecture on a new path, a path that was no longer regional, or even national, but European, and which it followed until at least the nineteenth century.

Bramante had done one thing definitively: he had shown that Brunelleschi's and Alberti's 'universally valid' architecture, free from intuition, artifice and personal choice, was no more than wishful thinking – almost itself an 'illusion'. That led to the uncertainties and ambiguities of Mannerism. Belief in the Classical models continued; attempts were even made to codify their features as 'laws'. But it was now only a fond hope of finding certainty, or as Vignola put it, of 'finding a rule with which I can acquiesce'.

Bramante's immediate collaborators and followers were soon treading the primrose path that he had pointed out to them, openly contradicting the rules. Half-way through the century, Vasari, in a vain effort to provide a theory for a situation where principles seemed to be disintegrating, proposed setting up 'a liberty which, not being regulated, may itself be made orderly within the rule'. But Serlio – closer to Bramante's direct followers – enthusiastically welcomed 'the strangeness [*bizzarria*] of things that are mixed and free [*miste e licenziose*]', which was going to satisfy the 'strange men seeking for what is new'.

Notes

1. G. Vasari, *Le vite . . .*, *Vita di D. Bramante*, published in 1568. See, of the many editions of the *Vite*, that by Milanesi, Florence 1878–85, IV, pp. 146 ff. The translation used here throughout is that of Gaston Du C. De Vere for the Medici Society, London 1912–14, IV.

2. E. Garin, *La cultura filosofica del Rinascimento italiano*, Florence 1961, p. 316. For an understanding of this fundamental historical change see also the following works by Garin: *L'Umanesimo italiano*, Bari 1952, *Medioevo e Rinascimento*, Bari 1954, and *Scienza e vita civile nel Rinascimento*, Bari 1967 (English transl. *Science and Civic Life in the Italian Renaissance*, New York 1969), all with bibliographies. Also, among the countless publications on both general and specific questions, the *Cambridge Modern History,* I, Cambridge 1957, and D. Hay, *The Italian Renaissance and its Historical Background,* Cambridge 1961.

3. For the culture and art of this period and the symptoms of crisis, see, in addition to the bibliographies in the works already referred to in n. 2, the following publications by A. Chastel: *Art et Humanisme à Florence au temps de Laurent le Magnifique*, Paris 1959, *Renaissance méridionale*, Paris 1965 (English transl. *The Golden Age of the Renaissance: Italy 1460–1500*, London 1965), and *Le grand atelier d'Italie*, Paris 1965 (English transl. *The Studios and Styles of the Renaissance: Italy 1460–1500,* London 1966), all with full bibliographies. Also E. Battisti, *L'antirinascimento*, Milan 1962, and H. Baron, *The Crisis of the Early Italian Renaissance*, Princeton 1966. On architecture in particular, the following recent general works may be singled out: L. Benevolo, *Storia dell'architettura del Rinascimento*, Bari 1968; P. Murray, *The Architecture of the Italian Renaissance*, London 1969, and *Renaissance Architecture*, New York 1971; M. Tafuri, *L'architettura dell' Umanesimo*, Bari 1969 and particularly L. H. Heydenreich and W. Lotz, *Architecture in Italy. 1400–1600*, Harmondsworth 1974—all with bibliographies.

4. On Bramante's birthplace, family and surname, see F. Sangiorgi, *Bramante 'hasdrubaldino'. Documenti per una biografia bramantesca,* Urbino–Fermignano 1970, which contains a discussion of the books cited so far.

5. Fra Bartolomeo di Giovanni della Corradina or Corradini of Urbino, known as Fra Carnevale, is a mysterious figure in the Urbino of the second half of the fifteenth century. An architect as well as a painter, he appears in early records as one of the architects at the court of Federigo da Montefeltro, along with Luciano di Laurana, Pippo Fiorentino, Scirro da Casteldurante and Francesco di Giorgio, but nothing can be attributed to him with certainty. His name also occurs in a number of other documents: in 1449 he was in contact with the Florentine masters working on the portal of S. Domenico, and he seems to have died in 1484. According to one document, in 1467 he painted the *Nativity of the Virgin* for the high altar of the church of the Confraternity of S. Maria della Bella at Urbino (mentioned by Vasari in his life of Bramante). The attribution to Fra Carnevale of the two famous Barberini Panels, while not impossible, is controversial and was challenged most recently by F. Zeri in *Due dipinti, la filologia e un nome. Il maestro delle Tavole Barberini*, Turin 1961 (with a bibliography). He also has been credited with the architectural background in Piero della Francesca's Brera Altarpiece, a project on which some believe he was assisted by Bramante.

6. The fundamental work on the palace is P. Rotondi, *Il palazzo ducale di Urbino*, Urbino 1950 (abridged English transl. *The Ducal Palace of Urbino*, London 1969). For new information and an up-dated bibliography, see Rotondi's *Francesco di Giorgio nel palazzo ducale di Urbino*, Novilara 1970.

7. F. Santi, *La nicchia di S. Bernardino*, Milan 1963 (with a bibliography); A. Bruschi, *Bramante architetto*, Bari 1969, pp. 53–75.

8. T. Yuen, 'The "Bibliotheca Graeca": Castagno, Alberti, and Ancient Sources', *The Burlington Magazine*, November 1970, pp. 725–36.

9. G. C. Argan, 'Il problema di Bramante', *Rassegna marchigiana*, XII, July–September 1934, pp. 212–31, reprinted in *Studi e note, da Bramante a Canova*, Rome 1970, pp. 9–23. Certain themes in this essay, which is still essential for a critical interpretation of Bramante's architecture, have since been developed in a number of excellent studies, such as those of Fiocco, Baroni, and Bonelli, cited in the following notes.

10. G. Fiocco, 'Il primo Bramante', *La critica d'arte*, I, 1936, pp. 109–14.

11. See especially Peter Murray's essay in *Studi bramanteschi. Atti del Congresso internazionale—Milano—Urbino—Roma 1970*, Rome 1974, pp. 27–34.

12. Franz Graf Wolff Metternich, 'Der Kupferstich Bernardos de Prevedari aus Mailand von 1481', *Römisches Jahrbuch für Kunstgeschichte*, 1967–68, pp. 9–97. On the engraving see also P. Murray, '"Bramante milanese"', *Arte lombarda*, VII, 1962, pp. 25–42; and my *Bramante architetto*, op. cit.

13. See C. Baroni, *Bramante*, Bergamo 1944, pp. 16–17.

14. G. Chierici, *Bramante*, Milan 1954, pp. 5–6.

15. See in particular P. Murray, *Renaissance Architecture*, op. cit., pp. 122–40, and, by the same author, 'Leonardo and Bramante', *Architectural Review*, CXXXIV, no. 801, November 1963, pp. 346–51.

16. See especially Brizio's contribution in *Studi bramanteschi*, op. cit., pp. 1–26. For the relationship between Leonardo and Bramante see also L. H. Heydenreich, 'Leonardo and Bramante: Genius in Architecture', *Leonardo's Legacy. International Symposium*, University of California, Berkeley and Los Angeles 1969.

17. The letter has often been published, e.g. in A. M. Brizio, *Leonardo da Vinci. Scritti scelti*, Turin 1952, p. 633. On Leonardo's project for the *tiburio* of Milan Cathedral, see especially L. H. Heydenreich, *Die Sakralbau-Studien Leonardo da Vincis*, Hamburg 1929, reprinted Munich 1971, pp. 25 ff.

18. *Bramantis opinio super domicilium seu templum magnum*; printed in *Annali della Fabbrica del Duomo di Milano*, Milan 1880, vol. III, pp. 62 ff.

19. A drawing formerly in the De Pagave Collection (now in the Biblioteca Civica, Novara), previously attributed to Bramante but certainly a late copy of an earlier drawing, bears an inscription that ascribes it to Bramante and to 1490: 'Dominicum Templum Ticini Fundatum—ab Ascanio Sfortia S. R. Eccl. Card.—Bramante Urbinate inven. MCCCCXC'. While the lower part of the building shown corresponds largely to the design as built, the upper part, especially the dome, is markedly different from it, and the drawing might therefore be a copy of a sketch by Bramante. See G. Struffolino Krüger, 'Disegni inediti di architettura relativi alla collezione di Vincenzo de Pagave', *Arte lombarda*, XVI, 1971, p. 292.

20. On Bramante as a poet see L. Beltrami, *Bramante poeta, colla raccolta dei sonetti in parte inediti*, Milan 1884; also E. Müntz in *Gazette des Beaux-Arts*, II, 1879, pp. 514 ff.; A. Berti, *Artisti-poeti italiani dei secoli XV e XVI*, Florence 1907, pp. 20–25; G. Natali, 'Il Bramante letterato e poeta', *Rivista ligure di scienze, lettere ed arti*, 1915, pp. 335–41, and by the same author *Vita di Donato Bramante*, Florence 1914; F. Malaguzzi-Valeri, *La corte di Ludovico il Moro*, II, Milan 1915, pp. 231–33; O. Förster, *Bramante*, Vienna and Munich 1956, pp. 139 ff. On Bramante as a writer see also Wolff Metternich, op. cit. For his contacts with other poets see R. Renier, in *Giornale storico della letteratura italiana*, 1885, p. 237, and by the same author 'Gaspare Visconti', *Archivio storio lombardo*, XIII, 1886, pp. 87–89; E. Percopo, 'Antonio Cammelli e i suoi "Sonetti faceti"' in *Studi di letteratura italiana*, IV, pp. 808–9, and by the same author *I sonetti faceti di Antonio Cammelli*, Naples 1908, sonnets 273–307. For Bramante's interest in Dante see A. Luzio, 'Le letture dantesche di Giulio II e di Bramante', *Corriere della Sera*, Milan, 11 September 1908.

21. Malaguzzi-Valeri, op. cit., II, p. 132.

22. Reproduced by Pedretti in *Studi bramanteschi*, op. cit. (above, n. 11), p. 199.

23. Förster, *Bramante*, op. cit.; also his entry on Bramante in the *Encyclopedia of World Art* (transl. of the *Enciclopedia Universale dell'arte*, 1958), New York, Toronto and London 1960, II, cols. 595–610.

24. Malaguzzi-Valeri, op. cit., gives almost all the documentary evidence for Bramante's absences.

25. Bramante's report is published in H. von Geymüller, *Les Projets primitifs pour Saint-Pierre*, Paris 1875–80, pl. 54, and in Malaguzzi-Valeri, op. cit., II, p. 126.

26. For a reconstruction of the piazza's appearance and a perceptive critical analysis of the original project, see W. Lotz in *Studi bramanteschi*, op. cit. (above, n. 11), pp. 205–21.

27. In *Studi bramanteschi*, op. cit. (above, n. 11).

28. This interesting suggestion was put forward by G. De Angelis d'Ossat in 'Preludio romano del Bramante', *Palladio*, n.s., XVI, 1966, I–IV, p. 92, and taken up by Doris Fienga in *Studi bramanteschi, op. cit.* (above, n. 11), pp. 417–26.

29. For a more extensive analytical and critical treatment see my *Bramante architetto, op. cit.*, pp. 245–90 and 822–36. New information, based on P. Marconi's restoration work in 1969 for the Soprintendenza ai monumenti di Roma e Lazio, was published by him in *Studi bramanteschi, op. cit.* (above, n. 11), pp. 427–36.

30. A. Schiavo was the first to point out this curious feature, though without going into it in detail, in 'Il chiostro di S. Maria della Pace', *Palatino*, VI, 1960, pp.103–5.

31. A. Venturi, *Storia dell'arte italiana. L'architettura del Cinquecento*, XI, pt. I, Milan 1938, p. 68; R. Bonelli, *Da Bramante a Michelangelo*, Venice 1960, p. 19; G. De Angelis d'Ossat, 'Preludio romano', *op. cit.*, p. 85.

32. P. Letarouilly, *Edifices de Rome moderne ou recueil des palais, maisons, églises*, Liège 1849–66, Paris 1868–74, pls. 64–66. This odd feature was first noticed by De Angelis d'Ossat ('Preludio romano', *op. cit.*); but during the recent restoration of the cloister no trace of it was found.

33. J. S. Ackerman, *The Cortile del Belvedere* (*Studi e documenti per la storia del Palazzo Apostolico Vaticano*, III), Rome 1954, p. 42. Ackerman's is an excellent critical and analytical study of the Belvedere as a whole. For its position in the complex of the Vatican palaces, see D. Redig De Campos, *I palazzi vaticani*, Bologna 1967. More recent information appears in my *Bramante architetto, op. cit.*, pp. 291–433 and 865–82. See also H. Brummer, *The Statue Court in the Vatican Belvedere*, Stockholm 1970.

34. For Julius II's activity see F. Rodocanachi, *Histoire de Rome. Le pontificat de Jules II. 1503–13*, Paris 1928, pp. 30 ff. On the city itself, see P. Romano, *Roma nelle sue strade e nelle sue piazze*, Rome 1947–49; G. Giovannoni, *Topografia e urbanistica di Roma* (*Storia di Roma*, XXII), Bologna 1958; R. Valentini and G. Zucchetti, *Codice topografico della città di Roma*, IV, Rome 1953; A. P. Frutaz, *Le piante di Roma*, I and II, Rome 1962; S. Muratori, R. Bollati, S. Bollati and G. Marinucci, *Studi per una operante storia urbana di Roma*, Rome 1964; L. Quaroni, 'Una città eterna. Quattro lezioni da 27 secoli', *Roma città e piani*, ed. 'Urbanistica', Turin, n.d.; L. Salerno, L. Spezzaferro and M. Tafuri, *Via Giulia, un'utopia urbana del Cinquecento*, Rome 1972.

35. *Scienza e vita civile, op. cit.* (n. 2), p. 44, also pp. 15 ff. and 33 ff.

36. 'Vita Nicolai V summi pontificis ex manuscripto codice Florentino', in L. A. Muratori, *Rerum Italicarum Scriptores*, Milan 1734, III, 2, pp. 923 ff.; for a modern critical edition of the Latin text, see T. Magnusson, *Studies in Roman Quattrocento Architecture*, Stockholm 1958.

37. The stone stands at the corner of the present Via del Banco di S. Spirito and Via dei Banchi Nuovi, near the Mint, founded by Julius II. The complete inscription reads: 'IULIO II. PONT. OPT: MAX: QUOD FINIB: / DITIONIS. S.R.E. PROLATIS UTALIAQ: / LIBERATA URBEM ROMAN OCCUPATE / SIMILIOREM QUAM DIVISE PATEFACTIS / DIMENSISQ: VIIS PRO MAIESTATE / IMPERII ORNAVIT / DOMINICUS MAXIMUS / HIERONIMUS PICUS / AEDILES. F. C. MDXII'. P. Portoghesi, in *Rome of the Renaissance*, London 1972, pp. 21–22, points out that the phrase 'occupate similorem quam divise' is taken from Book V of Livy, which is concerned with the rebuilding of Rome after its destruction by the men of Veii.

38. See above, n. 33. For the literary and archaeological allusions see also Ackerman, 'The Belvedere as a Classical Villa', *Journal of the Warburg and Courtauld Institutes*, 16, 1951, pp. 78–89.

39. Professor Frommel generously told me this, before the publication of his own study.

40. For a more detailed discussion of the illusionistic, proportional and other problems of the Belvedere, see my *Bramante architetto, op. cit.*

41. See J. S. Ackerman, 'Bramante and the Torre Borgia', *Rendiconti della Pontificia Accademia Romana di Archeologia*, XXV–XXVI, 1949–51, pp. 247–65, and De Angelis d'Ossat, *op. cit.*, p. 92.

42. 'Bramantes "Ninfeo" in Genazzano', *Römisches Jahrbuch für Kunstgeschichte*, 12, 1968; also my *Bramante architetto, op. cit.*, and C. Thoenes in *Studi bramanteschi, op. cit.* (above, n. 11), pp. 575–83.

43. See P. Giovio, *Le vite di Leon decimo et Adriano VI . . . et del Cardinal Pompeo Colonna*, Florence 1551, especially pp. 377–78 (the source of my quotation) and, by the same author, *Pompei Columnae cardinalis Vita*, in *Opera Omnia*, Basel 1578, pp. 130 ff.

44. Andrea Guarna da Salerno, *Scimmia*, Latin text edited and translated into Italian by Eugenio and Giuseppina Battisti, Rome 1970, especially pp. 117–21.

45. See Bruschi, 'Un intervento di Bramante nella Rocca di Viterbo', and E. Bentivoglio and S. Valtieri, 'I lavori nella Rocca di Viterbo prima e durante il pontificato di Giulio II', both in *L'arte*, IV, 1971, 15–16, pp. 75–109.

46. K. Weil-Garris Posner, in *Studi bramanteschi*, op. cit. (above, n. 11), pp. 313–38. On Loreto see also my *Bramante architetto*, op. cit., pp. 652–67 and 960–79.

47. For Bramante at Civitavecchia see my *Bramante architetto*, op. cit., pp. 938–45, with a bibliography, and, on the town-planning aspects, my contribution in *Studi bramanteschi*, op. cit. (above, n. 11), pp. 535–65.

48. L. H. Heydenreich, 'Studi archeologici di Leonardo da Vinci a Civitavecchia', *Raccolta Vinciana*, (Milan), XIV, 1930–34, pp. 53 ff.; also, by the same author, *Leonardo architetto, II Lettura vinciana, 15 aprile 1962*, Florence 1963.

49. The drawing is reproduced by Frommel in *Studi bramanteschi*, op. cit. (above, n. 11), tav. CXCIII. On the Via Giulia and Julius II's town plan, see the works cited in n. 34 above, especially that by Salerno, Spezzaferro and Tafuri, and my *Bramante architetto*, op. cit., pp. 609 ff.

50. F. B. Bonini, *Il Tevere incatenato*, Rome 1663, bk. IV; also A. Bacci, *Del Tevere*, Venice 1576, and my *Bramante architetto*, op. cit., pp. 632–33 and n. 40.

51. See my *Bramante architetto*, op. cit., pp. 436–527 and 986–1039, with a bibliography up to 1969, and the following more recent works: H. Günther, in *Studi bramanteschi*, op. cit. (above, n. 11), pp. 483–501, and P. Murray, *Bramante's Tempietto*, University of Newcastle upon Tyne 1972.

52. A highly significant sixteenth-century criticism of Bramante's decision, from which as we shall see a number of 'errors' or difficult architectural problems were to arise, appears in the second edition of the *Architettura di Pietro Cataneo senese*, Venice 1567, bk. III, chap. XI, p. 72. This passage, which as far as I know has hitherto been overlooked by Bramante scholars, is illustrated by a plan of the Tempietto and accompanied by measurements which confirm the close examination of the building which the author claims to have made—though, curiously, the illustration does not correspond to reality. This important addition to the 1554 edition is the result of what may be called an 'academic' point of view, but it contrasts well with the very well-known praises by Serlio and Palladio, in that it emphasizes an acute problem of planning.

53. The version of the history of St Peter's which was set down authoritatively (though not without errors) by late nineteenth-century historians, particularly H. von Geymüller in his *Les Projets primitifs pour Saint-Pierre*, op. cit. (above, n. 25), reached its climax, after about a century of research, in O. Förster's *Bramante* (op. cit.: above, n. 20). Now, with good reason, the whole subject has been thrown open to debate once more (see the bibliography and summary of the state of the problem in my *Bramante architetto*, op. cit., pp. 532–93 and 883–908), especially in the various contributions by Franz Graf Wolff Metternich, who is engaged upon a definitive book.

54. E. Battisti, *Rinascimento e Barocco*, Turin 1960, pp. 72 ff.

55. See especially Rudolf Wittkower's still essential book, *Architectural Principles in the Age of Humanism*, London 1949.

56. P. Murray, 'Observations on Bramante's St. Peter's', *Essays in the History of Architecture presented to R. Wittkower*, London 1967, pp. 53–59.

57. J. S. Ackerman, *The Architecture of Michelangelo*, London 1961, also D. Frey, *Bramantes St. Peter-Entwurf und Seine Apokryphen*, Vienna 1915, pp. 75–76, and D. Gioseffi, *La cupola vaticana*, Trieste 1960, especially n. 55.

58. C. Thoenes, in *Atti del Congresso*, op. cit. (above, n. 11).

59. *Architectural Principles*, op. cit.

60. See M. Dezzi Bardeschi, 'L'opera di Giuliano da Sangallo e di Donato Bramante nella fabbrica della villa papale della Magliana', *L'arte*, IV, 1971, 15–16, pp. 111 ff., including a bibliography and documents.

60a. New light has been shed on the history of this church by E. Bentivoglio and S. Valtieri, in *Santa Maria del Popolo a Roma*, Rome 1976.

61. op. cit. (above, n. 31), p. 30.

62. See Frommel in *Studi bramanteschi*, op. cit. (above, n. 11).

63. G. C. Argan, 'Sebastiano Serlio', *L'arte*, 1932, 3, pp. 190–91.

64. J. Shearman in *Studi bramanteschi*, op. cit. (above, n. 11), pp. 567–73.

65 See J. Schlosser Magnino, *La letteratura artistica*, Vienna 1924, expanded Italian version Florence 1967, pp. 114 ff. and 148 ff.

66. See U. Procacci, 'Postille contemporanee in un esemplare della vita di Michelangelo del Condivi', in *Atti del Convegno di studi michelangioleschi. Firenze-Roma, 1964*, Rome 1966, pp. 279–94.

67. N. Pevsner, *An Outline of European Architecture*, 7th ed., Harmondsworth 1963, p. 206.

Chronological list of works

Major works are marked with an asterisk. The chronological order is in some cases only tentative, when no definite information is available.

between 1472 and *c.* **1474** May have worked on the architectural background of the Brera Altarpiece by Piero della Francesca, formerly in S. Bernardino at Urbino (now in the Brera, Milan), as assistant to Piero or Fra Carnevale. (Very doubtful attribution.)

c. **1472? (before 1476)** Design, executed by others, for the arrangement of architecture and perspective in the Studiolo of Federigo da Montefeltro in the Ducal Palace at Urbino. (Doubtful attribution.)

1473 Architectural backgrounds for four panels of the *Nicchia di S. Bernardino*, formerly in S. Bernardino at Perugia (now in the Galleria Nazionale dell'Umbria, Perugia). (Doubtful attribution.)

c. **1474–76?** Design, executed by others, for the arrangement of architectural elements and perspective paintings in the library of the Ducal Palace at Urbino (destroyed), decorated with representations of the *Liberal Arts* (of which two are in the National Gallery, London, and two, formerly in the Kaiser-Friedrich Museum in Berlin, were destroyed in 1945). Possibly also designed the setting of the so-called *Lecture at the Court of Urbino* (now in the Collection of Her Majesty Queen Elizabeth II). (Doubtful attributions.)

c. **1474** Design for the main doorway of the Palazzo Schifanoia, Ferrara, executed by Ambrogio Barocci and others. (Doubtful attribution.)

date uncertain, between *c.* **1472 and** *c.* **1490** Project for S. Bernardino at Urbino. The detailed planning and building of the church are certainly due to Francesco di Giorgio. (Doubtful attribution, much disputed.)

before 1480, perhaps *c.* **1476** Project for the pair of chapels in the Ducal Palace at Urbino, the Cappella del Perdono or dello Spirito Santo, executed by A. Barocci, and the Chapel of the Muses or of Apollo. (Attribution probable, but not certain.)

***1477** Frescoes of philosophers in architectural frames, on the façade of the Palazzo del Podestà at Bergamo (fragments now in the Museo Civico). (Almost certainly the work of Bramante, but probably with assistance.)

probably after 1480–85 Frescoes on the façade of what is now the Casa Angelini, in Via Arena, Bergamo (now detached and preserved inside the house). Drawings by Bramante may have been used, in an altered form and without his supervision. (Very doubtful attribution.)

date unknown Frescoes including a *Pietà* in the church of S. Pancrazio, Bergamo. (Lost; referred to as Bramante's work by Marcantonio Michiel, 1525.)

***late 1481** Drawing of a *Ruined Temple*, engraved by Bernardo Prevedari (two known impressions, in the British Museum, London, and Perego Collection, Milan). (Certain attribution, documented.)

***c.* **1480 et seq.** S. Maria presso S. Satiro, Milan. (Certain. Perhaps begun by others before the appearance of Bramante, whose work is documented from 1482 to 1486. A 'Cappella di S. Teodoro', not executed, is referred to in 1497–98.)

date uncertain Design for church façade (Louvre, Paris), formerly mis-identified as S. Maria presso S. Satiro. (Disputed work, of uncertain authorship. Probably a copy of *c.* 1480 (?) after Bramante, who may have been responsible for the original design.)

date uncertain, 1480–84 or later? Designs for the architectural backgrounds in frescoes in S. Pietro di Gessate, Milan, possibly by Donato Montorfano. (Uncertain attribution.)

***date uncertain, between** *c.* **1480 and** *c.* **1490?** Frescoes of men-at-arms in the Casa Panigarola, Via Lanzone, Milan (now in the Brera, Milan). (Certain work, though not documented.)

date uncertain Frescoes of architecture and figures on the façade of the Casa Fontana (later Silvestri), Corso Venezia 10, Milan. (Doubtful work, much damaged, but with Bramantesque characteristics.)

September 1484 Drawing of the Ospedale Maggiore, Milan, probably only an elevation. (Lost, but documented.)

***1488 et seq.** Pavia Cathedral. Probably a work of collaboration, in which the design stage was dominated by Bramante, who is mentioned several times in documents in 1488. Partially altered during construction and never completely realized.

date uncertain, perhaps between *c.* **1480 and** *c.* **1490** Palazzo Carminali Bottigella, Pavia. (Doubtful.)

***1487–90** Model for the *tiburio* of Milan Cathedral (lost; probably made by M. Leguterio, 1487), and *opinio* or report on the *tiburio* (*c.* 1490).

date uncertain, perhaps between *c.* **1480 and** *c.* **1490** *Christ at the Column*, painting on panel formerly in the abbey of Chiaravalle (now in the Brera, Milan). (Attribution disputed but plausible.)

date unknown Fresco of the poet *Ausonius* and other figures on a façade in Piazza dei Mercanti, Milan. (Lost; ascribed to Bramante by Lomazzo in his *Treatise*, Bk IV, ch. XIV.)

date unknown Fresco of the *Four Evangelists* in S. Maria della Scala, Milan. (Lost; ascribed to Bramante by Lomazzo, op. cit., Bk V, ch. XIV.)

date unknown Fresco of the *Nativity*, in the courtyard of the Mint at Milan. (Lost; mentioned by Vasari—ed. Milanesi, VI, p. 511—and by others.)

***before 1493, probably not earlier than 1490–92** Fresco of *Argus* (?) in the treasury of the Rocchetta in the Castello Sforzesco, Milan. (Attribution disputed but plausible.)

May 1492 Theatrical designs in Milan. (Documented.)

1492? et seq. S. Maria di Canepanova, Pavia. (G. D. Amadeo, who may have been the original designer, is known to have been working here shortly after 1500. Doubtful work, to be compared with similar churches such as S. Magno at Legnano, S. Maria di Piazza at Busto Arsizio, etc., which seem to have been built after Bramante's departure from Milan but which may—like the Chapel of the SS. Sacramento in the parish church at Caravaggio—be based on ideas by Bramante.)

1492–93 Project for architectural frescoes in the transept and main chapels of the Certosa at Pavia. (Doubtful work, perhaps based on an idea by Bramante.)

***1492 et seq.** Eastern arm of S. Maria delle Grazie, Milan: architecture (partly altered during construction) and interior decoration. (Work not documented, but almost certainly based on a project by Bramante, made perhaps in collaboration with other architects.) This project was part of an unexecuted larger scheme for the total rebuilding of the church, the convent and the surrounding streets, in which Leonardo was probably also concerned. Other parts of the complex can be attributed to Bramante only very doubtfully, though they are Bramantesque in character or derive from his principles: the doorway of the church (1489–90), the sacristy and the adjoining cloister (*c.* 1492–97).

date uncertain; before 1498, perhaps 1490–95 or earlier? Pozzobonella Chapel, Milan. (Disputed, but very plausible.)

***1492 et seq.** Works in Vigevano: design for the piazza (subsequently altered) and painted decoration on its buildings; works at the castle, and interior frescoes there (lost); Palazzo delle Dame. Bramante's presence at Vigevano is documented in 1492 and in 1494–96, but it is impossible now to determine the extent of his contributions, which, according to the documents, also involved a 'Cappella della Concezione' for the Franciscans (1494, either never completed or destroyed) and an altar 'for relics' (1496?).

***1492 et seq.** Canonica of S. Ambrogio, Milan. (Certain work, extensively documented; unfinished.)

29 June 1493 Report on the fortifications of Crevola. (Extant, in Bramante's own hand.)

c. **1490–*c.* 1495** Work on the Palazzo della Cancelleria, Rome. (Begun already between 1485 and 1489, perhaps reworked in 1490–95, finished in the first decade of the sixteenth century. One or more contributions by Bramante, perhaps in 1492–93 and again in 1500 (according to Vasari), are uncertain and greatly disputed, though not unlikely.)

c. **1490–*c.* 1495** Reliquary of the Holy Lance (destroyed) in old St Peter's, Rome. (Early attribution, but very uncertain.)

date uncertain, between 1490 and 1500 Doorway of Casa Mozzaniga, Milan (now in the courtyard of Palazzo Trivulzio). (Attribution not confirmed.)

c. **1490–95** *Ponticella* of Ludovico il Moro, Castello Sforzesco, Milan. (Completed 1495–96; probably by Bramante, mentioned as his work by Cesariano in 1521.)

c. **1493–96** Porta Ludovica, Castello Sforzesco, Milan. (Plausible attribution.)

c. **1495** Designs for the architectural settings in paintings by Donato Montorfano in S. Maria delle Grazie, Milan—the Cappella Bolla and *Crucifixion* in the refectory. (Uncertain.)

***1497–98 et seq.** Convent and cloisters of S. Ambrogio (now Catholic University), Milan. (Certain work, extensively documented, but not completed by Bramante.)

***1497 (or a little earlier) et seq.** Façade of S. Maria Nascente at Abbiategrasso. (Not documented but almost certain.)

c. **1500?** Engraving of a street scene (various impressions and reprints in the Uffizi, Florence, British Museum, London, etc.). (Plausible attribution.)

late 1499 or early 1500 Fresco above the Porta Santa of S. Giovanni in Laterano, Rome. (Lost;

almost certainly by Bramante; mentioned by Vasari.)

*c.*1500 Fountain in Piazza S. Pietro, Rome (altered under Julius II, then dismantled and partly re-used), and fountain at S. Maria in Trastevere, Rome (subsequently much altered). (Not documented, but probably by Bramante; mentioned by Vasari.)

*1500 Cloister and convent of S. Maria della Pace, Rome. (Certain and documented work, probably finished in 1504.)

*c.*1500 *Antiquarie prospettiche romane*, a pamphlet with verses about Roman Antiquities, dedicated to Leonardo da Vinci. (Attribution uncertain.)

*c.*1500 Participation in plans for extending the church of S. Giacomo degli Spagnuoli in Piazza Navona, Rome. (Not documented, but not impossible.)

*c.*1500 Participation in plans for S. Maria dell'Anima, Rome. (Mentioned by Vasari; not documented but not impossible. Bramante's involvement in the project for the campanile is less likely.)

*c.*1500 et seq. Palace of Cardinal Adriano Castellesi di Corneto (now Palazzo Giraud-Torlonia) in the Borgo (now Via della Conciliazione), Rome. (Disputed, but very probably begun to a design by Bramante, between *c.*1499 and 1503; later partly altered, especially the façade.)

*1502? Tempietto of S. Pietro in Montorio, Rome. (Certain. Bramante's projected courtyard which was to have surrounded the Tempietto was never built, and the Tempietto itself was later partly reworked, particularly in the dome. The date 1502, given in an inscription but none the less disputed, should perhaps be regarded as the date when work on the crypt began, the upper part of the building being dated after 1505–06.)

*1504–05 et seq. Belvedere courtyard and statuary garden in the Vatican, Rome. (Certain work, extensively documented, not finished by Bramante; later greatly altered.)

*1505–06 St Peter's, Rome. (Certain work, extensively documented; not finished by Bramante, whose design was subsequently greatly altered.)

1505–07 Project for a complete rebuilding of the Vatican, Rome. (Mentioned by Vasari; few documents; must have involved several studies and projects; never carried out.)

1506 Works in Castel S. Angelo, Rome. (Difficult to ascertain, though Bramante is mentioned in documents. Previously, *c.*1500, he may have been involved in the works commissioned by Alexander VI.)

*1505–07 until 1509 (or begun between 1499 and 1503?) Eastern arm of S. Maria del Popolo, Rome. (Certain, documented work.)

1506–08 Project for the Rocca at Viterbo. (Documented, but not completed by Bramante.)

*c.*1506–08 Project for great stair in Palazzo d'Accursio (or degli Anziani), Bologna. (Plausible attribution.)

before 1509 West wing (*logge*) of the courtyard of S. Damaso, Vatican. (Almost certainly by Bramante, perhaps designed in 1507–08; completed by Raphael.) Bramante must also have been involved on minor works in the Vatican for Julius II.

*1507–08 et seq. Urban schemes for Rome: Via Giulia, Via della Lungara, widening of Via dei Banchi, etc. (Certain.)

late 1508 Project for a church for the Florentine community in Via Giulia, Rome. (Mentioned in archives, but not executed and subsequently lost.)

between 1507 and 1509 Project for S. Maria di Loreto, Rome. (Uncertain attribution. Work was carried on by Antonio da Sangallo the Younger and then by others.)

1508 et seq. S. Maria della Consolazione, Todi. (Disputed work, not documented. If the original design was indeed by Bramante, it was substantially altered during construction.)

1508 et seq. Coastal fortress at Civitavecchia. (Not documented, but almost certain.) Bramante may also have been involved in the design of the harbour, and possibly in the planning of the town, and was certainly concerned with the design of the dock in 1513.

*1508 et seq. Palazzo dei Tribunali and church of S. Biagio in Via Giulia, Rome. (Certain work, documented, but almost entirely destroyed.)

*1508 et seq. Works at Loreto. (Designs by Bramante are documented in the case of the 'Ornamento', or chapel built to protect the Holy House, and the Palazzo Apostolico. Neither was completed by him.)

1509 et seq. SS. Celso e Giuliano in Banchi (now Via del Banco di S. Spirito), Rome. (Uncertain; never completed, and since destroyed.)

*c.*1509–10? Project for S. Eligio degli Orefici, Rome. (Uncertain attribution. First Raphael and then Peruzzi were involved, and the building was subsequently greatly altered.)

*c.*1508–10 until summer 1513 Works at the papal villa of La Magliana, near Rome. (Documented.)

1509 et seq. Project for the church of Roccaverano in Piedmont. (Almost certainly by Bramante, although somewhat altered in execution.)

late 1509–early 1510 Architectural setting for Raphael's *School of Athens*. (Mentioned as Bramante's work by Vasari. Disputed attribution, but not unlikely.)

*date uncertain: 1510–12 or earlier? House of Raphael, formerly Palazzo Caprini, Rome. (Certain, or almost certain; destroyed. The identification with Palazzo Caprini was formerly controversial but is now almost certain.)

date uncertain: between 1501 and 1503 or, more probably, between 1508 and 1511 'Nymphaeum' of Genazzano. (Attribution not documented, but very likely.)

*c.*1512 or earlier Construction of the Borgo 'corridor', between the Vatican and Castel S. Angelo, Rome. (Mentioned by Vasari, who says that Antonio da Sangallo the Younger took part in the work.)

1513 *Tegurio* or temporary chapel protecting the papal altar in St Peter's, Rome, during reconstruction. (Certain. According to Vasari, completed by Peruzzi. Destroyed, but some fragments remain in the Vatican Grottoes.)

1513 (late in the year?) Project for Tiber embankment and canal, presented to Leo X. (Uncertain.)

Many other works have been attributed to Bramante without definite evidence. The following attributions are among the least improbable, though it is likely that the works are not by Bramante but by artists close to him or familiar with his work.

—Architectural decoration in fresco in the Sala Regia of the Palazzo Venezia, Rome (perhaps *c.*1490).

—Church of S. Sebastiano in Valle Piatta, Siena (*c.*1507? or earlier? or later?), and oratory of S. Giovanni in Oleo at Porta Latina, Rome (1509). Both are probably by Peruzzi.

—S. Maria delle Fortezze, Viterbo (begun 1514).

—S. Maria dell'Orto, Rome (first project, later completely altered; begun 1517?). Perhaps by a Roman follower of Bramante.

—Dome of the cathedral of Capranica Prenestina, above Palestrina (1520?). Perhaps by a Lombard follower of Bramante active in Rome.

Bibliography

THE importance of Bramante in the history of art and, in particular, of Renaissance architecture, has meant that his work has been described and discussed in encyclopaedias and dictionaries of art, in all general histories of art and of course in publications about the Renaissance. Of the latter, some of the most recent and important are listed above in note 3 (p. 190). However, there are also a number of other works which should be mentioned because they contain important information or critical comments about Bramante: N. Pevsner, *An Outline of European Architecture*, which has been translated into many languages (see particularly the Penguin Jubilee edition, Harmondsworth 1960); A. Venturi, *Storia dell'arte italiana*, especially VIII, pt. 2 and XI, pt. 1, Milan 1923 and 1938; A. Chastel, *Italian Art*, London 1963; J. Durm, *Die Baukunst der Renaissance in Italien*, Leipzig 1914; D. Frey, *Architettura della Rinascenza*, Rome 1924; W. J. Anderson and A. Stratton, *The Architecture of the Renaissance in Italy*, London 1927; W. Paatz, *Die Kunst der Renaissance in Italien*, Stuttgart 1953; B. Lowry, *Renaissance Architecture*, London and New York 1962; P. Portoghesi, *Roma del Rinascimento*, Milan 1971 (English transl. *Rome of the Renaissance*, London 1972); L. H. Heydenreich and W. Lotz, *Architecture in Italy. 1400–1600*, Harmondsworth 1974. Also, though it contains only brief references to Bramante, R. Wittkower, *Architectural Principles in the Age of Humanism*, London 1949, essential reading for an understanding of some of the characteristic aspects of Renaissance architecture.

MONOGRAPHS AND BIBLIOGRAPHIES
The most recent monographs on Bramante are: C. Baroni, *Bramante*, Bergamo 1944, G. Chierici, *Bramante*, Milan 1954, and *Donato Bramante*, New York 1960, and, more exhaustive, O. Förster, *Bramante*, Vienna and Munich 1956, and A. Bruschi, *Bramante architetto*, Bari 1969. There are also several useful entries in dictionaries or encyclopaedias, such as J. Baum's contribution in the Thieme-Becker *Künstlerlexikon*, IV, pp. 515–19, G. Giovannoni's in *Enciclopedia italiana*, VII, Milan and Rome 1930, pp. 680–84, A. Prandi's in *Enciclopedia cattolica*, O. Förster's in *Encyclopaedia of World Art*, II, 1958, cols. 595–610, and mine in *Dizionario di architettura e urbanistica*, *Dizionario biografico degli Italiani*, *Encyclopaedia Britannica*, etc.

These works, and especially the monographs by Baroni, Förster, and myself (in particular the latter, pp. 1063–82), all provide bibliographies of varying length, although none of them can be regarded as complete. Other bibliographical information, especially concerning Bramante's activity before his Roman period, will be found in F. Graf Wolff Metternich, 'Der Kupferstich Bernardos de Prevedari', in *Römisches Jahrbuch für Kunstgeschichte*, XI, 1967–68, pp. 9–97, and, on the most important works only, in *Bramante tra Umanesimo e Manierismo. Mostra storica-critica, Settembre 1970*, Rome 1970, pp. 219–24, and in *Dizionario biografico degli Italiani*, under 'Bramante'.

EARLY SOURCES, DOCUMENTS AND DRAWINGS
The most complete early biography of Bramante is Vasari's (*Le vite . . .*, *Vita di Bramante*, 1568, published in many editions and many languages (see above, note 1)). However, although Vasari is generally reliable on the Roman period, he gives practically no information on Bramante's earlier work, and what he does give tends to be inaccurate. It is therefore useful to consult works by other early writers, particularly regarding Bramante's activity in Urbino (still to a great extent shrouded in mystery) and his activity in Lombardy.

For the Lombard period in particular, see: C. Cesariano, *Di L. Vitruvio Pollione, De Architectura*, Como 1521 (photographic reprint of the original edition with an introduction, in English, and an index by C. H. Krinsky), useful for first-hand comments and observations on Bramante's Lombard activity by one of his pupils; Fra Saba (Sabba) da Castiglione, *Ricordi, ovvero ammaestramenti*, Venice 1549 and 1565, CXI, p. 139, for general information and for Bramante's early years in Urbino and Mantegna's influence on his style; G. P. Lomazzo, *Trattato dell'arte della Pittura Scultura e Architettura*, Milan 1584, and, by the same author, *Idea del Tempio della Pittura*, Milan 1590, informative on Bramante's activity as painter and treatise-writer.

On Bramante's Roman period, the following are key works: G. Burchard, *Diarium, 1483–1506*, ed. L. Thuasne, 3 vol., Paris 1883–85; P. De Grassis, *Diarium*, ed. M. Armellini, Rome 1884; Egidio da Viterbo, *Historia viginti saeculorum* (MS C.8.19, Biblioteca Angelica, Rome); F. Albertini, *Opusculum de mirabilibus novae et veteris Urbis Romae*, Rome 1510, ed. Schmarsow, Heilbronn 1886, also ed. R. Valentini and G. Zucchetti in *Codice topografico della Città di Roma*, IV, Rome 1953, a basic source of information on the Roman works before 1509; A. Fulvio, *Antiquaria Urbis*, Rome 1513, and *Antiquitates Urbis*, Rome 1527; Fra Mariano da Firenze, *Itinerarium Urbis Romae*, c.1517–18, ed. P. Bulletti, in *Studi di antichità cristiana del Pontif. Ist. di Archeol. Cristiana*, Rome 1931, which complements and updates the work by Albertini, above.

All these works, written by contemporaries of Bramante with first-hand accounts of his work, are indispensable to fill in gaps in Vasari's account of Bramante's Roman period, despite the fragmentary nature of their information. There are two further early sources for Bramante's Roman activity: S. Serlio, *Regole generali d'architettura*, Venice 1540, and, less useful, A. Palladio, *I quattro libri dell'architettura*, Venice 1570 (facsimile ed. Milan 1945). Other information can be found in G. B. Caporali, *Architettura con il suo comento et figure, Vetruvio in volgar lingua reportato*, Perugia 1536 (the author knew Bramante personally); in A. F. Doni, *Libraria seconda*, Venice 1555, which provides some (unverified) information about Bramante as theorist; in Michelangelo's letters, ed. P. Barocchi and R. Ristori, Florence 1965; in Condivi, *Vita di Michelagnolo Buonarroti*, Florence 1553; in Cellini, *Due Trattati*, Florence 1586, etc. A vivid portrait of Bramante's personality is provided by A. Guarna da Salerno, who must have known him personally, in his *Simia* of 1517 (ed. and transl. into Italian by G. Bossi, in *Del Cenacolo di Leonardo da Vinci*, Milan 1810, also ed. and transl. E. and G. Battisti, Rome 1970).

Additional information, especially on individual works, is provided by many documents which have been gradually discovered and published since about 1800. The most important are mentioned or quoted in Förster's monograph and in mine, usually with a note on the location of the documents and biblio-graphical references. For some of the documents on Bramante's works in Lombardy see C. Baroni, *Documenti per la storia dell'Architettura a Milano nel Rinascimento e nel Barocco*, I, Florence 1940, and II, Rome 1968. Some of the most important documents are referred to below in the bibliographies on individual works.

Various works are documented graphically by a number of early drawings in European and American collections, although none of these is definitely by Bramante himself. A few of the most important drawings are listed at the end of this bibliography. There are three especially rich collections of drawings associated with Bramante—in some cases copies or adaptations of designs by Bramante or his pupils, or else early drawings of works that had been built. These are a *corpus* in the Uffizi in Florence, the 'Coner Codex' in Sir John Soane's Museum in London (published by T. Ashby, 'Sixteenth-Century Drawings of Roman Buildings', in *Papers of the British School at Rome*, II, London 1904), and the sketchbook in the collection of Mr and Mrs Paul Mellon, attributed, perhaps incorrectly, to Bramante's assistant Menicantonio de'Chiarellis. The number of Menicantonio's drawings known and studied is small, but they are of basic importance: see N. Nachod, 'A Recently Discovered Architectural Sketchbook', in *Rare Book*, VIII, no. 1, New York 1955. Rudolf Wittkower was engaged in a systematic study of this sketchbook at the time of his premature death; a provisional report on his findings was made to the *Congresso internazionale di Studi bramanteschi*, Rome 1970, and will be included in the final volume of his *Collected Essays*.

Modern illustrations will be found in publications listed under individual works, below, and also in the monographs by Förster and myself; mine is the most fully illustrated. Still useful for elevations of some of the Roman buildings, though not always completely accurate, are P. Letarouilly, *Edifices de Rome moderne*, Liège 1849–66 and Paris 1868–74, and P. Letarouilly and Simil, *Le Vatican et la Basilique de Saint-Pierre*, Paris 1882.

GENERAL STUDIES

The earliest monograph was that of L. Pungileoni, *Memorie intorno alla vita e alle opere di Bramante*, Rome 1836. It covers Bramante's overall activity using relatively modern criteria, and is to some extent still valid. Even earlier, however, was an essay by V. De Pagave written at the end of the eighteenth century (printed in G. Casati, *I capi d'arte di Bramante da Urbino nel Milanese*, Milan 1870), which, despite inaccuracies, is important for Bramante's Lombard activity. Some acute critical descriptions of a number of the Roman works were provided by F. Milizia (*Le vite de' più celebri architetti*, Rome 1768, and *Roma nelle belle arti del disegno*, Bassano 1787 and Bologna 1826) and, later, by J. Burckhardt (*Der Cicerone*, Basel 1855). There followed a series of studies, especially of a philological nature, aimed at reconstructing Bramante's life and activity including the pre-Roman period, incorporating Vasari's information, written by various scholars throughout the nineteenth century. Then H. von Geymüller, the leading Bramante scholar of the late nineteenth century, produced his outstanding *Les Projets primitifs pour Saint-Pierre* (Paris 1875–80; German ed. Vienna 1875–80). Here and in the minor studies he published later, Geymüller wrote from his exceptional knowledge not only of the works themselves but also of the relevant documents and drawings.

Geymüller's patient work of historical reconstruction of Bramante's activity was carried further during the last years of the nineteenth century and the early years of the present century by various other scholars, many of whom directed their researches at specific problems surrounding individual works or groups of works. Among these scholars were L. Beltrami (who wrote especially about Bramante's Lombard activity, in a number of contributions including *Bramante a Milano*, Milan 1912), D. Gnoli ('Bramante a Roma', in *Annuario R. Accademia di S. Luca*, 1913–14, pp. 51 ff., and numerous other essays on specific topics, including one on the House of Raphael published in 1887 (see below) and another, *La Cancelleria ed altri palazzi di Roma attribuiti a Bramante* of 1892, in which he rejected, on chronological and stylistic grounds, Bramante's authorship of the famous Roman *palazzo*), and G. Giovannoni, who published various essays on individual works (and an overall study, still of major importance, in *Saggi sull'architettura del Rinascimento*, Milan 1931). Giovannoni was perhaps the most important Italian Bramante scholar in the first half of this century. Meanwhile, while several scholars such as Müntz were discovering new documents, a number of interesting attempts were made at reconstructing Bramante's personality, using painstaking philological research. The authors of these studies were critics and historians like F. Malaguzzi-Valeri (see especially his still important *La Corte di Ludovico il Moro*, in particular vol. II, *Bramante e Leonardo*, Milan 1915), A. Venturi (*Storia dell'arte italiana*, op. cit.), L. Dami (*Bramante*, Florence 1921), and, above all, D. Frey (in particular *Bramante-Studien*, Vienna 1915). Among more recent critical accounts are those by G. C. Argan ('Il problema del Bramante', in *Rassegna marchigiana*, XII, 1934, pp. 213–31, still of major importance), G. Fiocco ('Il primo Bramante', in *La critica d'arte*, I, 1936, pp. 109 ff.), P. Rotondi (whose studies concentrate mainly on reconstructing Bramante's early activity in Urbino as painter and architect: see especially *Il palazzo ducale di Urbino*, Urbino 1950; English version *The Ducal Palace of Urbino*, London 1969) and, although of a rather different nature, books by R. Bonelli (especially *Da Bramante a Michelangelo*, Venice 1960).

Among the many critical studies written in the last fifteen years or so, in addition to the monographs already referred to, the following must be mentioned: J. S. Ackerman (especially *The Cortile del Belvedere* (*Studi e documenti per la storia del Palazzo Apostolico Vaticano*, III), Rome 1954, and the very concise but illuminating description of Bramante's Roman work in *The Architecture of Michelangelo*, London 1961); P. Murray (especially 'Bramante milanese', in *Arte lombarda*, VII, 1962, and 'Observations on Bramante's St. Peter's', in *Essays in the History of Architecture presented to R. Wittkower*, London 1967, which also contains other important essays on Bramante by Metternich and Heydenreich); F. Graf Wolff Metternich (see especially his important studies on Bramante's St Peter's and a meticulous essay on Bramante's Lombard activity, 'Der Kupferstich Bernardos de Prevedari', op. cit.); C. L. Frommel ('Bramante's "Ninfeo" in Genazzano', in *Römisches Jahrbuch*, op. cit., no. 12, 1968, and other studies); L. H. Heydenreich ('Bramante's "Ultima Maniera"', in *Essays . . . presented to R. Wittkower*, op. cit.); G. De Angelis d'Ossat (in particular 'Preludio romano del Bramante', in *Palladio*, XVI, 1966, pp. 92–24); C. Tiberi, *Poetica bramantesca tra Quattrocento e Cinquecento*, Rome 1974.

Almost all these scholars, together with many others, presented papers to the *Congresso internazionale di Studi bramanteschi* which was held in autumn 1970, in Milan, Urbino, Loreto, Rome and the other places where Bramante was active. The proceedings of this congress, about fifty papers, were published in 1974 (*Studi bramanteschi*, op. cit.).

INDIVIDUAL WORKS

Prevedari engraving—Document in Milan, Archivio notarile (notaio Benino Cairati, 24 Oct. 1481) published in L. Beltrami, 'Bramante e Leonardo praticarono l'arte del bulino?; Un incisore sconosciuto: Bernardo Prevedari', in *Rassegna d'arte*, XVII, 1917, p. 155. Among the many critical analyses see P. Murray, 'Bramante milanese', op. cit.; F. Graf Wolff Metternich, 'Der Kupferstich Bernardos de Prevedari', op. cit.; and my *Bramante architetto*, op. cit.

Milan, S. Maria presso S. Satiro—Documents in Milan in the Archivio Curia Arcivescovile (Visite Past., S. Satiro), Archivio di Stato (Fondo di religione, Chiese e Benefici, S. Maria presso S. Satiro) and Archivio parrocchiale di S. Satiro, published in many places and, in most completely, by A. Palestra, 'Cronologia e documentazione riguardante la costruzione della chiesa di S. Maria presso S. Satiro', in *Arte lombarda*, XIV, 1969, pp. 154–60, and in *Studi bramanteschi*, op. cit., pp. 177 ff. All the monographs cited above include critical analyses.

Pavia Cathedral—Documents in Pavia, Archivio della Cattedrale, published by L. Malaspina di Sannazzaro, *Memorie storiche della fabbrica della cattedrale di Pavia*, Pavia 1816; C. Magenta, *Il Castello di Pavia*, Milan 1882, I, p. 538; Malaguzzi-Valeri, *La corte di Ludovico il Moro*, op. cit., II, 1915, pp. 83 ff. For references to critical analyses see my *Bramante architetto*, op. cit.

Milan, S. Maria delle Grazie—Documents in Milan, Archivio di Stato (Fondo di religione, Conventi), published in A. Pica and P. Portaluppi, *Il gruppo monumentale di Santa Maria delle Grazie*, Rome 1938 (with bibliography); C. Baroni, *Documenti per la storia dell'architettura*, II, Rome 1968.

Vigevano, Piazza Ducale and other work—Documents in Milan, Archivio di Stato (Piazzeforti; Missive; Autografi architetti), and Vigevano, Archivio, published in C. Barucci, *Il castello di Vigevano*, Turin 1909; F. Malaguzzi-Valeri, *La corte di Ludovico il Moro*, op. cit., I, pp. 601 ff.; II, pp. 158 ff.; W. Lotz in *Studi bramanteschi*, op. cit., pp. 205 ff.

Milan, S. Ambrogio, Canonica and monastery—Documents in Milan, Archivio Canonici di S. Ambrogio: see C. Baroni, *Documenti*, op. cit., I, 1940, pp. 43 ff.; P. Bondioli, *Il monastero di S. Ambrogio*, Milan 1935; F. Malaguzzi-Valeri, *La corte*, op. cit., II, pp. 215 ff.

Milan, Ponticella of Ludovico il Moro—Documents in Milan, Archivio di Stato, published in L. Beltrami, *La ponticella di L. il Moro*, Milan 1903.

Rome, S. Giovanni in Laterano, fresco above the Porta Santa—Recorded in a drawing by Borromini in the Albertina, Vienna (Arch. 388; above, Ill. 75): see H. Egger, 'L'affresco di Bramante', in *Roma*, 1932, pp. 303–06, pl. XI; and G. de Angelis d'Ossat, *Preludio romano*, op. cit.

Rome, S. Maria della Pace, cloister—Documents in Rome, Archivio Canonici Regolari Lateranensi di S. Pietro in Vincoli, S. Maria della Pace, published in C. Ricci, 'Il chiostro della Pace', in *Nuova Antologia*, I, 1915, pp. 361–67. Some indications as to chronology can also be found in inscriptions and coats-of-arms on the building itself. For critical comments, among the many contributions see G. De Angelis d'Ossat, *Preludio romano*, op. cit., my *Bramante architetto*, op. cit., and P. Marconi, in *Studi bramanteschi*, op. cit., pp. 427 ff.

Rome, palace of Cardinal Corneto—For documents, bibliography and critical comments see my *Bramante architetto*, op. cit., and C. L. Frommel, *Der Römische Palastbau der Hochrenaissance*, Tübingen 1971. A plan and a detail of the cornice appear in a drawing dating from before c. 1520 in the 'Coner Codex', in Sir John Soane's Museum, London: see T. Ashby, 'Sixteenth-Century Drawings', op. cit., pls 14 and 94.

Rome, Tempietto of S. Pietro in Montorio—A date (1502) is provided by a dedication stone in the crypt, which is mentioned by Fra Mariano da Firenze, *Itinerarium Urbis*, op. cit. (ed. Bulletti, pp. 97–98) written in 1517–18, but not by F. Albertini, *Opusculum de mirabilibus*, op. cit., written in 1509. For analytical and critical discussions and bibliographies, see my *Bramante architetto*, op. cit., and H. Günther's paper in *Studi bramanteschi*, op. cit., pp. 483 ff. There are many sixteenth-century drawings of the Tempietto; some are reproduced in my *Bramante architetto*, op. cit.

Rome, Belvedere—For documents (Vatican, Archivio di Stato in Rome, etc.), numerous early drawings (none by Bramante himself) and a complete critical study see J. Ackerman, *Il Cortile del Belvedere*, op. cit. For reconstructions of the project as a whole and in its details, and for more recent critical comments, see my *Bramante architetto*, op. cit.

Rome, St Peter's—Archive documents principally in the Vatican Archives. Many early drawings, especially in the Uffizi in Florence (department of drawings and prints: the collection includes Arch. 1, the first project, on parchment, rejected by Julius II, and Arch. 8v, 20 and 104, which are studies, perhaps in Bramante's hand), in the 'Coner Codex', already mentioned, in the collection of Mr and Mrs Paul Mellon (sketchbook attributed to Menicantonio de' Chiarellis), in the Albertina in Vienna, etc. The drawings are discussed and reproduced in the vast number of publications on St Peter's (see my *Bramante architetto*, op. cit., pp. 532 ff. and 883 ff.

The most important publications are: H. von Geymüller, *Les Projets*, op. cit.; K. Frey, 'Zur Baugeschichte des St. Peter', in *Jahrbuch der Königl. Preussischen Kunstsamml.*, 1909, 1911, 1912, 1916; D. Frey, *Bramante-Studien*, op. cit.; T. Hofmann, *Die Entstehungsgeschichte des St Peter in Rom*, Zittau 1928; O. Förster, *Bramante*, op. cit.; and, among the many studies by F. Graf Wolff Metternich, 'Bramantes Chor der Peterskirche zu Rom', in *Römische Quartalschrift*, LVIII, 1963, pp. 271–91, 'Le premier projet pour Saint-Pierre', in *The Renaissance and Mannerism. Studies in Western Art*, II, New York and Princeton 1963, pp. 70–81; 'Uber die Massgrundlagen des Kuppelentwurfes Bramantes für die Peterskirche in Rom', *Essays . . . presented to R. Wittkower*, op. cit.

Rome, S. Maria del Popolo, choir—Document published in E. Lavagnino, *S. Maria del Popolo*, Rome, n.d., p. 7; interesting remarks in F. Albertini, *Opusculum*, op. cit.; other analytical and critical discussion in my *Bramante architetto*, op. cit., and E. Bentivoglio and S. Valtieri, *Santa Maria del Popolo a Roma*, Rome 1976.

Rome, Vatican, logge of S. Damaso—Documents published in G. Hoogewerff, 'Documenti che riguardano Raffaello ed altri artisti contemporanei', in *Rendiconti della Pontif. Accad. Romana di Archeol.*, XXI, 1945–46, pp. 265 ff.; D. Redig De Campos, in *Studi bramanteschi*, op. cit.

Civitavecchia, harbour defences—Extracts from early accounts, documents and drawings published in A. Guglielmotti, *Storia delle fortificazioni della spiaggia romana*, Rome 1880, pp. 189 ff. Two medals of Julius II (Vatican medal collection) show Bramante's original project, on which see also my *Bramante architetto*, op. cit. Sketches by Leonardo da Vinci in the Codex Atlanticus (Milan, Biblioteca Ambrosiana, ff. 271r *f*, 97r *b*, 113v *b*) may illustrate Bramante's general scheme for the harbour and the town: see my paper in *Studi bramanteschi*, op. cit., pp. 535ff.

Rome, Palazzo dei Tribunali and church of S. Biagio—It is impossible to build up a complete picture from the accounts of observers at the time (such as Egidio da Viterbo, Andrea Fulvio and F. Albertini), from documents, early drawings (Uffizi, Arch. 136 (very important but perhaps only a first project), 109, 1898, etc.; also the 'Coner Codex', f. 11), and from the foundation medal of Julius II: see the bibliography in my *Bramante architetto*, op. cit., pp. 946 ff., especially D. Gnoli and G. Giovannoni. For further details and corrections see C. L. Frommel in *Studi bramanteschi*, op. cit., pp. 523 ff.

Loreto, Santa Casa, Palazzo Apostolico, façade and restoration of the church—Documents in Loreto (Archivio S. Casa), Recanati, etc., mostly published in P. Gianuizzi, 'Bramante da Monte Asdrualdo e i lavori per Loreto', in *Nuova rivista misena*, XX, 1907, pp. 99–117, 135–49; G. Giovannoni, *Saggi sull'architettura del Rinascimento*, op. cit., and *Antonio da Sangallo il Giovane*, Rome 1959, etc. Almost all the documents are also mentioned or summarized in my *Bramante architetto*, op. cit., pp. 960 ff. A project for the church façade appears on a medal of Julius II. The most important drawings are two plans in the Uffizi, Arch. 921v and 922. An essential analytical and critical study is that of Kathleen Weil-Garris Posner in *Studi bramanteschi*, op. cit., pp. 313 ff.

Rome, SS. Celso e Giuliano in Banchi—For early drawings and other evidence (notably the 'Coner Codex' (Ashby, op. cit., p. 19) and the sketchbook attributed to Menicantonio de' Chiarellis in the Mellon collection, ff. 56v, 57r), analytical and critical discussion, see C. Thoenes, 'Il problema architettonico da Bramante . . .', in G. Sequi, C. Thoenes and L. Mortari, *SS. Celso e Giuliano* (*Le chiese di Roma illustrate*), Rome 1966, pp. 29–52.

Architectural background of 'The School of Athens'—For Vasari's evidence (*Vita di Bramante*), comments, perspective reconstruction and basic bibliography see my *Bramante architetto*, op. cit., pp. 1036 ff.

Rome, House of Raphael—Façade documented above all by an engraving by Antoine Lafréry (1549) and by a drawing formerly attributed to Palladio (London, British Architectural Library, RIBA). For other drawings and prints, documents, analytical and critical bibliography (especially essays by D. Gnoli and by A. Rossi, with documents) see my *Bramante architetto*, op. cit., pp. 1040 ff., and C. L. Frommel, *Der römische Palastbau*, op. cit.

For other works of less importance or doubtful attribution see my *Bramante architetto*, op. cit., with bibliography.

DRAWINGS, PAINTINGS, ENGRAVINGS AND WRITINGS

As we have seen, there is no known drawing, architectural or otherwise, which can be ascribed to Bramante with any certainty. However, the Prevedari engraving does definitely derive from a drawing by him (see above, Individual Works), and he has fairly plausibly been credited with the drawings in the Uffizi already referred to, which are quick sketches in red chalk (sanguine) and are probably his early studies for St Peter's (though they also include a measured drawing of the plan of the Baths of Diocletian). Other drawings should almost certainly not be attributed to him, but should rather be regarded as copies of drawings by him, reworkings by other artists, etc. These drawings include a number in the Uffizi (Arch. 155, 1711, 1712, 1715, 1732, 1733, Paes. 401, etc.), in the Biblioteca Ambrosiana in Milan (f. 251, inf. 55; 145; 158; f. 252, inf. 62r, 176; 62v, 182; etc.), in the Louvre in Paris (church façade, formerly identified as S. Maria presso S. Satiro), and elsewhere. No systematic study of this problem has ever been made; but for some of the architectural drawings attributed to him, derived from him, etc., see my *Bramante architetto*, op. cit., *passim*, and bibliography. For other drawings which may possibly be by Bramante, as well as for his work as painter and engraver, see W. Suida, *Bramante pittore e il Bramantino*, Milan 1953.

On Bramante's activity before his arrival in Lombardy there is again no one systematic and conclusive study, though P. Rotondi has made a number of tentative contributions: see *Il palazzo ducale di Urbino*, op. cit., 'Contributi urbinati a Bramante pittore', in *Emporium*, XIII, 1951, pp. 109–29, 'Nuovi contributi a Bramante pittore', in *Arte lombarda*, year IV, no. 1, 1959, pp. 74–81, *Francesco di Giorgio nel palazzo ducale di Urbino*, op. cit., and his contribution to the 1970 Bramante Congress, in *Studi bramanteschi*, op. cit., pp. 255 ff. See also my *Bramante architetto*, op. cit., in particular chap. I, pp. 728–39, with bibliographical notes.

For Bramante as a painter, in addition to the above-mentioned book by W. Suida and the contributions of Rotondi, Peter Murray ('Bramante milanese', op. cit.) and Metternich ('Der Kupferstich Bernardos de Prevedari', op. cit.), see C. Gnudi, 'Bramante', in *Mostra di Melozzo e del Quattrocento romagnolo*, Forlì 1938, pp. 49–52, F. Mazzini, 'Problemi pittorici bramanteschi', in *Bollettino d'arte*, XLIX, 1964, pp.

327–42, and also P. Arrigoni, *L'incisione rinascimentale*, op. cit., and F. Mazzini, 'La pittura del primo Cinquecento', in *Storia di Milano*, Milan 1957, a work which is also useful for other aspects of Bramante's Lombard period.

For Bramante as treatise-writer and architectural theorist, see J. Schlosser-Magnino, *La letteratura artistica*, Florence and Vienna 1924 (subsequent editions up to 1967), pp. 144 ff. and 148.

For Bramante as poet, see above, note 20.

Further bibliographical references for some of Bramante's less important works and for problems and topics connected with his activity will be found in the Notes.

Acknowledgments for illustrations

Anderson 4, 5, 10, 12, 14; V. Aragozzini 17, 57, 72; L. Benevolo 66; Bergamo, E.P.T. (Wellsfoto) 21; Copyright Reserved 13; Giraudon 183; A. F. Kersting 58; Mansell Collection 2, 7, 20, 33, 59, 64, 128, 174; Georgina Masson 134; Milan, Archivio Fotografico del Castello 54; Milan, Civici Musei 32, 53; Pavia, Guglielmo Chiolini 48; Rome, Archivio Fotografico, the Vatican 109; Rome, G.F.N. 1, 60, 71, 74, 80, 89, 173, 177; from O. Förster, *Bramante,* Vienna and Munich 1956, by kind permission of Anton Schroll & Co. 23, 36, 72, 73; from P. Rotondi, *The Ducal Palace of Urbino*, London 1969, by kind permission of Professor Rotondi 16. The illustrations from the 'Coner Codex' are reproduced by courtesy of the Trustees of Sir John Soane's Museum, London: 78, 95, 103, 104, 108, 148, 166, 180.

Index

Illustration numbers appear in *italic* type